Case Critical

"*Case Critical* has become an essential manual for progressive social service workers, particularly social workers. . . . In every chapter, Carniol plants suggestions of the means for change — social movements, peer support, democratizing social work, listening to the powerless and aligning with them, working from the bottom up, progressive work at different levels of agencies."
— Anne Bishop, *The Canadian Review of Social Policy*

"We have used *Case Critical* for several years. Students have appreciated the candid and provocative review of social work and cite it as one of their favourite readings. Carniol's writing promotes critical thinking."
— Dianne de Champlain and Rosalie Goldstein, School of Social Work, University of Victoria

"This readable, synthesizing analysis of the profession offers social workers insight into the meaning of real change and provides them with the impetus to act accordingly in their day-to-day practice."
— Heather Barclay, *The Social Worker*

D1366979

Case Critical

Challenging Social Services in Canada

Fourth Edition

Ben Carniol

Between the Lines
Toronto, Canada

Case Critical, Fourth Edition

First published in Canada by
Between the Lines
720 Bathurst Street, Suite #404
Toronto, Ontario
M5S 2R4

Canadian Cataloguing in Publication Data

Carniol, Ben
        Case critical : challenging social services in Canada
4th ed.
Includes bibliographical references.
ISBN 1-89 6357-34-2

1 Social service — Canada.   2 Social workers — Canada.   0 I. title

HV105.C39 2000   361.3'.0971   C99-93 3108-6

Cover design and illustration by Lancaster Reid Creative
Interior design and page preparation by Steve Izma
Printed in Canada

Between the Lines gratefully acknowledges assistance for its publishing activities from the Canada Council for the Arts, the Ontario Arts Council, and the Government of Canada through the Book Publishing Industry Development Program.

THE CANADA COUNCIL | LE CONSEIL DES ARTS
FOR THE ARTS | DU CANADA
SINCE 1957 | DEPUIS 1957

Canadä

CONTENTS

Preface ix

1 Social Work and the Public Conscience 1
   homelessness — cuts to social services — social workers

   The Roots of the Social Work Crisis 5
   overview — hierarchy — social relations

   Definitions: Finding the Invisible Wall 7
   *wealth — patriarchy — anti-oppression practice —
   globalization — hegemony — internalized oppression —
   Social Work Code of Ethics — colonialism — racism —
   prejudice — sexualities & phobias — disabilism — ageism —
   multiple oppressions*

   Empowerment in Social Work 20
   expanding client choices — setting the stage

   The Challenge for Social Work 21
   *social change — progressive direction — regressive direction
   — developing anti-oppression approaches*

2 The Roots: Early Attitudes 24
   workhouses — displacing First Nations — social Darwinism

   Social Work: The Beginnings 29
   *Charity Organization Society (C.O.S.) — moral uplift —
   women's caring — the Depression — organized labour &
   social programs — social services expand*

3 Schools of Altruism 38
   choosing social work — altruism — social work skills

The Social Work Curriculum 41
*systems theory — ecological theory — feminist critiques —
addressing sexual orientation & racism — accreditation
standards — student voices*

Aboriginal Circles in the Classroom 48

Future Trends? 50

4 Social Workers: On the Front Line 53

Where Social Workers Work 54
social agencies — voluntary sector — public sector

How Clients Find Social Workers 56
voluntary & involuntary clients — agency outreach

How Social Workers Mean to Help 57
*interpersonal relationships with clients — racism —
lesbophobia & homophobia — sexism — disabled clients*

The Frustrations of Social Work 60
inadequate resources — illusory help — effective help

Cutbacks and Caseloads: The Professional Bind 63
*pressures to conform — efforts at radical practice — peer
support — doing more with less*

5 Managing Social Work: From Top to Bottom 69

The Stratification of Social Work 70
*bureaucracies & hierarchies — supervisors — senior
managers — public sector — voluntary boards*

Moving up in the Profession: Obstacles 74
*gender inequality — anti-racist practice — colonialism &
assimilation — destruction of families — residential schools*

Business Management Techniques 78
*employment assistance programs — management
prerogatives*

Privatization of Social Services 80
*private practice — workfare — private social services as big
business*

6 Unemployment to Welfare to Poverty: Clients Speak Out 86
*creating unemployment — reduced EI coverage — defining
"work" — cause of deficits — good jobs — bad jobs*

Globalization and Social Programs 92
structural adjustment programs

Entering the Welfare System 93
client voices

Social Services: A Major Disenchantment 95
client voices

Workers and Clients: Constraints and Contracts 99
self-determination — stigmatization — client voices

The Push to Workfare 101
*Canada Assistance Plan repealed — poor bashing — who
benefits?*

Broken Promises . . . and Their Consequences 103

In the Interests of the Young . . . and Old 106

The First Nations: No Use for Welfare Workers? 111
community accountability — suicide note

**7 Social Work and Social Change: Towards a Liberation
Practice** 114
*anti-oppression practice — feminist contributions —
withdrawing consent — structural social work*

Reconstructing Social Worker-Client Relationships 117
*power-sharing — reframing — social empathy —
individualism vs. individuality — participatory research —
Aboriginal insights — Afrocentric views*

Alternative Social Services 127
*women's shelters — less hierarchy — more co-operative —
disability services — First Nations self-government —
grassroots networks in Central & South America*

Alternative Social Services: Issues and Pitfalls 130
*consciousness-raising — funding issues — bringing
democracy to public services — Mondragon —
democratizing big business*

Social Action Groups 133

mobilizing diverse populations — social work support roles

Social Action Groups as Building Blocks 136

superficial changes? — breaking silence — interrupting top-down decisions — targeting corporate power

Labour Unions and Social Work 138

working conditions — social programs — protection for social service providers — student placements — community unions

Coalitions and Social Change Movements 141

working across constituencies — subgroups — political parties — resistance — invisibility of privilege — internalized dominance

Postmodernism 145

celebration of differences — identity politics — critiques — commonalities within differences

Bridging the Personal and the Political 149

liberation practice — naming one's privileges — re-entering one's pain — institutions as contested terrains — spirituality with radical politics — we are the majority — participatory democracy

Notes 156

About the Author 177

PREFACE

T HIS BOOK IS ABOUT the realities of both those who receive and those who deliver social services. It is about the experiences of social work and its caseloads. It had been my observation that much of the writing in social work was remote from the realities. In fact, social work students often complain that the theories they learn have little connection with their future work. Although social work textbooks are concerned about social conditions, they seem to evade the critical questions. Does the present system promote personal and community well-being? Or does it serve other priorities? Is social work being used in ways that contradict its official intentions?

The fourth edition contains new information and interview material, updated statistics, and substantially rewritten segments to better address the questions: How do we resist unjust practices? What are the alternatives? How can we get there?

To address these questions I have built upon the critical analysis developed by others, supplemented by my own experiences and interviews with social service providers and consumers. My experiences in social services and social work education span over thirty-five years in Cleveland, Montreal, Calgary, and Toronto; the interviews began during the 1980s in Halifax, Toronto, Calgary, and Vancouver, with more recent ones during the 1990s supporting the earlier findings.

Fortunately, the whole task was shared by many other people who played key roles in helping me bring the work to completion. Robert Clarke of Between the Lines patiently provided guidance and encouragement through all four editions of this project. With a sharp eye for the political implications of the evidence I was gathering, Robert helped me to become more explicit in perspective.

Barbara Riley: Wabano Kwe, a recognized First Nations elder from Walpole Island in Ojibwe territory in Ontario, offered support and encouragement during my journey of change by educating me about the healing ways of Aboriginal culture. Jim Albert, Aboriginal educator at Carleton University's School of Social Work, inspired me by how he lives his commitment of solidarity with the dispossessed. Dorothy Moore of Dalhousie University's Maritime School of Social Work strengthened my activism by sharing her extensive experience with grassroots initiatives and community coalitions struggling against oppression.

Although early drafts of the first edition contained insights from feminist analysis, it was Helen Levine who provided thorough and detailed feedback in this area and who thereby helped to place the role of women and women's conditions and struggles at centre stage. I am grateful for the time, skill, and care that went into her numerous excellent suggestions, most of which became integrated within the following pages.

Yvonne Howse (Saskatchewan) from the Cree nation and Malcolm Saulis from the Maliseet nation in the Maritimes are social work educators and active members of WUNSKA, the Aboriginal Network of the Canadian Association of Schools of Social Work; both Yvonne and Malcolm gave me valuable guidance on how to be inclusive of First Nations values and aspirations related to the social services and to social change.

For this edition, I appreciate the consultation I received from Susan Silver, Director of the Ryerson School of Social Work; Dennis Haubrich, Associate Director at the same school; and Sue Wilson, Chair of the Faculty of Community Services Research Committee. Their consultation strengthened my application for a research grant. I want to thank the Research Committee of the Ryerson Faculty of Community Services and the Dean of our Faculty, Judith Sandys, for helping me with a grant that enabled me to hire Suraya Faziluddin, a fourth-year Ryerson social work student, whose excellent research and communication skills made it possible for me to complete this project on schedule.

Helping me to track recent research and offering advice and support for my work on this book were: Paul Agueci, Donna Baines, Akua Benjamin, Sam Blatt, Catherine Brooks, Hannah Brown, Bonnie Brownstein, Jim Chang, Yisrael Elliot Cohen, Veronika Cohen, Sarah Collings, Dianne de Champlain, Pam Chapman, Sharon Chisholm, Janet Conway, Cathy Crowe, Emily Drzymala, Jeff Edmunds, Deb Frenette, Frieda Forman, Harry Fox, Rosalie Goldstein, Marci Gilbert, Shirley Judge, Sharole Gabriel, Josephine Grey, Nelson Gutnick, Gordon Hauka, Kira Heineck, Bill Howes, Lev Jaeger, Ronnee Jaeger, Saul Joel, Helen Kennedy, Miriam Kalushner, Ellen Katz, Joel Kurtz, Sonia Kurtz, Iara Lessa, David Lesk, Leiba Lesk, Heather Lockert, Gus Long,

Sylvia Lustgarten, Karen Malis, Georgina Marshall, Peggy Mayes, Tirzah Meacham, Monica McKay, Ken Moffatt, Anne Moorhouse, Ruth Morris, Eileen Morrow, Gordon Morwood, Mary Ann Murphy, Marvyn Novick, Patricia O'Connor, Stacey Papernick, Brent Patterson, Anne Parsons, Steve Pizzano, Lillian Pitawankwat, Catherine Phillips, Beth Porter, Alana Prashad, Luisa Quarta, Elizabeth Radian, Baruch Rand, Jackie Rand, Diana Ralph, Esther Rausenberg, Graham Riches, David Ross, Amy Rossiter, Laurel Rothman, Shalom Schachter, Shlomit Segal, Frank Sestito, Michael Shapcott, Hugh Shewell, Myer Siemiatycki, Bau St-Cyr, Karol Steinhouse, Sharon Dale Stone, Dennis Switzer, Ian Thompson, Judy Tsao, Tim Tyler, Ronny Yaron, June Yee, and Rima Zavys.

I have greatly appreciated the support from my publishers, Between the Lines, throughout the four editions of *Case Critical*. Paul Eprile, Peter Steven, Ruth Bradley St-Cyr, and Jamie Swift all provided me with encouragement and helpful suggestions for this edition.

Special thanks go to the women, men, and, in some cases, children who agreed to be interviewed and took considerable risks in being candid and in sharing painful realities. I am also grateful to the social workers who shed light on their work environment and on the pressures of their jobs. In most cases their names remain anonymous to protect their positions. Excerpts from these interviews occur throughout the book in italics.

This preface would remain incomplete if I did not express my appreciation to Rhona, whose affection strengthens my confidence; to Mira, whose sense of caring about others makes me hopeful about caring communities; and to Naomi, whose smile reminds me of why social change is urgent. My family, both immediate and extended, taught me not only to listen but also to hear and care about the well-being of others.

This book is dedicated to my parents, Elsa and Mathias Carniol.

1 Social Work and the Public Conscience

> If you really love us, how come you can't do nothin' about our conditions?
> — a teenage client

> I've gone out on calls in the middle of the night. I wasn't on duty at the time but when you get a phone call like that from a family in crisis you go and do what you can. It's as if social workers have become the conscience for the public so that the public can forget about these problems.
> — a social worker

DURING THE 1990s the level of homelessness in Canada had reached a critical stage. Across the country two hundred thousand people were homeless, with another two million at risk of becoming homeless.[1] It became obvious: Something had to be done. Then, it seems, someone within our higher levels of decision-making must have come up with a bright idea. If we could only make "the problem" less visible, it might just go away. Police departments received new directives. We may never learn all the reasons, but the results were clear: Police officers in a number of jurisdictions stepped up their efforts to get the homeless off our streets. For the men and women sleeping or begging in public spaces, it meant more harassment.

To oppose this harassment, anti-poverty activists in Toronto sent out a call. In the summer of 1999 a group of them invited people from social agencies, community centres, and housing support groups to show their solidarity with homeless people. We were invited to gather in a public park downtown, where volunteers would provide donations of tents, food, and blankets to the homeless. Together we would launch a "safe park" to provide poor people with a safe space, free from police harassment.

1

The mood was festive as I joined about five hundred people at the park on that bright and cool summer Saturday afternoon. I saw a few social workers I knew, as well as others from health services, various faith groups, and labour and community organizations. The good-natured crowd of women and men from a wide variety of ethnic and cultural backgrounds celebrated its diversity — and its cohesion — to the beat of Aboriginal drumming.

What was wrong with this picture? After all, this event was successful in bringing together homeless and non-homeless people to oppose the mistreatment of the poor by governments. Yet there was something terribly wrong when the powers-that-be in one of the world's richest countries were trying to minimize Canada's housing crisis, as if the real estate industry was doing a perfectly good job of producing affordable housing.

For weeks before this event, city councillors had criticized the idea of this "safe park." A social service manager had joined the backlash by claiming that the city had plenty of shelter beds for the homeless. What he did not say was that many shelters had appalling conditions. Elizabeth Mayer, a thirty-six-year-old shelter user in Toronto, told reporters: "The shelters are overcrowded. They are not safe places."[2] For example, when a shelter runs out of floor mats, people end up sleeping on a concrete floor, shoulder to shoulder, with others who are coughing and hacking in a large room with only one toilet for sixty people. Not surprisingly, some homeless people prefer to take their chances sleeping outside, even in sub-freezing temperatures.

No matter. The mayor was adamant: "No one will take over our public parks." When the police evicted the homeless and their supporters from the park at early dawn of the fourth day, the news coverage was extensive. Yet much of the media missed the main story — that the rising despair among Canada's poor was closely connected to more than a decade of political decisions by Ottawa and the provinces to slash spending on social programs.

But people who are connected to the social services, either as volunteers, staff, and users of the services, or as community activists, see what is happening. As a result more voices are insisting: Poverty and homelessness must not be swept under the carpet. For example, in the summer of 1999 local groups across the country joined together to form the National Housing and Homeless Network. Only months before, the mayors of Canada's largest cities had recognized that the level of homelessness had reached a critical stage. These mayors endorsed a "State of Emergency Declaration" calling on all levels of government to respond with humanitarian relief. The Declaration urged governments to use disaster relief funds, "both to provide the homeless with immediate health protection and housing and to prevent further homelessness."[3] To its credit, the Federation of Canadian Municipalities also endorsed this call for action.

Yet while various groups were urging government action, an opposite, more soothing message was being delivered to politicians from a different quarter. "Conditions are not so bad. You're doing the right thing. Do more of it." For years business groups and the business media had been escalating their demands that governments cut back on "big spending" — which mainly meant social programs. For example, *The Globe and Mail* was blunt in its message to the federal finance minister concerning his 1999 budget: "There is still much federal spending . . . that is wasteful."[4]

While politicians have generally caved in to the constant demands from business leaders to snip away at Canada's social safety net, there are exceptions. Libby Davies, Member of Parliament for Vancouver East, managed to conduct a cross-country inquiry into homelessness. Her report states: "In every community I visited I was struck by three basic issues: the lack of adequate incomes and high rents that drive people to poverty; the impact of the lack of new social housing construction; and the desperate need to improve and maintain the standard of low income market housing stock."[5]

Cathy Crowe, a nurse practitioner with years of experience serving homeless people, is an outspoken critic of government's failure to effectively address the issue of homelessness. "To be homeless is a daily life and death situation," Crowe says. "To be homeless is to risk tuberculosis infection. In Vancouver, the spread of HIV infection or AIDs is due to the consequences of homelessness. In Toronto, front-line workers report two to four deaths of homeless people per week."[6]

Despite this raw reality, social services are under attack. The focus on reducing the debt burden, the pervasive cry for tax reductions, and the new creed of "smart spending" mask a deep crisis. Social workers — like their clients — are caught in a crossfire. At times they feel beset from all sides: from dissatisfied clients, from their managers, from official policy, from business leaders pushing cutbacks in social services, from a sense of failure at having to confront — every day on the job — a bottomless pit of social problems. Yet their job is to provide help — "social security" — to people in need, the "clients."

As for the clients, evidence shows that they often find themselves blamed for the problems they face. They find they don't get the help they need, or they don't get nearly enough help to make a difference — or they get "cut off." Yet they are told in turn that this country has a solid package of social programs, at their service.

The wider community has long had an expectation that with all the money being spent on social programs the country would at least see a reduction of social problems. Yet the public has also long suspected that the problems are not in decline. On the contrary, they are worsening. According to Marjorie Bencz, executive director of the Edmonton Food Bank, "Government policies are being driven by purely fiscal considerations with no regard for the desperate plight of people — moms who can't afford formula for their babies — seniors — hungry children — single employables who are supposed to find work when no jobs are available."[7]

Not surprisingly, the public is highly ambivalent towards social work. There might be praise, for example, when a social worker protects children from violent abuse. But when it comes to their efforts to ensure that the poor get financial aid, social workers are sometimes seen as "bleeding hearts" using up taxpayers' money to help "lazy bums" get "something for nothing." Or when it comes to adequately funding First Nations social services there is an attitude of "Why should my taxes help those people?"

Part of the problem is that social workers and social services are functioning in ways that are very different from those described and publicized by the profession itself. In truth, because of the constant push of pressures and contradictions, social work in practice takes on a different hue than the picture that, for example, social work textbooks paint for eager students about to enter the profession.

Social services claim to offer effective help to the troubled and the needy. They are one of society's answers to the problems of poverty and social distress. They are aimed at the satisfaction and protection of basic human rights and needs: from living unmolested to having enough money available for housing, food, and clothing. Yet poverty persists, unabated. People have frozen to death on the winter streets of our cities for lack of a decent and secure place to stay. Studies show that the gap between rich and poor continues to increase, that wealth continues to concentrate. So too, women are still economically behind men, just as people of colour still suffer from the prejudices of mainstream society. A large segment of the population continues to lead broken or shattered lives, battered lives, lives without hope for the future. Not only social work, as a profession, but also the places in which it operates, namely the social services, are largely stymied by these problems.

By offering aid to a variety of client populations, such as the disabled, the unemployed, the poor, the ill, and the elderly, social work reinforces the impression that the organized society — the state — and its institutions care about and care for all the people within its confines. Yet, in my opinion, many social problems are aggravated or, indeed, created by the political, economic, and social conditions organized under the wide-ranging umbrella of the state — which then turns around and offers social work assistance.

All of this is not to say that for social workers themselves there is no job satisfaction. Very few social service jobs provide a totally negative experience. Social workers might help an old-age pensioner write up a claim for a financial supplement that eventually results in more money for her. We might help a child develop a better understanding of a difficult family situation or the inner strength to cope more effectively with a specific type of stress. We might listen to a lonely hospital patient express fears and doubts about the future, and be thanked for taking the time to listen. Some workers get a sense of straightforward personal satisfaction in skilfully navigating the perilous route of red tape necessary to achieve a client's goal.

These victories keep social workers going, but they also serve to shield us from our more critical feelings. Similarly they can shield us from analysing the role played by social agencies themselves in creating our powerlessness. Sometimes these satisfactions — not to mention the basic economic benefits of holding a steady job in a "worthwhile" profession — work to divert us away from the total, more disturbing, picture.

THE ROOTS OF THE SOCIAL WORK CRISIS

Many front-line social workers feel alienated from their work, with a sense of powerlessness and frustration. There is low morale, unsupportive management. As one worker said about her colleagues: *"If you ask any of these workers about how they see the future, they'll all tell you the same thing — I want to get the hell out of here."*

Conditions of work often militate against "getting the job done" — even if that were possible under the best of conditions. Why is this so? Why is it that social agencies, which have been established for the purpose of helping, end up by being part of the problem? Has social work failed to deliver on its promises? Most social workers know only too well that their services fall short. There are many reasons for this, including what happens inside their social services. As a report on the conditions faced by social workers in British Columbia's child welfare ministry states:

> Practitioners have reported that their work is inspected and scrutinized, but their views are not taken into account by policy makers; their work-load has increased substantially, but they lack adequate and appropriate resources; their competence is often questioned, but their requests for education and training are not heeded; their knowledge of practice is ignored, but they are aware of innovative approaches that would improve services. In short, practitioners feel devalued by their employer and pilloried by the media.[8]

These conditions are hardly new, though, so why have the problems never been solved? Is Canadian society really serious about its aid to its own citizens? If we really want to help people, shouldn't we also tackle some of the root causes of social problems?

My short response to these questions is that social services are often used to paper over the cracks that have appeared over the years in the walls of an unjust society. As a result the major sources of many social problems remain untouched. Typically social workers are expected to confine themselves to working with symptoms only.

To study — and, I hope, answer — some of the questions surrounding social work, this book looks at early attitudes towards "helping," and the emerging role of the welfare state; at who social workers are and how they are educated; at the work they do, in theory and practice, at how this work is organized, and at the people it affects — the "clients." From time to time the book also identifies innovations in social work, and the last chapter links those innovations to larger social change.

The hierarchical nature of social service organizations as they now operate means that clients almost always come lowest in the pecking order. This book means to give clients a stronger voice — at the expense, justifiably, of the mainstream "expert" voices of institutional management.

The other important theme that threads its way through this study is that the principles, management, and practice of social work are distorted — subverted — by structural conditions that have their roots nourished by the dynamics of colonialism, gender, racism, economic class, and other inequalities. These unequal social relations have become deeply entrenched in all of society's institutions, including social services. These services employ social workers, many of whom come from the middle class and are educated to be "professionals." Most social workers have also traditionally been women, and this has had its effects on the status, organization, and control of the work. Women social workers, as Jennifer Dale and Peggy Foster point out in their book *Feminists and State Welfare*, "have never exercised control over their profession nor over those organizations in which social work takes place."[9]

At the same time most clients are the poor and dispossessed: Aboriginal people, the unemployed or underemployed, or the unemployable, people suffering from depression and other debilitating conditions, the young and displaced, the elderly, the disabled. Most of these people again are women. Many of the clients are people of colour (once again with a majority of women). If a sense of powerlessness afflicts social workers, that sense is magnified greatly in the case of clients.

Why such a situation remains unchanged is directly linked to why our political system chooses to maintain questionable institutions rather than to change them. Despite the much-touted freedom of choice that we are supposed to enjoy, it is dramatic how un-free our thinking is, especially when we probe the causes behind the powerlessness and despair experienced by a large segment of the population. There is ample support for inquiries into the "pathologies" of the poor and the troubled, their personality deficits, their family stress, or their childhood traumas. Yet at the same time there is a taboo against asking: To what extent are unemployment, poverty, and basic inequalities directly or indirectly traceable to decisions made by a small group of people who possess the most power and wealth in the society?

DEFINITIONS: FINDING THE INVISIBLE WALL

The public has all along been encouraged to accept the welfare state as benign — that it is society's attempt to provide a minimum income and a "range of social services" for *all* members of society, that it attempts to reduce economic insecurity resulting from such "contingencies" as sickness, old age, and unemployment.[10] However, there is also another view. As Ian Gough points out, the welfare state:

> simultaneously embodies tendencies to enhance social welfare, to develop the powers of individuals, to exert social control over the blind play of

market forces; and tendencies to repress and control people, to adapt
them to the requirements of the capitalist economy. Each tendency will
generate counter tendencies in the opposite direction; indeed, this is precisely why we refer to it as a contradictory process through time.[11]

Many social scientists view this kind of contradictory process as stemming from the requirements of a patriarchal and capitalist society and
its dominant ideology. When the ownership and control of production
and reproduction along with power in political and cultural institutions
are largely confined to one gender and a small group of white people
— whether they are called the corporate elite, the ruling class, or the
rich (and famous) — the system creates and maintains its own built-in,
ineradicable inequalities. Viewed in this light, the institutions of the
welfare state are the dominant system's attempt to gloss over the very
inequalities it creates in the first place.

Despite the social services and their social workers, ostensibly
working for the well-being of the entire population, the system's distribution of power and resources remains profoundly unequal between
men and women, between whites and non-whites, and between the
economic classes. On the contrary, power has continued to further concentrate among the already powerful. In the late 1990s, for instance,
each of the ten richest chief executive officers in Canada was taking
home more than $10 million. A CEO's average increase in the years
1997-98 was over 50 per cent. Meanwhile average wages for the workforce as a whole increased by only 2 per cent in the period 1995-98.[12]

This unequal distribution of wealth has enormous human costs.
One study comparing neighbourhoods in Canada calculated that new-
born babies from the poorest areas had a life expectancy of about four
years less than those from the richest areas. The infant mortality rate
for infants under one year old was about twice as high in the poorest
neighbourhoods as in the richest. Aboriginal peoples living on reserves
averaged about eight fewer years of life than the population as a
whole. The reported disability rate was twice as high for young people
from the lowest income group as compared to families with high
income.[13] Small wonder that the United Nations Committee on Economic, Social and Cultural Rights criticized Canada: "For a rich country
like Canada, it is really quite shocking to know how women are so
poor and that they really suffer a great deal, especially single
mothers."[14] This picture is in stark contrast to the smug images that
portray Canada as a place in which social justice prevails.

In his groundbreaking book *The Vertical Mosaic,* published in 1965, sociologist John Porter recognized the role of class and gender in economic decision-making. He argued that economic power was concentrated in the hands of a small group of men he designated as the "economic elite." He also illustrated the role of sex and racism in this organization of power.

> In every society there are established mechanisms by which members are sorted out and assigned to particular social tasks. Often this process is based on biological or inherited characteristics. In most societies there are, for example, male and female roles. Sex has always been an initial basis of sorting and assigning people to their appropriate tasks. Hence, in this particular society, few women occupy positions of power because it is not "appropriate" that women should. Colour is another important biological characteristic which has been used as a basis of sorting people out.[15]

This sorting out process is also shaped by *patriarchy* — the systemic dominance of men over women through established social structures and social relations. This domination affects the treatment of women not only in society generally, but also more specifically in the production of wealth, and in the reproduction of new generations of human beings. Canadian sociologist Jane Ursel, for instance, defines patriarchy as "a system or set of social relations which operate to control reproduction through the control of women both in their reproductive and productive labour."[16] Dorothy Smith, widely recognized in Canada for her contributions to feminist theory and methodology, adds: "We have come slowly to the discovery that gender permeates all aspects of social, political and economic organisation; that what has been seen as not gendered is in fact largely an exclusively male arena of action and that from that viewpoint, gender relations are only present when women are. But from the standpoint of women, we are coming to recognise the pervasive effect or presence of gender."[17]

Another feminist theorist, Margrit Eichler, explains that one obvious reason for the relative invisibility of housework in our society is that the patriarchal family is the operative model for social organization. This means that the woman is defined as being economically dependent on her husband, which has had an impact on her work within the home: "Her work is, therefore, by implication seen as economically valueless, no matter what it may consist of and how much it would cost to replace it. Indeed this has been (and continues to be, to some degree) an explicitly accepted aspect of economic theory. In labour economics, the labour force is equated with gainfully employed workers, i.e., with paid labour."[18]

As a force patriarchy goes far beyond our national boundaries. As a United Nations report puts it: "Of the more than 1 billion people living in abject poverty, women are an overwhelming majority."[19]

Subordination by gender has also put women's safety at risk. For example, the Canadian Panel on Violence Against Women found that two out of three women in Canada have experienced what is legally recognized to be sexual assault.[20] Such figures — controversial as they are — reflect the pervasive and persistent historical subordination of women to men, which is further complicated by other divisions of power within societies. In *The Canadian Corporate Elite,* Wallace Clement took John Porter's work a step further by presenting detailed evidence showing that the various elites Porter saw as separate — the corporate, political, bureaucratic, church, intellectual — were tightly linked and homogeneous, forming a "power elite." Clement argued that this power elite determined the country's economic and political priorities and established its ideology through control of the mass media. This elite prevented the ideal of democracy from truly working in practice. It prevented Canada from fulfilling its promise of equal opportunity.

Clement stated that "the way society is organized provides some with the advantage to accumulate power and privilege [and] then transfer these to their children in the form of wealth, stockholdings, social 'position,' and access to education or 'inside' contacts for job placements."[21]

While an upper class largely influences our values, attitudes, and ideas, there is more to domination than the inequalities of class. Feminist writers have cautioned us against viewing the mode of production as the sole force in the making of history and society. One contributor to Canadian feminist thought, Mary O'Brien, calls attention to the fundamental importance of reproduction as a mode of production ignored by "malestream" thought because it has to do with women as workers and producers, as key actors in production. O'Brien points out that while class analysis is important, it is clearly insufficient because it ignores the role of male supremacy: "Reproductive relations, on the other hand, never do manage to make history in this interpretation. . . . This is pure patriarchal distortion; the act of biological reproduction is *essentially* social and human, and forms of the social relations of reproduction have as important an impact on the social relations of production as vice versa."[22]

O'Brien observes that gender conflict and class conflict produce forces for change that can be understood by analysing their different sources. She argues that the separation of the private life and the personal, on the one hand, from public life and the political, on the other, has come about through the historically developed structure of the social relations of reproduction: "The opposition of public and private is to the social relations of reproduction what the opposition of economic classes is to the social relations of production."[23]

It is important to recognize these differences in gender and class conflicts, as well as their common points. Indeed, when we consider the various oppressions that are not only based on gender and class but also on colonialism, racism, ableism, heterosexism, and ageism, it is the experience of unequal social relations that applies in common. Each of these dimensions has a privileged group that considers itself superior because of its greater power of labelling others as inferior. These superior/inferior divisions produce not only self-serving statements but also a host of prejudices. For example, the rich are "smarter" and the poor are "lazy." Men are "rational" and women are "overly emotional." Heterosexuals are "normal" and gays and lesbians are "perverts." The able-bodied are "capable" and people with disabilities are "crippled" or "stupid."

These prejudices serve to reinforce the privileges of what I will call the "ruling class," in which power is wielded mainly by white males. The pattern involves intricate cross-stitching of history, economics, ideology, gender roles, education, religion, the mass media — the list could go on and on. It can also be argued that because of foreign ownership of its economy, Canada has never had an independent ruling class: The holding of power has been complicated by a colonial relationship with, first, Great Britain, and more recently the United States.

The idea of white male authority within a ruling elite is also not a matter of simple, mechanistic systems of conspiracy and domination. As media analyst Todd Gitlin puts it, "Society is not a machine or a thing, it is a coexistence of human beings who do what they do (including maintaining or changing a social structure) as sentient, reasoning, moral, and active beings who experience the world, who are not simply 'caused' by it."[24]

To explain why a population more likely opts for maintaining the prevailing institutions over trying to change them, Gitlin points to Antonio Gramsci's theory of *hegemony*: the "name given to a ruling class's domination through ideology, through the shaping of popular consent." According to Gitlin: "Those who rule the dominant institutions secure their power in large measure directly *and indirectly,* by impressing their definitions of the situation upon those they rule and if not usurping the whole of ideological space, still significantly limiting what is thought throughout the society."[25]

Social work educator Bob Mullaly notes that hegemony leads people to internalize their oppression: "Through a process of cultural and ideological hegemony many oppressed people believe that if they cannot make it in our society, if they are experiencing problems, then it is their own fault."[26]

That kind of self-blame can create psychological depression among social service clients as they come to believe the societal prejudices about themselves, to the detriment of their sense of self-worth. At the same time, the Social Work Code of Ethics is clear that the social worker "shall promote social justice" and that social work's primary obligation is to "maintain the best interest of the client" based on "the dignity of every human being."[27]

To achieve those goals we need the knowledge necessary to address the oppressive labels that have been psychologically internalized by social service clients. As social service providers, we also need to know how these labels may have gained acceptance not only within social service organizations but also inside ourselves as individual practitioners. Working to promote social justice means working to change harmful attitudes and practices. This approach has been called *anti-oppression practice*: a form of practice that is pertinent to all of the helping professions. That practice requires an understanding of the nature of unequal power relations both within Canada and beyond.

On the international level the growth of inequality has been escalating in recent years, most notably through the nebulous force called *globalization*, a process in which transnational/global corporations have become increasingly more powerful. Dangling the carrot of new jobs and prosperity, transnational corporations shop around to find the nation or regions within a nation that can offer the lowest wages, levy the least taxes, and minimize other business costs. As a result, countries face an intense pressure to push down wages, taxes, and environmental standards in order to attract or satisfy foreign investors and businesses. The Ecumenical Coalition for Economic Justice has examined how the pressures for social cuts in Canada result from global economic activity, especially the threat of capital flight from nations that refuse to co-operate with international bond holders and currency traders. With the aid of telecommunications, businesses can shift huge sums out of a country in a matter of seconds, on a world stage where more than $1.5 trillion worth of international currencies are traded every day, much of it being speculation.[28]

Given the immense power and wealth wielded by these businesses, it is tempting to lose hope in social justice. But Howard Zinn, U.S. historian and activist, reminds us: "To be hopeful in bad times is not just foolishly romantic. It is based on the fact that human history is a history not only of cruelty, but also of compassion, sacrifice, courage, kindness. . . . We don't have to engage in grand, heroic actions to participate in the process of change. Small acts, when multiplied by millions of people, can transform the world."[29]

Indeed, there is more than one version of globalization; it is also a contested arena. A more democratic version of globalization consists of progressive grassroots initiatives around the globe offering a different vision of the economic good and organizing to oppose corporate control.

While such opposition has at times been successful, the trend today is ominously negative. Sometimes called the race to the bottom, the corporate version of globalization is increasing the gap between the rich and the poor around the globe. As researcher Armine Yalnizyan points out, "Today those people who find themselves in the richest 20% of the world's population have incomes that are, on average, 60 times as large as those on the bottom."[30] That gap is double what it was thirty years ago.

International organizations such as the World Bank reinforce this growing disparity by offering credit and loans on conditions that insist that governments offer "favourable" climates for international investment. To them, a favourable climate means cutting social programs and public services.

The history of global *colonialism* is the history of racism, leaving a legacy of poverty borne primarily by Southern nations. Colonialism in North America, while intertwined with racism, has a separate meaning for Aboriginal peoples. Racism has harmed people worldwide — people who, because of their different cultural backgrounds, are subject to discrimination in employment practices and to severe problems in housing availability and quality of education, to name a few blatant examples. But colonialism's bite has also had a lasting, especially painful hold on First Nations. It was official policy for the colonial authorities to systematically destroy the political, economic, and spiritual institutions of Aboriginal communities. This destruction included tremendous violence against First

Nations in order to displace them from their historic land and make room for European settlers.

In 1996 the Royal Commission on Aboriginal Peoples reported examples of colonialism by Canadian authorities:

> Violation of solemn promises in the treaties, inhumane conditions in residential schools, the uprooting of whole communities, the denial of rights and respect to patriotic Aboriginal veterans of two world wars, and the great injustices and small indignities inflicted by the administration of the Indian Act — all take on mythical power to symbolize present experiences of unrelenting injustice.[31]

Who benefited? Authors Tim Schouls, John Olthuis, and Diane Engelstad remind us that "all non-native Canadians have benefitted tremendously from racist policies, from theft of land and from defaults on solemn treaties."[32] To its credit, the Royal Commission engaged in extensive public hearings, giving voice to Aboriginal grievances, and it made proposals for correcting past and present wrongs inflicted upon Aboriginal peoples.

Although the terms prejudice, racism, and discrimination are often used interchangeably, they have different connotations. As authors Jean Leonard Elliott and Augie Fleras point out, *racism* is "a doctrine that unjustifiably asserts the superiority of one group over another on the basis of arbitrarily selected characteristics pertaining to appearance, intelligence, or temperament."[33] The authors of *Colour of Democracy* define *prejudice* as "a mental state or attitude of prejudging, generally unfavourably, by attributing to every member of a group characteristics falsely attributed to the group as a whole."[34] By contrast, *discrimination* is action based on prejudiced attitudes and beliefs. This action happens at both the interpersonal level and the level of societal institutions.

> Systemic racism is the name given to this subtle, yet powerful, form of discrimination which is entrenched within the institutional framework of society. With systemic racism, it is not the intent which counts, but rather the *consequence*. Policies, rules, priorities, and programs may not be inherently racist or discriminatory in intent. However, they have a discriminatory effect in that they exclude certain groups from access to equality.[35]

Systemic racism or *institutionalized racism* results in the exclusion of certain populations from access to quality education, good jobs and promotions, decent housing, or participation in an organization. "In all cases, racism reflects a pattern of intergroup relations," Elliott and Fleras note. "Those in positions of power are able to invoke a doctrine of superiority to ensure domination over those who are perceived as different and inferior."[36] According to U.S. cultural critic bell hooks, "White supremacy continues to overdetermine and shape the lives of most black folks, maintaining and perpetuating exploitative and oppressive forms of institutionalized racism."[37]

Although Canada has established human rights commissions and a constitution containing a bill of rights, researchers B. Singh Bolaria and Peter Li still conclude: "The evidence suggests that such changes have done little to ease racial tensions, much less resolve the problem of racism and discrimination."[38] This is evidenced, among other things, by Canada's restrictive refugee laws, which have been condemned by human rights and church organizations.[39]

Prejudices exist on the basis not just of skin colour, gender, or class, but also of sexual orientation. James Sears, co-editor with Walter Williams of the book *Overcoming Heterosexism and Homophobia*, defines *homophobia* as: "Prejudice, discrimination, harassment, or acts of violence against sexual minorities, including lesbians, gay men, bisexuals, and transgendered persons, evidenced in a deep-seated fear or hatred of those who love and sexually desire those of the same sex."[40]

Sears defines *heterosexism* as: "A belief in the superiority of heterosexuals or heterosexuality evidenced in the exclusion, by omission or design, of nonheterosexual persons in policies, procedures, events, or activities. We include in our definition not only lesbians and gay men but other sexual minorities such as bisexuals and transgendered persons as well."[41]

If social workers are to provide effective services, it becomes important that they understand the variety of prejudices that can undermine a person's self-esteem.

Lesbophobia is the mistreatment of or prejudice against lesbians, including belief in stereotypes such as lesbians being "undesirable women who can't land a man" or "man-haters." Feminist Bonnie Burstow challenges the helping professions to empathize with lesbians, to question coercive heterosexuality, and "to explore together the impact and possible ways of dealing with . . . the experience of being rejected, ridiculed, assaulted, or terrorized because of sexual preference." Burstow notes that helpful counselling to lesbians means "accepting and respecting lesbians as courageous, mature adult women who are affirming and defying."[42]

Bisexual activist Kathleen Bennett suggests that certain societal attitudes have arbitrarily created a series of forced choices and as a result have caused considerable suffering. We are not only expected to choose from a series of false "opposites," such as masculine/feminine, self/other, us/them, and intellect/emotion. We are also told that one of these opposites is positive, while the other is negative or stigmatized.[43]

When people are attracted both to the opposite sex and to same-sex individuals, the world of either/or becomes threatened. Karol Steinhouse applies the following definitions in her social work teaching and practice:

> Bisexuality consists of the ability, capacity, and interest in having sensual, sexual, and emotional relationships and responses to all genders. Bisexuality is fluid for every person and cannot be simplified into an absolute experience of a fifty-fifty split in attraction. Bisexual orientation is not a composite of gay/lesbian and heterosexual identities. Neither is it somewhere "in between" being gay and straight. . . .
>
> *Biphobia* is fear of anyone who identifies as bisexual or experiences bisexual feelings, relationships or sexual activity.
>
> It springs from *monosexism*, a belief system that single gender attraction is superior to dual attraction. Biphobia includes saying or doing hateful things in relation to bisexuals.[44]

Social workers, like other professionals, have choices: to either perpetuate prejudices or challenge them. A first step is to recognize the pervasiveness of negative stereotypes. For instance, prejudices can hound people with disabilities. Disabled writer Jenny Morris describes *disablism*:

> The way we live our lives is fundamentally influenced by other people's reactions to our physical and intellectual differences but also by society's reactions to the needs created by those differences. The common devaluation of our lives undermines our rights as citizens and as human beings to all the things which are an essential part of a reasonable quality of life. This devaluation is at the root of the prejudice we experience. This disablism, this prejudice, compounded of fear and ignorance, is an important determinant of our social, economic and personal experiences.[45]

That is why disability activist James Charlton concludes, "Disability is not a medical category but a social one. Disability is socially constructed."[46]

That society is also failing older people is evident through the existence of *ageism,* which applies negative stereotypes such as senility or inactivity to the elderly and often results in an abandonment of our older population because they are considered to be no longer "productive." As a larger proportion of Canadians live longer, ageism is increasing, and its effects are felt in socially constructed divisions such as gender and class. Writers Lynda Aitken and Gabriele Griffin note that older women "tend to be poorer than men, which affects the economically based decisions they can make."[47] Aitken and Griffin examine what happens when abuse is mixed with sexism and ageism: "The majority of abused older people are women. But old women are 'invisible.' Most have private lives only; few live extensively in the public domain. Their abuse goes on behind the closed doors of the home or the institution. Without adequate access to the public domain, it is difficult for older women to draw attention to the abuse they endure."[48]

In their book *Feminist Organizing for Change,* Nancy Adamson, Linda Briskin, and Margaret McPhail develop a synthesis of major forms of domination: "Neither class, gender, nor race is privileged as *the* primary source of oppression. Rather, the fundamental interconnections between the structures of political and economic power — in our society, capitalism — and the organization of male power — what we might refer to as 'patriarchal relations' — is emphasized."[49] That is why these authors highlight the term *patriarchal capitalism,* to illuminate "the class nature of women's oppression, the impact of racism and heterosexism, and the role of the state in reinforcing women's oppression."[50]

All of these factors — the roles of gender and racism, of disability, ageism, and sexual orientation, of political and economic power and ideology, of the uneven distribution of wealth and power — together create the social relations that dominate and confine our lives. These multiple dimensions of oppression, sometimes called *multiple oppressions*, are not separate islands unto themselves. On the contrary, they interact with and reinforce each other as they reproduce themselves in our daily lives. Donna Baines, a social work educator at McMaster University, analyses these diverse oppressions as ongoing experiences that are "dynamic, continuously changing social relations of domination and subordination."[51] These various social relations are part of a whole. Neil Thompson, writing for the British Association of Social Workers, puts it this way: "These are dimensions of our social location and so we need to understand them as a whole — facets of an overall edifice of power and dominance rather than separate or discrete entities."[52]

These primary structures of inequality are like invisible walls that accompany our every move, stretching on throughout our lives. The structures and relations of social work form one set of walls, for both worker and client. The larger structures and institutions of society — government, business, education, media, religion, family — form another set. Although these invisible walls do not by any means represent a unified system, they are closely linked, and together they take a heavy toll as we collide with them day in and day out and feel less and less certain about which way to turn.

A "welfare mother" expressed the sense of confusion — and anger — this experience creates:

"My daughter and I are both anaemic, so we should be buying vitamins but because I can buy them over the counter, welfare won't pay for them. I don't have the money so I said the hell with it! I've got a choice — either get the groceries I need or don't pay my bills. If I don't pay my rent, I'm out of my apartment. If I'm out of my apartment and can't find a place to stay, welfare will accuse me of being an unfit mother — and the government will take my kids. So what am I supposed to do?"

To get anywhere at all we have to first define and understand — locate — those invisible walls, and listen carefully and respectfully to the voices that manage to pierce through the cracks. Those voices provide their own analysis of how the society works. As a prisoner in jail told me:

"In the schools I found there was no equality there. If you're the son of a coal miner, the teachers pay no attention to you; if you're the son of a doctor, they'll help you all they can. Most kids have some trouble with school work, but you're not helped as equals. You sure notice that when you're a kid. You get told by everybody to get A's. Then when you start getting all D's, that really does something to you. You get pushed to the back of the class and you feel you don't belong, that you shouldn't be there, you feel awful as a kid but you don't know what to do. It's very bad, you start going downhill."

A young girl in a self-help group hesitantly described a different form of powerlessness:

"The incest usually happened when my dad came home from the bar. He'd be drunk and he'd come into the room and like we'd be in bed most of the time when he came home, because we knew he'd be drunk. So we'd go to bed and he'd come into the room and he'd sit on my bed and he'd put his hands on my breasts and my privates and I'd just — I'd wake up and I'd be really scared. And upset about it. And I'd wonder, well, what's going to happen? I don't want this to happen — and then he'd climb

under the covers and start committing the incest and I'd tell him to stop — that it hurt — leave me alone — that I didn't like it — but he just wouldn't go away."

As painful as it might be, once we begin to listen, to talk, to see things more clearly, we can begin to start rebuilding, from the bottom up, rather than papering over the cracks.

This bottom-up process has begun. It receives support and encouragement from individual activists and social movements. Professors Yvonne Howse and Harvey Stalwick, both from Saskatchewan, call on social workers to practice "participatory alignment" — that is, to listen carefully to what disempowered women and men are saying, and then to join on their side in their efforts to liberate themselves.[53] A heartening message — confident voices calling on social programs to change and be strengthened — also comes from Aboriginal leaders, women's groups, anti-racist advocates, AIDS workers, people with disabilities, refugee groups, gay and lesbian networks, and a host of other consumer and community organizations related to social services.

A basic part of anti-oppression social work depends on clarifying the meaning and nature of *oppression*. Mullaly, author of *Structural Social Work*, points out: "Everyone suffers frustration, restrictions and hurt. What determines oppression is when these happen to a person not because of individual talent, merit or failure, but because of his or her membership in a particular group or category of people."[54] When we reflect on what happens to people based on a series of inequalities created by the larger system, it is no accident that many people who are labelled one way or another as "inferior" end up in poverty and vulnerable to violence. One explanation links disadvantage to the various prejudices already described in this chapter. But it goes deeper.

I remember years ago, when I was a beginning social worker helping a variety of impoverished individuals, that the system's prejudices were blatant. It was clear that individuals were being mistreated either because of the colour of their skin, or because they were unemployed, or because of their membership in some other category. Yet what particularly struck me was the discovery that certain groups benefited from these prejudices and their resulting hardships. I began to realize how an affluent absentee landlord was benefiting from not repairing the broken plumbing in a low-income family's apartment. Or how a white corporate executive was profiting from low wages paid to Afro-Americans. The examples were plentiful. Mullaly puts it bluntly: "Oppression occurs because it benefits the dominant group."[55]

But what complicates matters is that each one of us has multiple characteristics. Each one of us has a particular cultural background, colour of skin, gender, class, sexual orientation, and age. Each one of us has particular abilities and other features. Some of these attributes serve to exclude us, while others might put us in a privileged position. As a result some part of each of us may experience oppression, while other parts might provide benefits. This mix of factors is important to sort out, not only for social workers but also for other helping professions, so that our communications will not create further barriers setting us off from the people we intend to help.

EMPOWERMENT IN SOCIAL WORK

The term *empowerment* has become a key for social workers, because it implies resistance to the various unjust power imbalances impacting upon clients, and it unmasks ways in which the system robs people of dignity. It puts an emphasis on client strengths, viewing them as allies in finding solutions to social stresses they face. That is how feminist counselling not only addresses immediate needs — for example, safe housing for women abused by men — but also explores larger questions, such as an awareness of abuse as being targeted not just towards a particular individual but towards a particular gender. Certain social services, such as transition houses, have helped abused or threatened women recognize that many other women experience a similar vulnerability to men who feel they should control "their" women. As a result women who have survived abuse can gain greater confidence and personal strength through a recognition of male responsibility in the larger context of changing gender relations.

Still, experienced helpers know: We cannot empower others.[56] Only the person who is disempowered can empower herself or himself. At best, social service providers can help set the stage for such empowerment. Instead of knowing what is best *for* the client, we can let go of the control inherent in the elitist version of professionalism. Instead of rushing in with our preconceived answers, we can listen, pause, learn from clients, and join with them in their struggles to alleviate distress.

A report on social services and child welfare from British Columbia describes many ways to set the stage for empowerment. In one case, after the social worker had listened and learned about an Aboriginal mother's struggle: "Her social worker provided her with the first glimmer that her struggles and those of her family and community were connected to generations of racism and oppression rather than caused by her own inabilities. She knew very little about her people's history before this encounter with a social worker and had internalized the racism and prejudices confronting her."[57]

By helping clients to empower themselves, social workers are revealing some of the previously invisible walls.

THE CHALLENGE FOR SOCIAL WORK

Social work is not only about patching up crises, but also about prevention. More specifically, it is about helping to prevent homelessness, hunger, poverty, and other social injustices — all of which connects to the idea of social change.

Today we receive mixed messages about the direction of social change in Canada. Due to the efforts of various social movements, some change is moving in a positive direction. For example, some professions and occupations are no longer closed to women. Land settlements are beginning to recognize Aboriginal claims to certain territories. In 1999 the Supreme Court of Canada ruled that gay and lesbian couples have the same rights as heterosexual couples in qualifying for support payments when common-law relationships break down.[58] Such examples suggest that our society is moving towards at least somewhat greater equality.

At the same time, and largely because of behind-the-scenes efforts by privileged groups, other changes are pushing us towards greater inequality. An example of this is the move to a more regressive tax system. In addition, the business sector's constant demands for tax concessions have resulted in companies paying less and less tax. In 1955 corporate taxes represented 25 per cent of all federal revenue. By 1973 they had fallen to 17 per cent, and by 1996 they were at 12 per cent of federal revenues.[59] At the same time the tax burden has shifted onto middle-income and low-income Canadians.

Given these simultaneous crosscurrents of social change, how can we tell which is the main direction of social change at any given time? One key way is to look at whether the gap between the rich and poor is getting wider (oppressive direction) or narrowing (progressive direction). In Canada the gap is widening. Research into market income — that is, income from sources such as salaries, and returns on investments, but excluding all government transfers — indicates: "In 1973, the top 10% of families with children under 18 earned an average income 21 times higher than those at the bottom. . . . By 1996, the top 10% made 314 times as much as the families in the bottom 10%."[60]

Meanwhile, the government programs that soften such gaps have been cut back. The main direction of social change in Canada is therefore towards greater inequality, more limited social justice, and greater hardships. This regressive direction means that the welfare state is failing dismally in its promises to protect the well-being of everyone in Canada.

The role and practice of social work are symptomatic of this failure — and of the continuing human loss. Although as a teacher of social work and as an experienced helper I am sympathetic towards at least some of the intentions — and some of the successes — of social work, I feel at the same time that it is vitally important to take a critical look at social work as a profession and as a method of intervention in the "cases" of people in need.

Challenging social services means helping to make them more democratically accountable. By democratic I mean making social programs subject to ongoing review by those most closely affected: both clients and social service providers. Democratizing social work also means becoming aware of power within client-social worker relationships, so that we can transform these relationships into more egalitarian and mutual methods of communicating. The general public must also be included in this process, so that everyone involved can have a more effective voice in shaping the future.

Decades of repeated cuts to social programs have taken their toll. Those most hurt have been the most vulnerable and the poorest of the poor. Along the way, social services have become members of the walking wounded, barely surviving the savage attacks orchestrated by business leaders and legalized by legislatures. As a result social workers have been left without the tools necessary to help their clients. A study has verified what social workers across the country know: "The lack of relevant resources that fit the particular needs of the family was one of the most frequently identified barriers to effective practice."[61]

So while clients experience a multitude of oppressions, social workers experience an environment that has become oppressive in its own way. Simply put, affluent and privileged elites are challenging social services to self-destruct.

At the same time, progressive grassroots networks and social movements are fighting back. They recognize that the types of changes being pushed by governments and their business sponsors are harmful and morally bankrupt. Such awareness is contributing to attempts by social workers to address the root causes of the exploitation and oppressive conditions that permeate our society.

This "anti-oppression" approach challenges social work practice to "walk the talk." These new and better forms of social work are emerging alongside other practical initiatives from grassroots networks and social movements. They are calling for a restructuring of our major institutions, so that they become answerable to the public rather than being strictly controlled from the top down. Without such transformation today's social problems will be perpetuated endlessly into the future, with band-aids being busily applied by a profession that should know better. The evidence of the need for such a transformation — as well as for a variety of progressive responses to this need — is in the following pages.

2 THE ROOTS:
EARLY ATTITUDES

Mary Dowding 514 King St. E. and husband. No children. says can't get work. fancy they don't want it. no reason why they should be in want. Recommend a little starvation until self-help engendered, probably drink.*

— from notes of a volunteer visitor, Toronto 1882

WHEN I WAS STILL a student in social work, the history of the welfare state was presented as a process of evolution whereby society gradually recognized its responsibility to the "less fortunate" or "underprivileged." Perhaps most Canadians also share this view about how social programs emerged. A closer examination, however, reveals a much different picture.

The professional relationship in social work — the historically developed link between help-giver and help-receiver — has been fraught with ambivalence from the earliest times. Historically the work of "charity" was a matter for churches and religious orders, whose teachings extolled the virtue of compassion towards the poor — while at the same time proclaiming that poverty was divine punishment for earthly sins. Compassion was key in the work of Vincent de Paul, who organized ways for people to visit the sick, the dying, the prisoners, and the poor in seventeenth-century France. The other side of the coin was state aid to the "needy," which took a decidedly punitive approach. It was as if needy people had committed a crime.

English law in 1531, certainly, was blunt about what would happen to the unemployed. A person considered to be one of society's ill-begotten group of "idle poor, ruffelers, sturdy vagabonds and valiant beggars" was "to be tied to the end of a cart naked and to be beaten with whips throughout the same market-town or other place til his

---

* Quoted in James Pitsula, "The Emergence of Social Work in Toronto," in *Journal of Canadian Studies,* vol.14, no.1 (Spring 1979), p.36.

body be bloody by reason of such whipping." As if this was not enough, this unfortunate would "also have the upper part of the grissle of his right ear clean cut off."[1] The poor in this case were far from being "blessed" in the eyes of the state.

At the same time as brutality was inflicted on jobless men, women were persecuted for being suspected of witchcraft. The accusation was focused mainly on spinsters and widows (that is, those women without male "protection") who might try to achieve a degree of personal independence. In doing this they posed a threat to the monopoly of male authority in intellectual, moral, economic, and religious spheres. Mary Daly documents the belief current in 1486 that "All witchcraft comes from carnal lust which is in women insatiable."[2] This belief, combined with the suspicion that some women were in league with the devil, served to justify witch-hunts and the subsequent torture and killings of large numbers of women.[3]

In time English law softened. Instead of being beaten and mutilated, the unemployed (or the "able-bodied" as they were called) were imprisoned and forced to work in jail-like institutions called houses of correction, "There to be straightly kept, as well in diet as in work, and also punished from time to time."[4] Influenced by the church, the state was somewhat less harsh to the "impotent poor," that is, the deserted mothers with children, the blind, the "lame," the "demented," the old, and the sick. These unfortunates could in seventeenth-century England receive limited assistance from officials who were called the "overseers" of the poor and who had been appointed to their positions by justices of the peace or magistrates. Two centuries later this division between worthy and unworthy poor remained, with both groups often ending up in workhouses or poorhouses, which had replaced the houses of correction. Charles Dickens attacked these workhouses in his novel *Oliver Twist*.

Mimi Abramovitz examined the impact of U.S. social welfare policy on the lives of women from colonial times to the present. Her book *Regulating the Lives of Women* notes that a patriarchal standard about what women should or should not do "has been used to distinguish among women as deserving or undeserving of aid since colonial times."[5]

In Canada, governments imported the traditions of France and England. While Quebec's government left it to the Catholic church to provide assistance and education to the poor, the colonial administration in the Maritimes saw to the construction of a workhouse in 1759, where "for many years whipping, shackling, starvation, and other necessary inducements were used to correct the behaviour of the idle, vagrant, or incorrigible inmates."[6] There were also public auctions of paupers. In 1816 in the Upper Canada village of Delaware, an indigent widow was auctioned off to the lowest bidder.[7] What happened was that paupers were "boarded out" in a sort of foster-home system. The auction was to see who would charge the municipality *least* for their keep; the successful bidder would expect to more than make up his cost by the work he would get out of the pauper.

Allan Irving, a social historian at the University of Toronto, has documented the introduction of welfare to Upper Canada in the 1830s by Sir Francis Bond Head, the lieutenant-governor, who believed that "workhouses should be made repulsive . . . if any would not work for relief, neither he should eat."[8] Although workhouses were not developed everywhere in English Canada, the local jails served the same purpose: "Jails became a type of poorhouse — a catch-all for a variety of social problems — the homeless poor, the insane, the offenders, both petty and serious, young and old."[9]

This history of Canada's responses to the poor and less fortunate evolved on the heels of the horrific dispossession of Aboriginal peoples. A 1992 report issued by the British Columbia government states:

> Europeans did not only bring cultural chauvinism to North America. They also brought concepts of land use and ownership that thinly veiled the most systematic theft of land in the history of human existence. Because Europeans had a view of Nature as a thing to be brought under human control, lands that were not so dominated were considered unused. Coupled with that view was the concept of private land ownership. Consequently, "undeveloped" land was unused land and unused land was unowned land. Based on this cultural justitivation, Europeans were to engage in, and condone, a violation of their own international laws regarding the relations between nations. They confiscated virtually all the territories of the Aboriginal Nations of North America.[10]

Colonialism, racism, and exploitation not only shattered the economic self-sufficiency of First Nations, but also created havoc with their communal and family life:

> Under the authority of the Indian Act, the federal government established a system of residential schools for our people and enforced attendance and residency in those schools. The government's goal in creating them was to separate our people from our culture, and to instill European culture values in us. This was to be accomplished by creating the

greatest possible separation between our children and their extended families, minimizing the opportunities of our cultural values being passed on to our children. For many victims of the residential school system, not only were cultural values lost, but the experience of normal family relationships and the natural process of parenting were lost as well. In their place was substituted an example of child care characterized by authoritarianism, often to the point of physical abuse, a lack of compassion, and, in many cases, sexual abuse.[11]

The cruelty of European authorities towards First Nations was echoed by England's treatment of its poorer citizens. England in the nineteenth century had brutal factory conditions, including long hours of child labour. Trade unions were illegal, women had no vote, and the living conditions of the working class were abysmal. The owners of industry and commerce felt that it was their superior moral character, not their economic structures, that was responsible for the widening gap between rich and poor, men and women, whites and non-whites. Such was their smugness, that some of the well-to-do genuinely felt that the pauper class needed only proper moral instruction to be raised out of their woeful condition.

If poor men had few rights during this era, women were seen as chattels, or as the property of men, with no separate existence of their own. Pat Thane summarizes: "If the husband entered the workhouse, the wife would have no choice but to follow. A destitute wife could be refused entry to the workhouse if her husband would not enter, or [could be refused] permission to leave if he would not leave. If a male pauper was officially classified 'not able-bodied,' so was his wife, whatever her personal physical condition."[12]

Just as the position of the poor was a subordinate one, the same was true of people of colour. During an age when many people still supported slavery, there were ample theories to justify assumptions about the superiority of the upper class and indeed of the growing middle class, and the "natural rights" of the men in these classes to subordinate others.

One form of justification was the growing emphasis on "scientific thinking," which by the nineteenth century was used to explain why people occupied different ranks and status. Theories such as the survival of the fittest, with arguments about the extinction of certain animal species and the continuation of other species, were applied to thinking about people and economic status. Aristocratic men, as a consequence, were viewed as the "fittest," possessing the most desirable of human traits. This group of "superior" beings included men rather than women, whites rather than non-whites, the physically healthy rather than the sick, property owners rather than servants. The evidence for the aristocracy's "moral superiority" was, presumably, their extraordinary wealth and their ability to have their commands carried out.[13]

Conversely, it followed that the poor and the powerless possessed the least desirable traits. Those who were paupers, due to either illness or physical disability, or to old age, low-paying jobs, or unemployment, became viewed as "inferior" — a designation still very much with us to this day.

Social progress was seen as the promotion of the most desirable of human traits. Since the traits of the poor were considered not worth preserving, it was logical for Thomas Malthus, writing in the early nineteenth century, to conclude that no aid whatsoever should be given to the have-nots. He felt that if all relief were withheld, either the poor would develop proper moral qualities to equip them for survival, or they would die. In short, the poor, Malthus argued, should be abandoned and "nature" allowed to take its course. True, mass death would follow, but such a fate would be borne by the poor as "evils which were absolutely irremediable, [which] they would bear with the fortitude of men, and the resignation of Christians."[14]

While such prescriptions may have sounded perfectly "natural" to those who possessed abundant wealth, they were not exactly welcomed by the potential victims. In any case these more extreme ideas and programs were not implemented because most of the poor (including, especially, women and children) were needed and exploited as factory workers. Their labour was indispensable to the very same system that was keeping them poor. And with servants and women in the private sphere, their sexual and domestic servicing of their masters made the Malthusian logic too ludicrous to be acted upon.

The brutalities of the workhouses in England brought agitation for change by the working class and reformers in England. But a Royal Commission, established in 1834 to study the conditions of the poor, strongly recommended the continuation of workhouses for the poor, including the continuation of their harsh conditions. The reason the commissioners gave: "Every penny bestowed, that tends to render the condition of the pauper more eligible than that of the independent laborer, is a bounty on indolence and vice."[15] The Royal Commission believed it had discovered a way both to aid the needy and protect the system. It would accomplish this by extending benefits to the poor at a level that was clearly less than the wage of the poorest-paid employee. There was to be no room for questioning whether the lowest wage was a fair wage. The net effect was to legitimate these lowest wages by focusing on the incentive of the working poor. In addition, this approach also created the illusion of freedom. The poor were to be given "choices." Work at abysmal wages, or enter the workhouse, or die of starvation.

To implement that report, six hundred more workhouses were built throughout England between 1834 and 1850.[16] It was the kind of thinking, fashioned by men of privilege, that today still haunts our social services and influences how helping professionals see their work and their relations with clients.

SOCIAL WORK: THE BEGINNINGS

In the late nineteenth century, when social work began as an embryonic profession in London, the main movers of charity accepted the established division between worthy and unworthy poor. There was a certain sympathy for the worthy poor, but for the unworthy — the able-bodied poor or the unemployed — it was still felt that the full rigour of the workhouse should be applied. Welfare state expansion tended to focus on these unworthy poor, often women: "unwed" mothers, "promiscuous" ladies, "irresponsible" wives, and so on. This left the worthy to be aided by the more traditional charitable organizations, outside the purview of the state.

The idea of more systematic social assistance took on an added sense of urgency when members of the affluent class noticed that socialism was becoming more appealing to their factory workers. Furthermore, the rich donors resented being pestered for donations to the many separate charities. Along with this resentment, there was the suspicion that many paupers were lying about their circumstances in an effort to collect greater amounts of relief from more than one charity.

As a result, a new organization was formed in 1869 in London: the Society for Organizing Charitable Relief and Repressing Mendicancy. It was soon renamed the Charity Organization Society (C.O.S.). It offered to co-ordinate the various charities and advocated a thorough investigation of each application for charity. Such co-ordination and investigation came to symbolize "scientific charity," which borrowed ideas from the emerging social sciences and from factory management. With these innovations, charity leaders held out the promise of imposing efficiency upon the charity process. Through investigation of applicants, fraudulent claims would be weeded out. And for the truly needy, the cause of their poverty would be discovered.

The C.O.S. approach became popular and spread to other locations. At the operational level, the C.O.S. provided "friendly visitors" from the upper class, women who volunteered to visit poor families. So much importance was placed on developing a co-operative, helpful relationship between the help-giver and the help-receiver that it was the relationship itself that came to be viewed as the best form of assistance to the poor. Not that these well-off philanthropists expected the pauperized masses to rise above their wretched state. The goal of friendly visiting was to provide paupers with a life of dignity, but only within the confines of their continuing poverty. And since the C.O.S. leaders believed that financial aid would be wasted on the poor, their motto became "Not alms, but a friend."

The very organization of the C.O.S. reflected the subordinate position of women. Although most of the visitors busily assessing the means and morals of the poor were women, the C.O.S. was led and controlled by men. In fact, there was only one woman on its first council. The men, as Jennifer Dale and Peggy Foster put it, "were happy to inaugurate areas of work for women" in which the women "could in effect be the helpmates of men."[17]

Conveniently, for rich white men at least, this solution to poverty's problems was inexpensive. It also nicely camouflaged the connection between their growing wealth and the subordinate status of women, poor men, and non-white unfortunates. Happily for the rich, friendly visitors confirmed their own views about being superior mortals and gave them a clear conscience about their relationship to the poor.

In the late nineteenth century the C.O.S. was transplanted to North America.[18] The following advice was given to friendly visitors on how to develop co-operative, helpful relationships with the poor: "You go in the full strength and joy and fire of life; full of cheer and courage; with a far wider knowledge of affairs; and it would be indeed a wonder if you could not often see why the needy family does not succeed, and how to help them up."[19] Given the assumption that the poor were morally inferior, it was logical that assistance became defined as moral advice on how to uplift the poor into becoming better individuals. It was conceded that as time went on morally uplifted individuals might even escape their poverty.

Throughout this period the personal link between help-giver and help-receiver was maintained even while the message shifted from the previous religious uplift to moral uplift. With the emergence of social work, the content of the message would change again, but the centrality of the relationship between professional and client would remain.[20]

Social workers, however, did not directly replace the well-to-do volunteer. There was an intermediate step, stemming from the nature of the C.O.S. Again, at the operational level, the C.O.S. format consisted not only of wealthy volunteers, but also of paid employees called "agents" who were often from the working class.[21] These "agents" were poorly paid and low-status technicians. Initially they were few in number, but as the quantity of cases grew and far exceeded the number of volunteers, more agents were hired and they all carried larger parts of the workload. This group of employees was the forerunner of the modern social worker.

In Canada the C.O.S. influenced how charity was dispensed during the nineteenth century. For example, in Toronto, before someone could receive charity (fuel or groceries) from the municipality's main charity organization, a visitor went to the applicant's home and conducted an investigation. These visitors were volunteer business and professional men who recommended whether to grant or withhold relief. As seen from the comfortable position of the visitor, poverty could be avoided by anyone who really wanted to shake it off. As a result the "help" offered often consisted of withholding material aid. This punitive approach was rejected by the early social workers who took over from the volunteers in the 1910s and 1920s.

Many of these early social workers were women who were finding an outlet for their creative energies outside the home. Carol Baines, a social work educator at Ryerson Polytechnic University, writes about how women's caring for others in the home and community influenced social work just prior to the turn of the twentieth century:

> The unpaid work of women as members of voluntary organizations, coupled with the poorly paid work of church deaconesses and social service workers, expedited the development of services for poor women and children through city missions and fledgling social service organizations. These institutions assumed a range of social service roles as they attempted to put in place a feminine vision of a caring society. In promoting an ethic of care, women were fund-raisers, managers, planners and policy-makers as well as providers of concrete services to poor women and children. A maternal mission of service and a feminine consciousness united these women as they formed networks of support and alliances.[22]

Baines points out that this caring was seen as women's "natural work" and therefore unvalued. She also describes how a move towards social work professionalism at the turn of the twentieth century meant more reliance on male supervisors and more specialization, and less emphasis on support networks with other women.[23] These early social agencies found themselves answerable to wealthy male philanthropists or politicians. The result, according to Dale and Foster, was that "the new professions were made up of middle-class women who were very much involved in the social control of working class mothers."[24] Meanwhile, Aboriginal peoples received little or nothing of these "benefits," but were controlled on Indian reservations by white Indian agents.

This social control was reflected in the attitudes of Canada's early social workers. Although less punitive than the friendly visitors, they did not support the idea of government increasing financial aid to the poor. In the 1920s and 1930s Canadian social workers opposed measures such as family allowances out of a fear that the result would be an increase in the family size of an "undesirable" class of people. As one social worker stated at the time, people who earned low wages were "frequently physically and mentally unfit" and therefore certainly not to be trusted.[25]

The model adopted in social work, as social historian Terry Copp puts it, was "stern charity, charity designed to be as uncomfortable and demeaning as possible." Copp analyses the case of Montreal, which in 1901 was home to a great variety of charitable institutions organized along ethnic and religious lines: "fifteen houses of refuge, thirteen outdoor relief agencies, fourteen old age homes, eleven orphanages, eighteen 'moral and educational institutions,' and more than a score of other miscellaneous charitable agencies."[26]

Most thinkers on social questions at the time thought that the proper role of the state was to be minimal — to maintain public institutions for the insane, the criminal, and the "absolutely unfit." Those who were simply poor or unemployed or "handicapped" in some way were to be left to the charitable institutions or, more likely, to their own devices. The prevailing attitude was that most of the poor who, for instance, resorted to begging were out-and-out frauds, and that it was harmful to aid these people.[27]

Along the same lines, when the Depression created massive unemployment in the 1930s, social work leaders were suspicious of granting relief payments to the poor. One leader, Charlotte Whitton, argued that instead of paying money to needy parents, the state should remove children from their homes. She believed that many of the mothers were unfit as parents, and so: "The dictates of child protection and sound social work would require cancellation of allowance, and provision for the care of the children under guardianship and authority."[28]

There was also fear. At a January 1932 meeting one of the local branches of the Canadian Association of Social Workers reported: "Social workers are paid by the capitalist group, for the most part, in order to assist the under-privileged group. Thus organized support of political issues would be very difficult if not dangerous . . . because of the danger of attempting too radical changes, since we are paid by the group who would resent such changes most."[29]

Despite such resistance by many social workers, the expansion of the welfare state occurred in Canada due to several converging factors. The dislocation during and after the First World War — with the need for support both of injured soldiers and of families left behind — brought some initial forays into expanding state intervention. A greater force was increasing labour turmoil and worker dissatisfaction with brutally unfair conditions, as the urban population grew and industrialization continued. In the first three decades of the century, as Copp writes:

> All of the accepted norms of society were being called into question by the growing complexity and disorder of the industrial system. Montreal was being transformed into a sprawling ugly anthill. Frequent strikes and the growth of labour unions seemed to foreshadow class warfare on a European scale. . . . The fundamental social problem was poverty, massive poverty, created by low wages and unemployment. For individuals, direct assistance limited hunger and prevented starvation, but the small section of the working class which regularly came into contact with organized charity was too often confronted with the "alms of friendly advice" and too seldom helped to achieve security.[30]

In 1919 Winnipeg experienced a general strike when thirty thousand workers left their jobs to fight for the principle of collective bargaining, better wages, and the improvement of working conditions. In this case the state proved only too eager to intervene, refusing to talk with unions but sending in Mounted Police and federal troops. The state clearly came down on the side of the manufacturers, bankers, and businessmen, and revealed a distinct distaste for ideas and actions involving workers' rights.

Police forces were also used against the institutions of the Aboriginal peoples — who were portrayed as savages lacking in culture and possessing no worthy structures of their own in the first place. The

House of Commons Special Committee on Indian Self-Government offered an illustration of this in its 1985 report:

> The Iroquois (as they were known by the French) or Six Nations (as the English called them) or the Haudenosaunee (*People of the Longhouse,* as they called themselves) have a formalized constitution, which is recited every five years by elders who have committed it to memory. It provides for a democratic system in which each extended family selects a senior female leader and a senior male leader to speak on its behalf in their respective councils. Debates on matters of common concern are held according to strict rules that allow consensus to be reached in an efficient manner, thus ensuring that the community remains unified. A code of laws, generally expressed in positive admonitions rather than negative prohibitions, governs both official and civil behaviour. . . .
>
> The Canadian government suppressed the Haudenosaunee government by jailing its leaders and refusing to give it official recognition. In 1924, the council hall at the Six Nations Reserve was raided by the Royal Canadian Mounted Police (RCMP). All official records and symbols of government were seized and have never been returned.[31]

With the Depression of the 1930s, working-class militancy spawned a series of protests, including the famous On-To-Ottawa Trek, when four thousand angry workers marched across Canada to present their grievances to parliament. Left-wing political groups were openly calling for an end to capitalism.

As a result of these kinds of opposition, leading industrialists began to grant concessions to the labour movement's advocacy for old age pensions and unemployment insurance. Reluctantly they supported some expansion of the state into social welfare, provided it was understood that capitalism itself would not be threatened. Sir Charles Gordon, president of the Bank of Montreal, wrote to Prime Minister R.B. Bennett in 1934 to support the idea of unemployment insurance: "May I suggest to you that for our general self-preservation some such arrangement will have to be worked out in Canada and that if it can be done soon so much the better."[32] Not everyone in power agreed, but enough of them were persuaded to endorse an expansion of social welfare. When the federal government decided it was time to adopt unemployment insurance and other social programs, the same prime minister reminded business leaders why an expansion of the welfare state was necessary: "A good deal of pruning is sometimes necessary to save a tree and it would be well for us to remember there is considerable pruning to be done if we are to save the fabric of the capitalist system."[33]

To further camouflage this "pruning" of the capitalist system, business and government officials began to argue that our civilization had developed a capacity for compassionate responses to the needy, that "humane values" constituted the foundation of Canadian society, and that social programs were the manifestations of the society's concern for helping one's "fellow man" (they were perhaps less certain about women).

Within this rationale, political support was consolidated for Canada's social security programs. The first old age pension was introduced in 1927. Its payment of $20 a month was subject, as Dennis Guest puts it, "to a strict and often humiliating means test — proof that poor-law attitudes still influenced Canadian political leaders in the 1920s."[34]

In following years, workers' compensation for injuries, public assistance, child welfare, and public health programs were created or expanded. The 1950s and 1960s saw a substantial growth in social programs, with the federal government playing a key role in the funding of new, universal, old age security payments, an expanded unemployment insurance program, an evolving medicare approach, and additional social services geared to low-income Canadians.

Outspoken social workers also identified the ever-present opposition to social welfare. Bertha Capen Reynolds, a radical social worker in the United States, wrote in 1950:

> We have noted that the interests which oppose really constructive social work constitute only a small minority of the whole population, but influence a much larger sector through their ownership of newspaper chains and control of radio broadcasting. Many hard-working folk who sincerely want people in trouble to have a fair break are frightened by propaganda to the effect that the country is being ruined by taxes to support a "welfare state," and that people on relief are "chiselers" and social workers "sob sisters."[35]

Yet even the years of welfare-state expansion saw severe shortages of social services. Bridget Moran, a social worker based in Prince George, B.C., during the 1950s and 1960s, has documented her experience. In 1963 she wrote to the premier of British Columbia:

> I could not face my clients for yet another year without raising my voice to protest for them the service they are going to get from me. I have no excuse except desperation for what follows. . . . Every day, here and across the province social workers are called upon to deal with seriously disturbed children. We have no psychiatrists, no specially-trained foster parents, no receiving or detention homes to aid us. We place children in

homes that have never been properly investigated, we ignore serious neglect cases because we have no available homes.[36]

Partly in response to such advocacy, social services expanded. This growth was also a response to the new sense of guiding "humane values" and of the need for a "modern" nation to make steady progress towards a just society. Social workers, it was said, viewed themselves as having an essential role to "ensure that citizens will have access to those materials, services and resources of society that will permit them to develop their potential as individuals."[37]

Critics, however, have a different point of view. They argue that the development of beliefs about helping are expressions of the system rather than challenges to it, that the welfare state was and is shaped by capitalism, colonialism, patriarchy, and other power relations based on inequality. One team of social work researchers states: "Male supremacist ideas influenced the lines along which capitalism developed. To preserve the basis of male supremacy in the family it became necessary for men to discriminate against women in the labour market. Women became a vulnerable and manipulatable segment of the labour force used in factories."[38] These researchers also argue that "Forms of discrimination against Blacks and women in the employment sector are similar": "Both groups are confined to low-skilled, low-paying jobs, wage differentials for similar work, separate lines of seniority and advancement, exclusion from managerial and supervisory jobs, etc. All of these can be seen as methods of keeping each group in its 'proper place.'"[39]

But social services provided by the state are more than a means of social control. They also represent battles fought and won over the years by working people. The welfare state stemmed in part from a militant labour movement and a consequent fear of revolution that prompted concessions to a population needing to be convinced that capitalism was capable of caring for its social casualties and of curbing its worse excesses. In this sense the welfare state played the role of legitimizing a political and economic system under attack.

One early critic, U.S. community organizer Saul Alinsky, argued over fifty years ago that social workers "come to the people of the slums under the aegis of benevolence and goodness, not to organize the people, not to help them rebel and fight their way out of the muck — NO! They come to get these people 'adjusted'; adjusted so they will live in hell and like it too."[40]

An extreme view, perhaps, but one shared by many critics who see the traditional values of the past — the values of the poor laws, for example — simply perpetuated under the guise of modern professionalism.

The new forms of social assistance represented, as Terry Copp puts it, the middle class's attempt "to devise plans to re-organize society without altering any of the fundamental economic relationships."[41] In the process the middle class not only ensured a measure of gainful employment to some of its members but also, through the emergence of this new profession, social work, seemed to offer indisputable proof that we do live in a caring and just society.

3

SCHOOLS OF ALTRUISM

Social workers are dedicated to the welfare and self-realization of human beings; to the development and disciplined use of scientific knowledge regarding human and societal behaviours; to the development of resources to meet individual, group, national and international needs and aspirations; and to the achievement of social justice for all. . . .
— Canadian Association of Social Workers, Code of Ethics

AN IMMENSE EMPHASIS on altruism pervades social work. Most students who enter social work have a strong desire to help others. In Canada over five thousand students a year attend about thirty schools of social work, and as a reason for choosing this course of study they frequently say, "I want to help people." There is a selfless quality that views the client's needs as priority for action.

In my own case, I was a foster child at the age of five and was later adopted. My childhood years were characterized by abrupt dislocation and a repressed sense of loss. With the help of some caring adults, I somehow managed to keep a sense of balance: so much so that in later years I was frequently able to offer emotional support to others. When I entered social work I felt I had found a haven of sanity in a world filled with conflict and injustices.

When I went to university, in the 1960s, most social work students were from the middle class. That situation has changed over the past thirty years. Today many students hold part-time jobs, many more are on student loans, and many of them graduate with debts that reach over $25,000.[1]

Still, the social work curriculum has a long history of being grounded in middle-class values, operating on a view of the system as acceptable and as working well in general. This tendency is being challenged, but until recently schools of social work saw themselves as turning out graduates who could fit nicely into social service organizations. Minor criticisms of social agencies and of training courses were tolerated, even welcomed. But there was also a high premium placed on students being able to carry out assignments with a minimum of conflict and dissatisfaction.

Writing about her student experiences in the masters of social work program at the University of Toronto, Joanne Darlaston says: "The 'mainstream' perspective presented in class is not objective. It is a white, middle class, heterosexual, able bodied, male perspective." When she spoke out in class, Darlaston says, she found that she "often felt silenced." Her comments were "sometimes followed by quiet whispers 'there she goes again' or body language that implied lack of interest or irritation."[2]

Most social work students and teachers used to be female. There was a marked shift in this after World War II and, as professor Joan Turner points out:

> By the later 1960s and the early 1970s, social workers were keenly working to improve their status as professionals, looking to medicine, psychiatry and law as models of successful (and, of course, male-based) professions. Without much thought to the sexism inherent in the move, schools of social work sought to recruit more male students and more male faculty. It was anticipated that the presence of more highly educated (Ph.D.) male educators in social work would enhance the status of the schools in the eyes of the university administrators and in the communities.[3]

The effect reinforced the tendency for men to hold senior positions. Today most of the heads of Canada's schools of social work are still men. A Task Force on the Status of Women established by the Canadian Association of Schools of Social Work in the 1980s saw a pattern of discrimination against women in social work education. More specifically, it found that women in schools of social work across Canada earned less, received fewer promotions, and enjoyed less job security than did their male counterparts.[4] This pattern was confirmed by Colleen Lundy and Gillian Walker of Carleton University. They found that "women continue to face what has been called a 'chilly climate' or 'poisoned environment' in academia when it comes to sexual and gender harassment," and "The resistance of a male ordered academy to scholarly approaches which include gender issues and women's voices is borne out in the experiences of women who took part in our survey."[5]

Despite the inequalities in their structures, schools of social work continue to attract students who genuinely want to become professional helpers. This attraction is common to other human service professions. Whether it is nursing patients back to health or teaching children to read and write, or understand algebra, a deep sense of satisfaction often comes from one person helping another. Some researchers suggest that altruism has a biological basis and that mutual aid may be as much an instinct towards survival as the need to locate food.[6]

Psychoanalyst Erich Fromm, differentiating between selfishness and self-love, offers another approach. According to Fromm, selfish people are interested only in themselves, want everything for themselves, feel no pleasure in giving but only in taking. By contrast, self-love allows you to love and care for others, as you do for yourself. Caring for others can provide an ultimate meaning to life: "The affirmation of one's own life, happiness, growth, freedom, is rooted in one's capacity to love," Fromm writes. And, "Giving is more joyous than receiving, not because it is a deprivation, but because in the act of giving is the expression of my aliveness."[7] Perhaps because such "giving" does strike a responsive chord, it has become fashionable to advertise the "helpful" side of our major institutions. And so we hear about the "helpful" bank offering to arrange our loans or about the U.S. military "helping to bring democracy" to any number of countries.

What about social work help? What makes it unique? Schools of social work mix in material from psychology and psychiatric theory, offering a gateway to the world of personal motives, subconscious drives, family dynamics, pathological responses, and on and on. It is exciting stuff. Students can and do apply these concepts to themselves, their peers, and to others. But it doesn't end there. There's also the focus on the societal level. Materials and approaches from sociology, political science, and economics are selected, condensed, and applied to social welfare. Students learn about various social security schemes, law-making processes, and political pressures. Again, it is heady stuff. And with Canadian governments spending billions per year on health and social programs, including social security payments, students quickly get the feeling that they have arrived in the big leagues. Students can also feel important because they see they are jumping into an arena connected with one of the biggest issues on the national agenda — social welfare reform.

The standard range of study provides the foundation for what is usually deemed the "primary" area of social work training. In this primary area, attention is concentrated on training students to develop practical, professional skills. As students proceed with their training, their desire to help others becomes focused more strictly around acquiring practical skills. "I want to learn how I can conduct better interviews," says one. "I want to improve my assessment skills," says another. "I'd like to learn more about family therapy."

Most students want to learn how to do counselling with individuals and families. A minority have a major interest in research, agency administration, community work, or policy analysis. This reflects the reality of the job market. The majority of social work graduates become employed in the provision of direct services to individuals and families.[8] To tailor students for such jobs, social work training includes instruction on how to listen to and clearly understand what clients are saying, how to observe non-verbal cues, how to get clients to communicate their thoughts and, especially, their feelings. Such skills are sometimes referred to as "professional relationship skills." A standard text articulates the importance of these skills to social work students: "Professional relationships between clients and social workers are the heart of social work practice. Social workers' ability to develop working relationships hinges on their interpersonal effectiveness and self-awareness. Social workers must be skillful in communicating empathy, genuineness, trustworthiness, respect and support."[9]

With this emphasis on professional relationship skills, social work has zeroed in on the psychology of human interaction, although increasingly attempts are being made to introduce political questions as a focus.

THE SOCIAL WORK CURRICULUM

Social work training needed a unifying theory or a framework that could make sense out of the variety of personal-environmental processes within the society. The answer, supposedly, was to be provided by *systems theory*.

Systems theory, still popular in social work textbooks, was developed by sociologists who had in turn adapted it from the physical sciences. According to the theory, individuals, families, neighbourhoods, workplaces, and other institutions are all examples of systems, all with their own boundaries within which they carry out their particular function. Each system is understood as being interdependent with the other systems that make up its environment. By such means as inputs, outputs, and feedback with its environment, each system is viewed as striving to retain sufficient equilibrium to grow and change to better carry out its functions. In other words, the survival and development of social systems are seen as hinging on stability — which invokes a social control function, so that the various parts can be better "integrated" into the larger order. For social work, systems theory has also been used as a way to understand interactions between clients, workers, and their respective environments.

Systems theory appeared to be an advance in thinking because it discouraged social workers from giving exclusive attention to the internal psyche of individual clients. But despite its promise it contains several flaws. For one thing, it ignores the power gap between social work professionals and clients. U.S. social critics Richard Cloward and Frances Fox Piven write:

> The systems theory approach invites social workers to view clients as "interacting" with a variety of "systems" in which we should ostensibly "intervene." The very blandness of the language denies any recognition of the realities of power. We learn that inmates "interact" with prisons; that mental patients "interact" with state mental hospitals; that recipients "interact" with welfare departments; that children "interact" with foster care agencies; that slum and ghetto dwellers "interact" with urban renewal authorities. But most clients do not "interact" with these systems, they are oppressed by them.[10]

But while the proponents of systems theory concede defects within the specific *subsystems* of our society, these same proponents are careful to avoid any suggestion that there may be fundamental flaws within the very core of the system. In other words, their theory allows social work students to consider how to help change a specific subsystem, but the reconstruction of the entire system is considered out of bounds.[11]

The consequent aversion to basic change serves to reinforce the widespread suspicion that large-scale radical change in our society must lead to state dictatorship. By contrast, there is a different school of thought within social work, a perspective held by a growing number of teachers who view the need for alternative structures to be based on the development of more democracy rather than less. This perspective also contains the yeast of altruism, but it is a form of altruism recognizing that real help will be stifled so long as there are built-in structures of inequality within a given society.[12]

At the operational level, this egalitarian approach to people — consumers and providers of social services — attempts to redefine social work practice. Such redefinition integrates the personal and political aspects of social problems and their remedies. This approach retains the importance of relationships but believes that relationships flowing in hierarchical patterns (top-down) are as ineffectual as those based on assumptions of moral superiority. Feminist social workers have pioneered ways of using this alternative form of practice. Helen Levine writes:

> Personal stress and distress are seen as a barometer, a kind of fever rating connected to the unequal and unhealthy structures, prescriptions and power relationships in women's lives. There is a rejection of the artificial split between internal feelings and external conditions of living and working, between human behaviour and structural context. A feminist approach to working with women involves weaving together personal and political issues as causes of and potential solutions to women's struggles. Women's troubles are placed within, not outside their structural context.[13]

Feminism is also challenging traditional social work research. As Sharon Taylor, a feminist activist and professor of social work at Memorial University of Newfoundland, puts it:

> Traditional research methods are "scientific," meeting criteria of objectivity, observability and measurability of empirical data, and using logical interpretation and explanation. Research developed through feminist process, in contrast, challenges assumptions about the nonattachment and objectivity of the researcher. Such research becomes contextual, participatory, inclusive, experiential, involved, socially relevant.[14]

Noting the importance of emotions, not only in knowledge-building but also in teaching, Taylor adds: "Feminist educators do not distance themselves from the sources of their knowledge, for they identify knowledge and its source as empowering. Traditional academics dismiss intuitive knowledge as primitive, but feminists are learning to listen to and trust their 'inner voice' as the source of women's wisdom." As well, feminist process includes administration: "Feminist process values shared leadership, consensus building and creating community. A feminist leads through facilitation, to enable others to make their contribution while simultaneously making their own."[15]

Despite a wide range of available feminist scholarship and activism, as Joan Gilroy of Dalhousie University's Maritime School of Social Work says, "The dominant models of theory and practice are inherently sexist and oppressive to women. . . . In spite of increased awareness of inequality and oppression, significant changes in social policies and services and in agency and professional practices are yet to occur."[16]

Similarly, major changes are yet to occur with respect to anti-racist social work. Dorothy Moore, professor at the same Maritime school, is an advocate for affirmative action in her school as a means of counteracting Nova Scotia's historic racism, which had excluded Aboriginals, Afro-Canadians, and Acadians from equal access to university education: "A school which simply concentrates on cross-cultural counselling and not on diversifying its student and faculty population, is only training dominant group members to 'social work' the oppressed — and therefore only reinforcing structural racism." But Moore recalls that in the early days many of her colleagues responded to affirmative action policy proposals with "outright resistance." They "held that it was not needed or that recruitment to the school was an inappropriate solution." Still, she persevered, giving informal leadership to the development of alliances both inside and outside of the school, which gradually did result in the adoption of affirmative action in the recruitment of students. Despite this, obstacles continue: "Affirmative action in theory can quietly become exclusion in fact, when barriers to admission are erected. Requirements such as the prior completion of some general university credits, supposedly to avoid possible problems of study skills, very effectively reduce the pool of eligible candidates from disadvantaged communities."[17]

While various schools are contesting admission and hiring practices, the social work curriculum on anti-racism remains limited. As Lena Dominelli observes about the situation in England, "Social work educators have done little to challenge the racism inherent in the theories and practice." As a social work educator, she observes that this "training does not prepare white students to be effective anti-racist practitioners in an ethnically diverse society. They are seldom actively encouraged to confront racism in either the classroom or their practice placements."[18] In the United States, social work educator Doman Lum examined professional journals over a recent twenty-five-year period, and concluded: "Cultural diversity has been largely neglected in practice journals and professional journals."[19] He also concludes that social work textbooks have also failed to explicitly include people of colour in social work practice.

Social work education has also provided a limited response to the needs of people with disabilities. According to the report of a discussion involving the Persons with Disabilities Caucus of the Canadian Association of Schools of Social Work: "Many participants had experienced social work education as devoid of content concerning people with disabilities."[20]

Similarly, when social work educator Brian O'Neill reported on interviews with thirty-seven gay men from eleven schools across Canada, he found that those men "perceived the climate within their schools of social work to be unsafe for open discussion of same-sex sexual orientation" and that the curriculum lacked "appropriate content on the topic."[21] While the general picture is bleak, a few schools are now addressing the prejudices, isolation, hopelessness, and fear experienced by lesbians, gays, and bisexuals. Jill Abramczyk, a graduate from Carleton University's School of Social Work, notes:

> If the learning environment is a safe and respectful one, teachers and students alike will feel more comfortable being themselves, being honest about who they are, whether lesbian or gay or heterosexual. Coming out is especially important for lesbians and gay men, whether teacher or student, who may otherwise be hiding or denying a very significant part of their lives. A safe, liberating and loving learning environment allows them to be true to themselves and each other.[22]

Professor Roopchand Seebaran of the University of British Columbia observes that some social work teachers "talk redistribution of power but hoard it to stay in control" in the classroom.[23] When students at York University's School of Social Work decided that they wanted to take the racial diversity of clients into account, one professor responded, "We're not going to discuss multiculturalism in this class!" Another professor said, "Social work is a North American practice suitable for everyone. . . . This is the way you talk to clients. You make eye contact with them, and you find out how they really feel."[24] A part-time student holding a full-time job in an agency pointed out that most of the clients there were not from European backgrounds. If you looked at those clients in the eye, she said, many of them would think you were being rude and they would feel threatened.

Ultimately the York social work students decided to do something about their learning situation. What triggered the revolt was not only what they saw as patronizing attitudes and a lack of respect on the part of the faculty for both students and clients, but also their sense that many faculty were far removed from the realities of practice within social services. They wondered: How relevant is this education for my future possibilities?

The York students had heard about a small network of activist social workers that I belong to. After York students contacted us, we met with them and listened to their grievances: They were demoralized and at least one was considering quitting social work. We listened, brainstormed, came up with tactics, and helped the students take action. Students documented their grievances in detail, then went above the school's director to the dean, giving him a copy of the grievances and offering to meet with him. He was appalled at the situation and cautiously supportive. The students initiated a petition, demanding changes within the school.

The school suddenly found itself on the defensive. The more conservative professors began intimidating student leaders, branding them "intellectual terrorists." In response student leaders met with a reporter from the campus newspaper and got swift and dramatic coverage.[25] Some of the professors tried to defend their position in an open letter to the newspaper. Our network responded with our own open letter. By now the school was scrambling to salvage some of its lost credibility, and students were no longer feeling as powerless. My guess is that the school's more sympathetic faculty probably had an internal showdown with the school's old guard, because the director left, others retired, and promising revisions were made in the school's mission statement and curriculum.

These positive results included a new curriculum, with courses focusing on an anti-discriminatory approach to social work. Narda Razack, who teaches one such course, says, "Students are encouraged to explore their role as both oppressor and oppressed in order to understand the context for working with a diverse population." She adds: "Teaching a course around oppression creates emotional and politically charged situations. . . . As a racial minority woman teacher, the tension is doubly uncomfortable for me, since I represent the group that faces forms of 'everyday racism.' "[26]

Razack talks to the class about her own "structural location" in society and works at building a measure of mutual respect and community spirit among her forty students. She notes that, based on student evaluations and feedback, "the outcome of such courses is generally positive," but some issues remain: Students display anger as well as guilt; the feelings of the minority students clash with the "subtly superior attitudes" of some classmates; and a few students have a "blatant disregard for change."[27]

The wider arena of Canadian social work education parallels the healthy ferment in these classrooms. For example, in June 1999 the annual meeting of the Canadian Association of Schools of Social Work approved new accreditation standards, which would apply to all schools of social work in Canada as a condition of being accredited by the national organization. The new standards include these points:

> The curriculum shall ensure that students achieve . . . an understanding and analysis of oppressions and healing of aboriginal peoples and implications for social policy and social work practice with aboriginal peoples in the Canadian context . . . transferable analysis and practice skills pertaining to the origins and manifestations of social injustice in Canada, and the multiple and intersecting bases of oppression, domination and exploitation.[28]

Still, we should be careful not to assume that the move to adopt the right words necessarily means action. Those words are a helpful first step — not insignificant in moving towards social progress — but significant change comes through implementation.

Despite the possibilities contained in practice aimed at optimizing egalitarian relationships and structures, social work education too often prefers to emphasize the more conventional assumptions, such as: Try to help your clients to adapt, to function "better," but, because social workers cannot by themselves produce social change, make no unrealistic claims about changing social conditions.

In this way the existing social structure is understood as "given." The professional task is viewed as helping people as much as possible within the confines of present institutional arrangements. One student said: *"We are taught that 'help' happens in the interaction between clients and systems. If we can strengthen that interaction, then things will get better. This doesn't deal with larger problems of inequalities and capitalism. We are taught to accept the larger structure."*

Despite the tolerance of systems theory for some reform, there is still an emphasis on the adjustment of the individual client or family to cope better within existing social conditions: shades of an earlier era.

So when government agencies establish their policies, procedures, and rules for providing aid to clients, social workers normally see it as their job to carry out these expectations. Similarly, students are trained to carry out what these agencies expect. This is one reason why there ends up being a fatal gap between social workers and the clients. For example, a group of clients were asked to address students at the University of British Columbia, and one of them recalled:

"When we told students in social work about our experiences, they were stunned. They figured it's a rainbow out there and all they have to do is say to clients 'I'm on your side.' But it's not that easy. They were

stunned to find that families on welfare were bitter, frustrated, and degraded. They didn't realize the strains, the hatred. Maybe they thought all clients liked social workers. They were surprised to hear about all those applications we're expected to fill out, all the lecturing we get about getting jobs. They didn't know that the jobs we could get pay so poorly they don't even cover the costs of day care and transportation. From my experience, social workers don't get down to the core — why children on welfare are feeling the way they are. Social workers are fast to blame the family but they don't go to the roots of these frustrations. And a lot of it has to do with not having enough money."

Although being on welfare may be foreign to most students, this is not always the case. Some social work students do come from low-income families. Others have been through child welfare institutions. A small number are from First Nations. Some are people with disabilities or from recent immigrant populations. Nevertheless, despite this mixture of backgrounds, the general tone in many schools of social work remains one of supporting the status quo. A student reflected on this tone: *"The school didn't deal with cultural differences or about differences in cultural attitudes. We didn't touch on Native, immigrant or refugee issues. . . . We are taught to work within the system and don't create too many waves or you'll be seen as unprofessional."*

ABORIGINAL CIRCLES IN THE CLASSROOM

Although Canadian social work education has its lingering legacy as a white and middle-class domain, Aboriginal approaches have been added to more and more curriculums. For many years the Saskatchewan Indian Federated College has had Aboriginal social work educators teach Aboriginal students. Laurentian University in Sudbury, Ontario, offers its social work education in three programs or streams: Aboriginal, French, and English. Schools of social work are building new links to First Nations in the Maritimes as well as in other parts of Canada.

Some social work educators are learning from Aboriginal ways of helping. For example, during the annual conferences of the Canadian Association of Schools of Social Work in Calgary in the 1990s a respected Ojibwe elder, Barbara Riley, presented the caring and sophisticated insights of the Anishnabek Traditional Counselling Wheel:

Unlike mainstream culture, spirituality is at the base of all (our) teachings and values. This view emphasizes balance, harmony and unity amongst all things — in particular within humankind and between each race. Aboriginal people are not an ethnocentric people. We are taught respect, kindness, generosity and humility. Because of our holistic world view, we see the interdependency, inter-relatedness and interconnectedness of all things among human beings, animals, plants, elements, and the universe.[29]

Aboriginal teaching circles invite participants to sit in a circle, and each person in rotation takes a turn at speaking. Barbara explained that no one should interrupt the person speaking. When it's your turn, you can choose not to speak. Barbara, as teacher or elder, began by speaking first, addressing the topic personally and politically and setting the tone. After everyone had a turn, Barbara, as teacher, made some concluding comments.

Strangely enough, though I had experienced Barbara's teaching a number of times and was deeply impressed, it never occurred to me to use learning circles in my own teaching until one day, when we were having supper after a meeting, Barbara asked me point blank: "Do you use learning circles in your teaching?" The question completely threw me, and I fumbled for an answer, finally coming out with, "No . . . um, I don't . . . I see it as belonging to your culture."

Barbara, not at all taken aback by my answer, said that in her experience the circles were an excellent way to teach self-discipline, respect, risking, humility, and caring for others. We talked about what I had learned from the circles she had led. She said: "You know, we can't do it all by ourselves. There are too few of us. We'd wear ourselves out running all over the country, doing workshops here, there, everywhere. Other races can help us. White people in my tradition are doers. And we can teach whites how to do it — for the good of all. But humility is important, and also acknowledging your teachers." She convinced me to introduce learning circles in my own teaching.

In recent years schools of social work in different parts of Canada have hired Aboriginal teachers. Fyre Jean Graveline, an Aboriginal social work educator, describes how she introduced an Aboriginal perspective to social work students:

> In most Aboriginal Traditions, prior to ceremony, procedures are followed in order to prepare the mind and the body to be receptive to knowledge and insight, which may come from anywhere. Smudging, the use of burning herbs for purifying space and one another, has many effects on the individual and collective psyche. It serves as a demarcation of time, notifying everyone that "Circle Time" is beginning. It is a signal for the mind to be still and in present time; it provides everyone in the group with a shared embodied experience. As the sweet-smelling smoke

encircles the area, it is easy to feel the calming presence of our plant sisters, entering and filling all of those present.[30]

Having participated in smudging at the opening of numerous circles led by Aboriginal teachers, I can attest to this "calming presence," which opens a pathway remarkably different from mainstream teaching-learning. Graveline points out the significance of telling personal stories in these circles: "Sharing 'personal' stories of oppression and change helps to promote the consciousness necessary for activism to occur. Collectivizing our understanding of oppressive experiences helps to depersonalize racist trauma and refocus our energy on an external target."[31]

Graveline's teaching provides ample evidence of changed consciousness. For example, one of her students, reflecting about Aboriginal circles, wrote about having "developed new ways of thinking aside from my white middle class perspectives. Most of all I have gained an understanding about my white privileges and how I can use my own voice to help change society's racist attitudes and actions." An Aboriginal student in Graveline's class reported, "As class ended tonight, I reflected on the wonderful experience that it was! I was so happy to finally be able to express my Native identity as part of my being. It was the first time that my Voice was actually being heard, not only by others but by myself."[32]

The circles also provide a springboard and support for social action. Graveline reports on student activism that included:

> challenging racial slurs with friends, family, co-workers and teachers; writing letters of protests to papers, magazines, companies, agencies and the School [of Social Work]; organizing and/or facilitating race relations training (including sessions on White privilege) for peers, agencies and children; lobbying for change in policy, service provision and staffing of agencies; revising core curriculum in Schools; joining existing community groups working for change; working for change at School through committee work, workshops, video production and Open circles.[33]

FUTURE TRENDS?

A number of schools of social work are beginning to apply challenges to other systemic inequalities as well. One result is a growing debate within social work education, because academics who continue to favour the status quo are still very much around. I heard one social work dean saying, "There's nothing wrong with our economic system because it has served the majority of Canadians very well."

Attitudes of denial or sheer ignorance about the desperately critical conditions experienced by so many Canadians can still be found in social work education. A social work textbook published in 1999 offers glib assurances: "Canadians have a sense of pride in having created a social welfare system that guarantees a basic standard of living for all its citizens."[34]

Guarantees? What kind of guarantees exist when already stingy welfare allowances can be reduced even further in a rich province like Ontario, for instance? When social work students are misled by illusions that "all is well" with the system, they tend to side with the social agency and its problems rather than with the clients. Many students are in for a mixture of shock and confusion when they confront the actual conditions in social services:

"I went to the welfare office. The waiting room smelled of urine. It was smoke-filled with no ventilation, a small room holding eighty people. The walls were kicked in. There were cigarette butts everywhere. I had to go through locked doors to get to the offices and I felt like I was a prisoner. When I asked about the locks, they told me the staff was threatened — if clients can't get their cheques some go berserk. . . . There was no dignity there. The place made you feel like scum. It was as if the whole structure was accepting it. When I talked about it with other students, they were concerned — but only for the staff. These students were not upset by it and were accepting of it. They were too caught up in carrying out their role in handing out cheques."

Social work's official aspirations of achieving social justice — and practical ideas for bringing this about — are still not receiving priority, then, within all schools of social work. Granted that the schools and their deans are part of larger institutions and heavily influenced by the policies of universities and colleges, nevertheless these schools also have some autonomy. Within their range of autonomy, values of social justice are often contradicted by the school's own practices.

By being part of the larger university or college, schools of social work are themselves subject to a host of rules and policies governing items such as fee schedules, grading criteria, and course design.[35] The expectations to conform to these rules apply generally to university education, as do the pressures on professors to spend more time on research (and therefore less time with students). As a consequence the social relations between professors and students are often experienced as impersonal and alienating. Furthermore, realizing the importance of good grades to their academic success, students have a strong incentive to feed back what professors want to hear.

More specific to professional training are the field-work courses that place students in social agencies as part of the curriculum. Students are assessed not only on how well they relate to clients, but also on how well they respect the agency's mandate (and its limitations) and fit into the agency's work. Assessments of student performance are still rooted in those social work theories that value "helping" clients adjust to existing conditions. Not that students are expected to issue directives for clients to follow. The process is far more subtle. Students are encouraged to ask about what clients want, to empathize with their problems, to explain what the agency can or cannot do, and to offer help only on terms acceptable to the particular agency. In this way students learn to replicate professional roles that provide help based on socially acceptable or officially defined options.

Students are taught that the best way to act upon their concerns is to develop their technical skills in an objective manner. They are also taught that by acquiring these technical skills, they will be capable of enhancing their clients' interpersonal relationships and enriching their clients' interactions with specific systems within our society. As a result, many students develop an excessive faith in their own "objectivity" and in the power of their emerging technical expertise to overcome problems that are essentially of a political and structural nature.

The sense of professional elitism is partly created, and certainly nourished, by the educational experience of social work students. It springs as well from history and from the prevailing political, economic, and social relationships. And finally, in professional practice, the power relationships are firmly buttressed by the institutions and agencies that end up employing the graduates of social work schools.

4 SOCIAL WORKERS:
ON THE FRONT LINE

The pressure of working with people in crisis is extremely drain-
ing. I had an excellent supervisor who understood this. She insti-
tuted a change which helped our morale. We'd work one day with
clients and one day following up with paper and arrangements;
the second day felt like a "day off" even though we were all working in terms of the paper follow-ups. But you knew the difference
and as a result we became quite efficient. Then, I understand this
supervisor got flak from the other managers. Before you knew it,
we were back to every day seeing clients in crisis, with a new
supervisor wanting twenty-minute interviews.
— a social worker, British Columbia

I F BOTH SOCIAL WORKERS and their sense of altruism are under pressure, it is clear that as much — or more — of this pressure comes
from above, from government policies and managers, as from
below, from the clients. Part of the pressure too has come from the
unprecedented expansion of social work in the post-World War II era.

Membership in the Canadian professional social work association
grew from 600 in 1940 to 3,000 in 1966 to almost 16,000 in 1999.[1]
The profession has enlarged its operations in a host of new fields, ranging from gerontology to drug addiction, from child welfare to social
security payments.

This tendency towards professional expansion has not proceeded
without challenge. Governments wishing to justify cutbacks have
accused social workers of drowning clients with an overabundance of
services. They have been accused of doing too much for troubled families, thereby weakening the family as an institution.

Part of the pressure on social workers also comes from the role
they adopt and practise — as professionals. The average salary levels
for social workers are modest, but after all, money isn't everything.
Social work's capacity to make professional judgements, to channel

53

clients along one path instead of another, to offer advice to decision-makers about what social programs should be doing: These are elements of professional power. They are partly why we want to go into a profession, whether consciously or unconsciously. According to John McKnight:

> Professional services define need as a deficiency [in the client]. . . . As *you* [the client] are the problem, the assumption is that *I,* the professionalized servicer, *am the answer.* You are not the answer. Your peers are not the answer. The *political, social and economic environment* is not the answer. Nor is it possible that there is no answer. I, the professional, am the answer. The central assumption is that service is a unilateral process. I, the professional, produce. You, the client, consume.[2]

This criticism, however, overstates the extent of social work power while understating the extent to which professionals are serving power groups other than themselves. True, the social worker is in a stronger power position than the client. But social workers, like other professionals, are not a power unto themselves. Social work also exists as part of larger institutions, which are in turn shaped by larger forces.

Most social workers are employees of *social agencies* (also known as social services), which in turn are influenced directly or indirectly by the welfare state, and the practice of those agencies is an integral function of the overall system. In Canada the state includes a wide range of government commissions, departments, and agencies supposedly organized for the purpose of enhancing the public's general welfare — by which is meant our social as well as economic well-being. One way of promoting these goals is the deployment of social workers within social agencies, both within and outside government.

WHERE SOCIAL WORKERS WORK

Social workers find themselves plying their trade in a number of different social services. They may work in the *voluntary* (or private) *sector* for agencies such as the YWCA/YMCA, Elizabeth Fry Society, or John Howard Society. The terms "voluntary sector" and "voluntary agency" are sometimes misunderstood to mean that the services are provided by volunteers. But while volunteers do offer services in some of these agencies, in others most if not all of the services are delivered by paid social service providers. The agencies in this sector are designated "voluntary" because they are governed by voluntary boards of directors made up of individuals who are often "prominent" and moneyed people in the community and who receive no direct remuneration for their activities on the boards. These boards in turn hire service providers, including social workers, to carry out all or part of their programs.

Sometimes the voluntary agencies are established by religious or cultural/ethnic groups that raise their own funds to finance, for example, the Catholic Family Services, the Jewish Homes for the Aged, the Salvation Army, or the Caribbean Immigrant Services. Many of the agencies in the voluntary sector receive funding from donations collected through local charity appeals, such as the United Way. It is mainly from within this sector that much of social work evolved into a profession during the early part of the century. Increasingly, however, these agencies are also obtaining supplementary funding from government and are thus becoming more and more influenced by government policies and organization.

A small but growing number of social workers also work in private practice, running their own offices much as lawyers do, with clients paying fees for service. Or they work in the quasi-government sector, in settings that have voluntary boards and are partially autonomous as organizational structures, but are at the same time governed by state legislation and regulations, and have funding that originates from the state. Hospitals, which often employ social workers as part of their staff, fit into this category.

Perhaps the best-known example of the quasi-government sector is the Children's Aid Society in Ontario, in which social workers obtain their authority from provincial legislation. Each Ontario Children's Aid Society, in different locales throughout the province, has its own volunteer board of directors, which establishes further policies and standards for social workers to follow. (Most provinces, it should be noted, maintain child welfare agencies within the public sector, that is, operated directly as part of the government.)

But undoubtedly the largest single area for social work is in the government or *public sector*, with social workers employed directly by the welfare state. These social programs carry out services that are often statutory. Their tasks and the decisions they make are specified by government regulations and policies. An example is public assistance — better known as "welfare" — or "workfare." These programs provide for the payment of limited amounts of money to people who have little or no financial resources. Social workers interview applicants for welfare, assess their needs, and decide whether the client qualifies for assistance based on the agency's regulations and policies. Increasingly automated and depersonalized, today these programs allow less and less time for counselling and various job training projects. A greater emphasis on welfare clients finding jobs is reflected in new names for welfare departments. For example, Nova Scotia calls its department "Income and Employment Support Services." In Ontario it is "Ontario Works." Quebec calls it "Ministère de l'Emploi et de la Solidarité," while in the Northwest Territories it is "Productive Choice."[3]

Although social work has often been equated with welfare or public assistance, social workers are employed in numerous other agencies within the public sector. A partial list includes probation services within juvenile and adult correctional branches, alcohol detox centres, mental health clinics and psychiatric services, and outreach programs for homeless youth.

How Clients Find Social Workers

The needs that bring clients to a social work agency — or bring an agency to the client — are many and complex. The problems can range from wife battering to poverty, child abuse to alcoholism, drug addiction to marital strife, or conflicts in the paid workplace or at school.

If you have had a serious illness that prevents you from returning to your job, you might have to seek out a social agency to get financial help or advice. An AIDS patient in a hospital or a student having difficulty might be referred to the hospital's social service department or the school's social work counsellor. You could get a visit from a social worker if you are a parent and someone (a neighbour, teacher, or doctor) suspects you have violently abused your child and reports you to a child welfare agency. If you have been convicted of a crime you might be ordered by the court to report to a probation officer, who is a social worker. The *official* message to clients is: We are here to help you.

If you are experiencing severe interpersonal problems (within your family, for instance) you might seek out social work counselling. That would probably bring you to a social agency in the voluntary sector. Or, you might find yourself going to a private practitioner's office.

In some cases the social agency takes the initiative. The agency may identify individuals and families who it feels are most likely to experience social problems. This means, for the most part, the poor. In turn most of the poor are women and children. Rich people who need help can afford to use private services, and as a result their problems and needs remain more hidden.

There is a marked contrast between a client voluntarily seeking help — say, with an alcohol problem — and an involuntary situation in which a court compels the client to receive social services. A rough rule of thumb is that involuntary social services are provided by government agencies, whereas the voluntary sector tends to offer services that clients are free to accept, reject, or approach on their own initiative. Thus the term "voluntary" applies to more than the social agency's board. It can also apply to the level of client choice in accepting the social worker's services. To the degree that client choice is reduced, the welfare state moves in with its own definitions and solutions.

How Social Workers Mean to Help

Depending on the agency and on the client population, most social workers offer access to financial and other resources and provide various types of counselling. Providing access to resources might include helping a client get access to subsidized housing, searching out a decent nursing home for an ailing parent, or seeing that a disabled child is able to get to the right summer camp.

One of the hallmarks of social work competency is the ability of workers to establish effective interpersonal relationships with clients. This requires that the worker attempts to enter the world of the client psychologically, to create enough of a sense of empathy and establish sufficient rapport to elicit a description of the problem as seen by the client.

All of this, needless to say, is not an easy task, and certainly it can be argued that it is impossible for a social worker to ever fully understand the world of the client. This difficulty is compounded when a social worker is from a different culture, class, or gender than the client. Black social work researchers in Nova Scotia found:

> It is obvious that many clients experience some discomfort in accepting help from a Black professional social worker. We have been questioned about our qualifications and many clients seem shocked (and sometimes a little skeptical!) to learn that we have graduate training from an accredited School of Social Work. We are also frequently asked about our place of birth. We are both Nova Scotian Blacks — from East Preston and Halifax respectively. Many whites, especially those from the lower socio-economic groups, find it difficult to believe that a Black Nova Scotian could have attained such a position. They find it equally hard to be in a position of having to receive help from one.[4]

Later on the same authors also reported, somewhat sadly: "As we reflect on our experience of the past 10 years, we realize that little has changed. We must still work twice as hard to build our credibility, to prove our competence, to attain whatever goal we have in sight, and then to hold on to it."[5]

Clients often feel ashamed or confused about their problems, whether it is alcoholism or unemployment or violence in the home. Therefore social workers consider it important to be skilled in asking the appropriate questions, observing, listening, and focusing on painful topics. In theory we try hard to be non-judgemental, to refrain from criticizing or blaming clients for their situations. All these skills and attitudes, at least on paper, are aimed at obtaining an accurate picture of client perceptions. Again, however, it is questionable whether social workers try to get accurate pictures of client perceptions. In actual practice we more likely focus primarily on our own perceptions, our own assessments, and our own definitions of problems, of what is "normal." This very condition is what is called "professional," and much of the time it is a one-way process.

For example, considerable lesbophobia and homophobia exist among many social work educators, students, and professionals who accept the prevailing stereotypes that dehumanize lesbians, gays, and bisexuals. In practice the implications of this tendency are serious, because social workers "will see clients who have had same-sex encounters or relationships; they will see clients who are concerned about issues of sexual orientation; they will see parents struggling with the sexual identity of their children; they will see lesbian mothers fighting for custody of their children. Some people who seek the services of social workers may even be seeking 'cures' for their homosexuality."[6]

Jill Abramczyk notes that efforts to "cure" lesbians and gays or to "convert" them to heterosexuality are "nothing less than more oppression," which arises from the belief of "professionals" that it is not mentally healthy to love members of the same sex in a complete way. "Clearly it is imperative that social workers understand the positive aspects of being lesbian and gay, and be able to convey this knowledge to their clients."[7] But while this is indeed imperative, it is not happening. Instead, as social worker Ron Clarke points out with reference to the moral panic generated by HIV/AIDS, there is a "conspiracy of silence which surrounds human sexuality at the personal and professional levels."[8]

At times this silence is broken. A few services are based on gay-positive and lesbian-positive values and reflect the standard that Bonnie Burstow calls upon us to meet when counselling lesbians: "It is our responsibility to help our clients understand the profound disentitlement involved in being 'in the closet' and the entitlement and pride that become possible when out." But Burstow cautions:

> Coming out can mean loss of jobs, loss of friends, ridicule, violence and being subject to that nauseating "liberal" tolerance that always misses the point. We need to be up-front about the difficulties involved in coming out — especially of being out before one is ready. We need to assure the client that it is not only all right but preferable for her to take her time. Taking time is a way of caring for self. She may need our assurance that absolutely nothing is wrong with coming out selectively and that in some situations selectivity is wise.[9]

Such knowledge is essential for social service providers. Also needing understanding and support are bisexuals, who face immense difficulties when coming out of the closet, given society's deeply entrenched "either/or" duality. In Kathleen Bennett's view, many bisexuals "did not originally intend to be crusaders against dualism. They began their quest for a bisexual identity with the raw data of their own emotions, urges and experiences. Only after that, if at all, did they face the understanding that our culture requires too many either/or choices." As Bennett points out, "The realities of bi-oriented love and lust speak to our souls long before we become inclined to theorize about them."[10]

Much of social work practice today flounders when it attempts to address different forms of oppression, even though in theory social work skills and values are meant to serve all clients. The skills of social work practice are rooted within social work values, such as the value and importance of the individual's dignity. The worker's expression of this value, in theory, helps to communicate to the client that the worker empathizes, respects, and understands the pressures on the client.

Very frequently, however, these theories and intentions break down in practice. When caseloads of individuals and families number in the hundreds, it becomes impossible for the worker to know clients except on a superficial level: *"From a service point of view, I don't even have time to listen to clients. In one recent month my total caseload was over 215 cases! I burnt out last August. During one hour then I had as many as five cases of evictions to deal with. It got to the point that emotionally I gave as little as I could to each client. Of course clients realize it and get resentful."*

Meanwhile, textbooks offer guideposts to social work with individuals, groups, and families as if this overload was not happening. These texts typically emphasize the importance of client feelings. One of them, for instance, states, "Clients are frequently blocked from taking constructive action to resolve or relieve the stress of their problem situation by unacknowledged feelings that freeze their ability to act."[11]

At the same time social workers are taught that within the psychological realm it is not enough to merely develop empathy and caring relationships with clients. The social worker is also expected to be clear about the mandate of the social service. This means that the worker must make demands on the client, even if it is a voluntary relationship. Daphne Statham, experienced in the British social work system, writes of the social worker/client relationship: "Help is conditional. The pattern of tell-me-your-problem, or, alternatively, behave-well-and-I-will-give-you-material-help, is by no means extinct in practice."[12]

An influential social work educator, Lawrence Shulman, refers to the social worker's demand for work as "the worker's confrontation of the client to work effectively on her or his tasks and to invest that work with energy and affect."[13] But this approach is one-sided and presumptuous. It seems to demand work from the client but only empathy or caring from the social worker. The worker is in control, in power — leaving the relationship open to serious abuse. A better approach would surely be to acknowledge that demands for work need to come from both participants — from client as well as worker — to initiate a process of mutual demands and negotiation.

A redefinition in the client-worker relationship is being demanded, for example, by organizations of disabled people who "reject the charity and the medical models of disability, asserting that the services we require should be provided as a civil right and that it is society which disables us rather than our physical condition."[14] Social workers who take this challenge seriously will see "the person first, before their disability," rather than the medical labels that typically dominate the service. Similarly, in working with other groups of people who have been heavily medicalized, such as older people, service providers who make sure to see the person first will be taking a large step towards establishing a more mutual relationship with those clients.[15]

THE FRUSTRATIONS OF SOCIAL WORK

Most social work textbooks spend their time elaborating how the demands of the work and the accompanying skills of creating empathy can be applied by professionals to help their clients. These elaborations include a variety of techniques from which social workers can choose, depending on the client's problem and on the type of service being offered by the agency.

Such an approach, like the idea of "demand for work," presents social work in an idealized form and assumes that the professional's relationship with the client will be governed by an unqualified concern for the client's well-being. Unfortunately, this is often very distant from the truth.

Social workers may try to temper agency practices in light of what they think a client needs or wants. But the fact remains that social workers are employees who are expected to follow the agency's rules and policies. These rules in turn often place social workers at odds with clients. Supervisors are usually nearby to remind social workers about the agency's expectations. A social worker in British Columbia described such expectations within a public assistance agency: *"As a social worker, you know it's impossible for a family to stay within the food budget. But you find your supervisor is putting pressure on you — to put pressure on the client to keep within the budget."*

In this way the benign-sounding "demand for work" opens the door to demands by the state, via social workers, that clients accept, conform, and adjust to the rules. This puts a squeeze on clients. It also creates discomfort for many social workers who try to maintain a sense of personal accountability, of decency and respect for others, as distinct from the requirements of the agency. As one social worker put it:

"The rates for welfare are so inadequate that you'll often find a mother, father, and child all living in one room in a run-down hotel; it's the only place they can afford because the rent elsewhere is too high for them. The place has no cooking facilities, so they eat by going to a greasy restaurant and buying things at 7-11 and corner stores. You find mothers trying to toilet-train their child where there's no toilet in the room, so they have to go down the hall — to a toilet shared by several tenants."

From a feminist perspective, Jennifer Dale and Peggy Foster see the limited aid extended by social workers as reinforcing inequalities: "By acting as the rationers of scarce resources welfare professionals provide a useful buffer between women's demands and a State which will not meet those demands. Welfare professionals, rationing resources on a personal and individual basis, help to disguise the collective nature of women's oppression."[16]

Knowing that as a professional helper you are not really going to be helping clients get on their feet produces a sense of demoralization — primarily among clients but also among social workers. After all their training, social workers discover that while their social services do provide some help to clients, at best they can barely scratch the surface of the problem. Within agencies, tensions can build and explode. A social worker in Vancouver told me this story:

"This rather large fellow comes up to the receptionist. You can see he's not drunk — he's stoned. He's about six-foot-five, I mean, he's big! And he asks for something. He's told by the receptionist he can get it from his own welfare office. He asks for some coins for the bus. The reception-ist, an eighteen-year-old woman, starts to look in her purse to give him some change.

"I was in the middle of a conversation with another social worker who overhears the client asking for change. She stops talking with me, turns around and tells the receptionist, 'No! Don't give it to him!' Well, that big fellow — he just blew! He swung both arms across the reception desk — the typewriters, phone, papers all went flying all over the place.

"As if this isn't enough, this social worker now tells him that I walk that distance once each day! I felt this was all crazy, that the social worker should have just shut up. I was looking around the waiting room to see if anyone else was looking to join a fight. You can get a few clients all getting angry and you can get into some pretty heavy duty stuff! Luck-ily everybody was still calm.

"I wanted to defuse the situation fast. So I tried to change the tone by saying, 'Actually, I don't walk once, I do it twice.' This fellow did see the humour of it, but added his own by hissing at me — 'Thhhaatssss your tough luck!!!' Meanwhile somebody had called the police. He turns to leave but before going, he points his finger at the social worker and says, 'YOU'RE FUCKIN' DEAD!!!' She wilts. He walks out."

Bob Mullaly explains the response of some social workers: "We may use our professional role to gain a sense of power. Rather than empowering the people with whom we work, we may actually rein-force their victim status by playing the role of benefactor and exploit-ing the power differential between ourselves and service users."[17]

When abused and mistreated people explode in anger — either individually or as a total community — we may react with fear. Or we may become defensive and ourselves lash out in retaliation. But, as anti-racist educator Paul Kivel suggests, "Rather than attacking them for their anger, we need to ask ourselves how many layers of compla-cency, ignorance, collusion, privilege and misinformation have we put into place for it to take so much outrage to get our attention?"[18]

More typically, clients know they are being mistreated but believe they have no choice but to conform. There are additional barriers for someone whose first language is not English. One workfare participant complained: "I went into the office and she want me to sign something . . . but sometimes I don't understand the words and I don't want to make mistake, and I was by myself. I said I want to take home, and she said NO! You have to sign here."[19]

An executive director of a Halifax employment project set up to aid prisoners from federal penitentiaries found herself working on a shoestring budget that had been cut back: *"If a prisoner isn't able to find a job after release from prison, what happens? He can go on welfare but many are too proud, so where can they get money to pay for food and rent? Crime becomes very tempting and the next thing you know, they're back in prison. Our society spends a lot on punishment, jails and the like but little on positive help."*

Though often bleak, the experience of clients receiving social services sometimes hits an oasis of caring. When clients experience such exceptions, they recognize the help: "She started from a place of concern, compassion and interest in knowing about my life. That helped."[20] But even when social workers seem to have made positive contributions, all too often they witness their work being undone. A social worker in the Maritimes, for instance, had developed a program for school drop-outs who were in conflict with their families and the law. The program consisted of building solid relationships with the youths and taking them out to work on fishing boats:

"After a couple of weeks the kid would return home and the mother would tell me — 'My son looks great! I don't recognize him! He's got a tan, developed a bit of muscle, the lines under his eyes are gone, the tension is gone, he looks great!'

"But it was all a mirage. Those changes meant nothing . . . nothing! Because these kids went right back into their old situations, there were no other choices. We had a temporary program and when it was gone, the kids were left with nothing, no jobs, just like before."

CUTBACKS AND CASELOADS: THE PROFESSIONAL BIND

No matter how appropriate the social workers' "demands" on their clients, no matter how sensitive their communication skills, the core of the problem seems to remain beyond their reach as professionals. Realizing that social agencies should develop better ways of working with clients, some social workers cope by trying to cut through the red tape. Usually, it's an uphill struggle. As a parole officer working with offenders inside federal prisons said: *"When you visit the pens as a parole officer to plan for conditional releases, you discover more injustices. You try and do something about it but others in the bureaucracy are afraid. So people do their jobs and the bureaucrats can always say 'Sorry, but that's the rule.'"*

As a consequence, social service workers experience a sense not only of powerlessness — at least with respect to management and control of the job — but also of futility as they face the inertia of their institutions. Of course, this may not be the case with all social agencies. But it is the case very frequently and holds true for most client populations regardless of province or region. An apt description focuses on the working conditions in British Columbia's child welfare ministry:

> Workloads were frequently described as impossible, overwhelming and a major cause of increased stress and pressures which in turn creates "assembly-line social work." . . . High workloads lead to crisis management which means that only families who are in an absolute crisis situation can receive attention from Ministry staff. Parents reported that they had to be "drowning" in order to receive service.[21]

As a result, while it is possible that social services to individuals, families, and groups may be offered in a useful and humanitarian manner, social workers find their competency undermined by the very contexts they work in. Is it any wonder that some professionals drop out? It begins with a yearning to escape, as one social worker told me: *"The other day I heard about someone on the west coast, he built himself a small house on top of a tree, overlooking the ocean. I really like that idea, imagine letting the wind come and swaying you in that tree and just being free. I might go and find a tree like that. . . . "*

Most of us, however, have been trained to hang in, for various reasons. The job does have its satisfactions, after all, and sometimes these satisfactions work to prevent us from grasping the total picture.

The major distortions advanced by some social work textbooks don't help, either. For example, Francis Turner, in *Social Work Practice*, writes that Canadian social work practice is admirably tolerant of a wide diversity of approaches to helping people. He suggests that a factor in this tolerance could be "Canada's long tradition of multiculturalism."[22] That "long tradition" failed to impress the 1996 Royal Commission on Aboriginal Peoples, which offered graphic evidence of the distance between "multicultural tolerance" and the harsh reality of the even longer tradition of colonialism in Canada. Other examples abound.

In that same social work book, Ray Thomlison and Cathryn Bradshaw examine pressure-group politics and indicate that the disabled, the poor, and professional and labour groups are the "special interest groups" that lobby governments to try to influence policies.[23] Nowhere do Thomlison and Bradshaw name the most powerful, most effective "special interest groups" on the Canadian scene — namely, the ones that promote the goals of powerful corporations, whether propelled by industry, by think tanks, or by associations such as the Business Council on National Issues (BCNI), whose very special agenda has been adopted by one government after another in Canada in the past two decades.[24]

When social work textbooks downplay or ignore corporate influence of public policy, they contribute to social work's floundering in the face of cutbacks and high caseloads. Gaining knowledge about the negative impact of arbitrary corporate power on social services is a first step in joining with others to do something about it.

Pockets of social services across the country do contain more progressive forms of practice that include substantial influence "and direct decision-making by consumers/constituents." In one instance, a report indicated, a drop-in program for parents in Halifax was started by "professionals who nurtured the initial leadership (by consumers) and then withdrew to a support role," thereby supporting consumer control over the service.[25] Another example came from Central Alberta, where clients of mental health services in nine communities carried out leadership roles in conducting a survey of service needs. According to Elizabeth Radian of Red Deer College, the clients were effectively involved in the project from beginning to end — "from the initial planning to the presentation of the project at a conference."[26]

Sandra Frosst headed another research project, *Empowerment II: Snapshots of the Structural Approach in Action,* involving thirty-one progressive social workers who had graduated from Ottawa's Carleton University. In reflecting on their practice, the workers gave out comments such as: *you need to feel comfortable not being in control . . . you need to be able to join the client versus treat the client . . . you have to involve yourself in challenging the agency without shafting yourself in the process . . . you have to have an acute awareness of society and politics and see this and from there pull the skills.* The authors of the report conclude that, based on this sample, "There is a shared feeling that social analysis is key to assessment and for many this informs the use of skill."[27]

Two child protection offices in British Columbia initiated another project, an experiment in power-sharing (between workers and clients): "Clients reported that one of the most exciting features of this project was the fact that workers actually listened to their ideas and acted upon them. Being heard is one thing; taking action together on the basis of these messages is the next, and very powerful step."[28]

Such joint actions were empowering for both clients and workers. Power-sharing is also being implemented in some other counselling agencies, for example at Vancouver's Pacific Spirit Family and Community Services:

> Because we believe horizontal, circular structures are more effective than top-down relations, we work as a team, with weekly meetings and a rotating chair. . . . We believe that for many people, creativity has been stifled, and we seek to regenerate and renew this vital service. Over the past four years we have increasingly recognized that emotions, thoughts and visions can be expressed in many languages, and thus we provide access to art, play and music as mediums of discovery, in addition to verbal explorations.[29]

These examples reveal an overlap in the skills used by progressive workers and by status quo professionals. As Australian social work educator Janis Fook notes: "Interpersonal and communication skills, for example, may be used by a worker to either help clients accept their own inadequacies, or to identify structural causes of their problems."[30]

What sustains progressive practice in face of immense pressures to conform to top-down practice? Mullaly suggests, "There is consensus in the literature that the most important way of protecting ourselves, not only from agency reprisal, but also from burnout, is to have peer support."[31] My own experience has also shown that support from people both in and out of my workplace helps give me the energy to stick with an anti-oppression approach over the long haul. Wanda Thomas Bernard, Lydia Lucas-White, and Dorothy E. Moore also provide an example of interpersonal and political support in Nova Scotia: "The ABSW (Association of Black Social Workers) is a voluntary group of Black social workers and human service workers who offer solidarity and mutual support to colleagues who would otherwise be isolated in their workplaces. It is empowered to act as a collective voice to advocate on behalf of the Black community on critical issues."[32]

In a similar vein, feminist Joan Pennell of Memorial University in Newfoundland argues: "The absorption that might occur when social movement aims are incorporated into social agencies, is reduced when social workers continue to engage directly with women and other oppressed groups."[33]

Despite examples of effective help, the fallout from a failed economic system means less funds for social services and fewer social workers responding to more clients with greater problems. As client contacts become shorter, more rushed, and more superficial, workers are left with less autonomy and less opportunity to be caring.[34]

Typically, the satisfactions of the work are outweighed by the stress generated by overwork:

"During the time I'm supposed to write up my clients' files, my day is interrupted by walk-ins — homeless families with nowhere to go, crises of all sorts, phone calls from anxious clients I haven't had time to call for two or three months. There've been some days I haven't gotten near my files. So I have to do it on my own time. It's difficult, some husbands get angry when you bring work home. But if you don't your supervisor is on your case. The clients are angry too because they haven't received their cheques because you haven't had time to write up their file.

"We're talking basics here. It could be a family that's been evicted with five or six children; there's no groceries so they're hostile. That's why our casework is critical to their well-being. Yet the demands go beyond our energy or time. Talk of pressure! I'm developing allergies and my doctor tells me it's stress-related. Other social workers have migraines. There's been three marriage breakdowns among my co-workers. I've seen social workers becoming hysterical, breaking down and crying at the office."

Another source of conflict is the difference of opinion held by social agency managers and supervisors about the reasons for the front-liner's stress. For instance, when I was working in Alberta seasoned social workers there were carrying what they found to be excessive workloads and had to use overtime to complete the work. The provincial department they worked for decided arbitrarily to cut back on their overtime allowances — but not on their caseloads. The explanation given to these social workers was clear: The department's budget had to be cut back; therefore do the work within regular working hours; if you can't we will have to conclude you are incompetent.

Such tactics by management have left front-line social workers feeling vulnerable. Neither the social work professional associations nor the labour unions' negotiations with management have been able to counteract such forms of intimidation effectively.

Another social worker in Alberta recalled what happened when she had some questions about a client in a difficult situation. She went to her supervisor for some advice. She told me that what happened to her had also happened to other workers: *"Now the supervisor turns on me and says — what's the matter with you? Don't you know what to do?*

"The thing is, the supervisor sometimes doesn't have the answer either. But instead of admitting it, the supervisor scares away the worker. After being treated that way, the worker learns not to ask again. Especially since it's the supervisor who evaluates the performance of the front-line worker."

Again, not all supervisory relations with front-line staff are like this. But such incidents happen too often to be simply dismissed as exceptions to the rule. No wonder some social workers become bitter:

"It's rather irksome when social workers are criticized, say by people outside the department, and yet management never tries to defend the quality of commitment by social workers. Meanwhile, we're sweating it out . . . "

5 MANAGING SOCIAL WORK:
FROM TOP TO BOTTOM

The organization chart of a social agency shows the positions occupied by employees, illustrates the hierarchy of power, and clarifies proper channels of communication.

— *Canadian Social Welfare,* a textbook

A S AN ACTING DIRECTOR of a social development agency in Montreal a number of years ago, I was concerned about the inadequacies I saw in welfare services. When I let it be known to my co-workers and superiors that I intended to speak out on these problems, to go on public record, I received quiet yet clear messages about my "short-sightedness." Furthermore, when I joined welfare clients who were staging a sit-in at a welfare office to protest low welfare rates, many members of the agency's board saw my attitude as "unbecoming of a professional."

After that, had I wanted, for instance, to become executive director of the agency, there would probably have been sufficient opposition from the board to block the appointment. Most of the board members came from the upper echelons of society, from high positions in business and the professions. They believed in general that things were being taken care of efficiently and properly, to the basic good of all concerned. The few problems they saw were limited to "abuses" of the system, usually emanating from the client end of things. Sometimes they saw problems as being caused by "bad apples" or malcontents: social workers who were not trying hard enough to make things work; or clients who were not trying hard enough to pull themselves up by their bootstraps. At the most the problems needed some careful, judicious, and "realistic" mediating.

Such board attitudes, unfortunately, are typical of established

69

social agencies. This is as true today as it was in the past. Elspeth Latimer, a noted scholar of social work history, observes, "Throughout the profession's history, with very few exceptions, social workers have functioned as employees of social welfare agencies under the management of lay boards," an arrangement that "simply rules out social reform activity as an integral part of the regular employment of the social worker."[1]

The reason that reform is ruled out by lay boards is that they are personally and professionally divorced from the problems that social work sets out to address. These boards see the issues from the perspective of a male dominant class that at best patronizes the predominantly female client class, at worst works to protect its own interests and to prevent any inkling of significant change. The top-down flow of power — via gender, cultural and other prejudices, and hierarchy — has a major impact on the maintenance of inequalities inside the social work profession.

THE STRATIFICATION OF SOCIAL WORK

Social services are stratified in ways similar to most of our government bureaucracies and business hierarchies. Among the reasons given for such a stratification are greater efficiency and accountability of the organization — a rationale widely accepted by the public, including the professionals within our social services. We also assume that those at the peak of the social agency's pyramid are the most qualified and competent. According to this theory, a measure of a person's competence in social work is the ability to rise up the career ladder.

Social service workers are taught that the current structures of authority are necessary and desirable, with little consideration of whether alternative organizational structures might better serve clients. A textbook states:

> An authority structure is needed to allocate responsibility and coordinate tasks. It provides a chain of command through which decisions are made about what is to be done, who is to do it, and how and when it is to be done. Authority is vested in stratified positions and legitimized through the dispensing of rewards and sanctions.[2]

Such hierarchies are offered as "natural," and the descriptions of them tend to downplay the aspect of social control embedded in the structure. While these hierarchies offer rewards for "professional competency," and while they expedite the work in certain ways, at the same time they reproduce power relations that maintain the haves and have-nots, the privileged and the subjugated, in an unequal society.

Overwork, speed-ups, cutbacks, and their effects on clients are therefore not the only reasons for demoralization among social workers. Front-line workers also experience a sense of powerlessness and frustration because of their subordination to directives issued from above. The top-down flow of power becomes, among other things, a channel for punitive actions against social workers, leading to a profound sense of alienation. This was illustrated some years back in Alberta after a series of scandals involving foster parents abusing foster children. In response the provincial government decided that social workers in its child protection divisions must visit each foster child and each family on their caseloads once a month.[3] As one of the social workers said, at first glance it sounded like *"an improvement over just letting situations drift endlessly."* But, the worker added:

"Now comes the catch, with 90 or 120 children on your caseload, plus all the paperwork, tell me how it's possible to carry out this policy? It can't work! It's impossible! Now if something blows and a child is harmed, the managers can say, 'We have a policy, why aren't the workers carrying it out?' A classic case of blaming the victim! You answer, 'But there aren't enough hours in the day,' and they can't hear that. The managers will pass down the blame to the supervisors — why can't you manage your units? And the supervisors will bitch against the line workers — why can't you manage your cases?"

This top-down process is not confined to government. A service provider in a voluntary sector agency serving youth and families describes an appalling imbalance in power because *"when the person who supervises you clinically is the one who hires you, is the one who fires you, is the one who disciplines you and is the one who overrules you."*

If the constant demand for conformity doesn't wear us down and if we retain our abhorrence of arbitrary power, promotions create other hazards. We become divorced from front-line colleagues and client realities. Even if we remain part of the union, as supervisors we begin representing management. A level of mistrust towards us develops among front-line workers, and we react to that mistrust. According to a supervisor in a welfare office:

"You find you now have two levels, your previous colleagues who are still line workers and your new colleagues who are also supervisors. You find yourself talking to other supervisors about 'they' at the line level, as if somehow 'they' were not quite as wise as you supervisors. 'They don't know.'"

Gradually the separation becomes solidified. As you attend certain meetings, you have access to information and decisions that the line staff does not have. Misunderstandings can easily develop, with line staff suspecting or knowing that you are holding back information. Many supervisors do try to be open with front-line workers, and some succeed. But such openness occurs despite the agency hierarchy, not because of it.

Harassed by overwork and feeling isolated from each other, several social workers in one child welfare agency decided to improve the situation. When phone calls to the office reported potential child abuse, these workers decided to make home visits in pairs instead of alone. All the work still got done. The team approach proved to be rewarding for the workers and created a fresh level of energy and responsiveness in relation to clients. Work pressures became more manageable and morale improved. But one of the participating social workers got a severe reprimand from her male supervisor:

"At first I thought he was joking. He went on to say that he was supposed to be in charge of the unit and that I had too much control. After I left his office I was ready to quit. It was horrible because I doubted my own capabilities and he had convinced me at least for the moment that I was in the wrong place. He never directly mentioned the changes in our unit working together and it was only later I realized that was what bothered him. He could be supportive as long as he felt he was in charge. When we took the initiative and tried to improve how we worked, he panicked, he felt he was losing control."

Such incidents might be explained away as mere reflections of insecure supervisors, but such a rationale avoids looking at the part played by the agency structures themselves. In fact, the problem is very much part of a larger pattern. Conflict between different levels of the organization exists all the way up to the senior managers, who in turn are subordinate to top authorities. Managers are sometimes social workers, but in the public sector they often come to their positions from other fields or disciplines, such as public administration or business management. For social work managers, conflict stems not only from their efforts to protect budgets but also from priorities established higher up.

An example of this tendency was an attempt to reorganize the Federal Correction Services in Ottawa. The goal was to better integrate parole services with correctional services. However, according to one social work manager, integration made the work much more difficult because it brought the parole officers into an organization primarily concerned with "security":

"Most of the administration in Ottawa is preoccupied with security, with pens and with cutting down on escapes and on hostage incidents. The whole idea behind parole is very different, we try to help the ex-prisoner make it back into the community. As it is now, there's no dis-tinction made between our goals and the goals of the prison."

The social worker pointed out that it is not only the goals of the work that are in conflict, but also ways of implementing them:

"Let's face it. Social workers are not 'paper-oriented,' we have a dif-ferent approach from a bureaucrat who wants us to fill out forms, statis-tics, and reports. The main approach now in correctional services is 'what's the cost?' instead of 'how well are you helping prisoners?' In Ottawa they can tell you how much it costs per square foot of prisons, but what difference does that make when it comes to helping prisoners after release?"

While the crosscurrents of differing approaches must be navigated by social service managers, there's not much doubt about whose inter-ests ultimately prevail. While managers may privately disagree with goals or ways of implementing them, their actions on the job usually reflect what is expected of them by top management as incumbents of these positions.

Despite some discomfort, many social work managers become apologists for the system. One experienced social worker, a woman who had succeeded in becoming a manager, said she had seen this hap-pen with many of her colleagues, especially after they had assumed positions of authority within a welfare organization: *"They seem unable to separate themselves from their employer and they find themselves jumping to the defence of the system. I believe this happens when social workers become senior bureaucrats and they really want to keep their authority."*

So, for workers scaling the professional ladder, what may have begun as a career with the goal of improving conditions for clients ends up by perpetuating the status quo. The reasons are clear. Higher pay, more influence, more prestige, a sense of personal security: These are considered normal goals of other occupations. Why should it be dif-ferent for social work?

Similar hierarchies exist in the voluntary sector, with the main dif-ference being that social work managers or executive directors are accountable to voluntary boards rather than to a government minister.

Another difference is size: The voluntary agency is usually smaller than a government agency. Voluntary boards, however, are influential in giving direction to social agencies and in promoting their credibility in the eyes of major funders. As in the public sector, social work executives strive to provide their operation with effective management. This includes financial management and supervision of either departments or front-line staff, depending on the size of the agency.

While social work executives in the voluntary sector are in strategic positions to speak out about the effects of unjust social conditions upon clients, they usually don't. It's not so much that they are told to keep quiet. There's a much more subtle process at work, as administrators learn that boards prefer a smooth operation, free from community or public controversy.

Boards are usually also active in a monitoring role. As part of this role, the board has the power to hire and fire its executive director. Social work executives, therefore, realize that the board plays a crucial part not only in relation to funding bodies but also in evaluating the executive's performance. In other words, there's not only the question of the agency's financial position, there's also the matter of the executive's professional survival as manager of the agency.

MOVING UP IN THE PROFESSION: OBSTACLES

Agency hierarchies may reward certain competencies, but their patterns of promotions and salaries indicate that another priority is also being served, that the management of social work is governed by the larger, structural relationships of society as a whole.

Researcher Carol Baines notes that the "more lucrative administrative positions of leadership" in social work have continued to be disproportionately filled by men. While women make up about 70 per cent of the profession, Baines says, "They remain concentrated in the lower-paying direct service positions committed to an ethic of caring about and for marginal populations."[4] By the late 1990s a survey of members of the Ontario Association of Social Workers revealed that women workers were earning only 80 per cent as much as their male counterparts.[5]

Given the patriarchal structure of our society, such an outcome is not surprising, even when it applies to social work, long considered a female profession. Because the most basic caring and nurturing of others has been systematically defined as women's work — whether paid or unpaid, whether in the home, community, or workplace — male social workers benefit by being favoured for managerial positions. While the women's movement has challenged discrimination against women managers, the question remains as to whether the minimal numbers of women in managerial positions are required to assume authority according to entrenched male patterns of domination.

As with the subordinate position of women, non-white social workers' on-the-job relationships are influenced not only by competencies and personalities but also, and more importantly, by the dominant (white male) society's relations with people of colour. Black women social workers in Nova Scotia outlined some of the obstacles they face in their work:

> We have had to establish our credibility with co-workers as a prelude to building good working relationships based on mutual respect. Several of our peers are uncomfortable discussing racial issues although they must work with Blacks and other minority groups from time to time. We have both had the experience of hearing co-workers or supervisors discuss minority groups (other than Blacks) in a negative manner. Our suspicions are that similar attitudes toward Blacks may be expressed at other times.[6]

Along similar lines, a study in Toronto found a disturbing separation within social agencies:

> The health and social services "system," at least for members of diverse cultural and racial groups, could be characterized as a situation of "two solitudes." Two subsystems, mainstream and ethno-specific . . . exist side by side, live somewhat separate existences, hardly take account of one another in their effort to plan and deliver service, and do not account to one another for their plans and activities.[7]

The devaluation of different cultural/ethnic groups began with the dispossession of the First Nations from their land, accompanied by racist missionary attitudes towards the "red savages." Later examples include the exploitation of Chinese railway workers, the treatment of Japanese Canadians during the Second World War, and the denial of immigration to Jews seeking refuge from Nazi regimes, to name a few. Deep racism continues to permeate Canadian institutions, including the social services. To practice anti-racism within social services means inviting people of colour to help monitor our social services' progress in dealing with the issues of everyday life, including the building of non-racist practices — though Lena Dominelli warns about the possible backlash for social workers pursuing those goals: "Such work contains risks which can affect the whole of their careers and place their promotion prospects in jeopardy. Thus, white social workers committed to anti-racist social work must prepare themselves for a rough ride in pursuing their goals." Dominelli advises "white anti-racist social workers to develop alliances with other workers, management, politicians, trade unionists and others sharing their anti-racist goals."[8]

But anti-racism does not mean only being concerned about racism. On the contrary, it offers a doorway through which we can enter and address a host of other systemic inequalities ranging from heterosexism to class privilege — because addressing any one oppression can pave the way for addressing all of them. Indeed, one of the goals of anti-oppression practice is to widen the scope of practice to include the entire cluster of systemic inequalities.

For their part, Aboriginal peoples have experienced particularly harsh treatment by the economic, political, and cultural institutions of our society. The high rates of unemployment, poverty, and suicide among the First Nations are well documented.[9] These "social problems" have been largely caused and aggravated by public policies that have run rough-shod over Aboriginal cultural values and traditions. The welfare state has aimed at converting Aboriginal peoples into whites. This assimilationist approach, historically spearheaded by the federal Indian Affairs department, has carried a clear message: Aboriginal cultural values are inferior to the values of mainstream society.

In a number of provinces a high proportion of social work clients, especially in areas such as child welfare, come from Aboriginal communities. Once again, a high proportion of these clients are women. Typically, Aboriginal children have been removed from their homes and communities to be placed in non-Aboriginal foster homes. As a result many of these children, during adolescence especially, experience confused and conflicted feelings about their personal and cultural identities.

When these separations induced by social services are added to the separations created by residential schools, it is hardly surprising to find "the alienation and separation of the children from their Indian tribal beliefs, languages and cultural ways."[10] Sid Fiddler, former dean of the Saskatchewan Indian Federated College, Saskatoon Campus, concludes:

> The parenting skills, sense of responsibility and initiative, knowledge and kinship relating, communicating skills and ways of life have also decreased with each succeeding generation that has been in the residential school system. The incidence of child abuse and family violence among Indian people today is in part attributed to the early experiences

of physical, sexual and psychological devaluation and abuse of many Indian parents who themselves grew up in these authoritarian institutions.[11]

Aboriginal teachers Lauri Gilchrist and Kathy Absolon view the personal damage (such as alcoholism, addiction, violence, sexual abuse, poverty, and unemployment) as symptoms that First Nations people carry as a result of the pervasive colonialism and racism to which they are still subjected. As a method of dealing with these problems, Absolon and Gilchrist call for a kind of reversal of the prevailing pattern: "Healing the symptoms is about a process whereby our emotions, spirit, mind, and body are decolonized."[12]

Fiddler elaborates on this same process of healing and recovery: "Taking responsibility and control has its roots in cultural revival and Native spirituality. It is a means to regain Aboriginal sense of history, development, pride, identity as well as dealing with the pain, anger, oppression that results in multi dysfunctionality among many Native people."[13]

There are people from Aboriginal communities who also hold social work jobs — usually the lowest paying and least secure jobs — but advancement into senior positions proves to be difficult. In fact, it is difficult for them to get into these jobs in the first place, just as it is difficult for them to enter and complete a social work education.

A major hurdle for Aboriginal social workers is facing the accusation from family and friends that they are abandoning their people to join the "white man's" world. The bitterness of this accusation becomes more understandable when you consider the historical and current grievances of the First Nations against white society. Whether it is the hidden or blatant prejudices of white townspeople or urban employers, or the trivialization of Native cultures by Hollywood movies and TV programs, the institutions of the dominant society have left little room or respect for the expression of authentic Aboriginal values. When Native students find themselves confronting these realities through their social work training, they face another painful question: Should they continue to train in a field that is responsible for such attacks on their culture? Will they inevitably be collaborating with a white welfare state that is perpetuating a colonial relationship with their people?

Despite these poignant questions, some Native students find they have an overwhelming desire to do social work. They feel that despite the damage inflicted on their own people by the social service delivery system, surely they can contribute something worthwhile — and, indeed, who better than they?

Of those who graduate, some become disillusioned as they experience racism within the social services. Others become active in developing new services with and for Aboriginal people, services based on First Nations' cultural traditions. From those social workers who remain in mainstream social services, a small number find that they can gradually receive promotions, though very few are allowed to reach the most senior posts. Meanwhile, if they have retained their credibility in their Aboriginal communities, the personal and political tensions remain, because the questions that face all social workers can become brutally stinging when one Aboriginal person asks another: Whom are you working for? Our people? The white man's agency? Or just for yourself?

BUSINESS MANAGEMENT TECHNIQUES

Today's social programs face persistent pressure to apply business philosophies and techniques in the delivery of social services. These techniques, along with their computerized programs, are presented as scientific and as a means of providing more efficient services. There are also strong claims that such approaches can improve staff morale. Those who raise concerns about the new techniques find themselves on the defensive. After all, how could anyone be against scientific progress, against more efficiency, or against better staff morale?

Therefore most social service managers have welcomed business methods into their organization. To facilitate this process, two decades ago the Canadian Association of Social Workers explored how a technique known as "Management by Objectives" could be applied in social work agencies.[14] This project required the splintering of social work processes into detailed job tasks. The hope was that everyone within a social agency would participate in discussions to reach consensus on who should do what specific tasks in delivering social work services. The approach also promised more democracy in decision-making within the social services.

This optimism was not shared by everyone. Neil Tudiver of the University of Manitoba warned that splitting social work into small bits and pieces would separate the "thinking parts" of the job from the "doing parts." Further, the result of skimming off the "thinking parts" from front-line workers would be an intensified form of control exercised by social service managers. Tudiver predicted that such developments would further reduce the range of judgements exercised by front-line workers. He believed that the promise of democratic participation merely masked the interests of management in exercising complete control over the work process.[15]

A study in England shows that such fragmentation of social work is already well underway. The British trend involves a detailed specification of service inputs and outputs, with each part measured and costed out. Researchers Lena Dominelli and Ankie Hoogvelt analyse this trend as part of a shift towards viewing the caring for others as a commodity to be bought and sold as a business transaction. In these exchanges social services are increasingly quantified and price-tagged in competitive bidding for contracted-out services. Dominelli and Hoogvelt note that such contracted-out projects often result in lower rates of pay for service providers. Moreover, this business approach, they explain, is part of worldwide restructuring led by global corporations aimed, in part, at lowering labour costs.[16]

A U.S. text, *Quality Performance in Human Services*, also shows a distinct preoccupation with the measurement and fragmentation of social services.[17] In their enthusiasm for this approach, the authors of the book overlook the mixed results of this technique when used in private industry. Within manufacturing enterprises, the term in vogue is "lean production," which includes collapsed job categories, increased flexibility of worker deployment, outsourcing, and the promise of labour-management co-operation. While business, not surprisingly, has heralded lean production as a means of achieving greater efficiency, feedback from autoworkers in the "leanest" plants indicated that they experienced not only the heaviest and fastest work, but also "the highest degree of physical health risks, exhaustion, and stress."[18]

Even though business techniques have been widely introduced in Canadian social agencies, most social service workers have not experienced greater democracy in their workplaces. If anything, staff morale has deteriorated, due partly to the greater job insecurity that results from permanent positions being replaced by short-term, poorly paid contract positions. Clearly, such business techniques have not delivered on their promise of providing more effective services. What they have succeeded in doing is further entrenching power within management, leaving social work staff even more dependent upon directives from above.

Beyond social work a whole new industry has sprouted up, promising to improve communications and teamwork within government and corporate bureaucracies. Professional consultants, industrial psychologists, and employee assistance co-ordinators are a few examples of a whole new breed of human relations experts who use creative techniques to induce employee acceptance of hierarchies and to divert or repress challenges of management control. Given tensions arising from job insecurities in a climate of high unemployment, management-sponsored services have grown to address certain problems experienced by employees in the private and public sectors. Under the umbrella of "Quality of Working Life," Employment Assistance Programs (EAPs) try to address problems of alcoholism and poor mental health of employees. Tudiver observes that counsellors in the program end up identifying with management, so when emotional stress is caused by the workplace itself, counsellors fail to address these matters. "They take a bandaid approach, offering to repair the wounds inflicted by the employer, with little promise of preventing future inflictions."[19]

In class terms, just as the interests of managers in private enterprise become identified with the owners, managers of social agencies (and most of their consultants) identify primarily with the interests of those in control of the social service delivery system. In both cases, front-line employees emerge as a separate group, subordinate and subservient to the power of the managerial group. Managerial techniques, then, by intensifying this division, ultimately serve to further alienate the relatively powerless front-line workers.

Given the leverage of social agency managers, it appears that social work is being granted professional status only in a symbolic sense. Although social work professional associations can discipline their own members for unethical conduct, these associations have no clout when it comes to protecting a practitioner from authoritarian directives issued by social agencies. The day-to-day control over practice is not exercised by the profession but rather by a smaller group of agency and welfare state managers.

PRIVATIZATION OF SOCIAL SERVICES

Efforts by corporations around the globe to funnel more and more human activity into "free"-market financial transactions have had an impact on social services. Whether it is within the voluntary social service sector, where agency boards and managers have become preoccupied with financial management at the expense of responding to community needs, or within the public sector, where services are being contracted out to commercial firms, the "corporate model" has quickly become a stronger presence within social services. Privatization of social services means that more and more of these services are provided by the private sector on a for-profit basis.

One example of privatization is reflected in the gradual growth of private social work practice, sometimes called "independent" practice. Ironically, one reason for the growth of private practice was the disenchantment by professionals at the social control over their practice by agency managers.

As a result, some social workers decided to manage their own social services by setting up private offices, much like dentists or lawyers, and charging fees for their services. Sometimes several social workers have joined together in partnerships or other arrangements, or have formed consulting firms seeking contracts — for example, to carry out staff development programs for established social agencies. These private social work businesses are not viewed as "social agencies," because that term normally refers to a non-profit approach to social work.

Social workers who have opted for private practice do succeed in escaping the regulations and policies of social agencies. One private practitioner expressed relief at no longer having to work for what he saw as a government monopoly over certain social services. Yet, although these social workers are no longer constrained by bureaucratic rules, they create a different kind of constraint by bringing the principles — and necessities — of capitalism directly into their delivery of services.

To generate profits these workers must charge a fee for their service. Who will be able to pay? Almost always, it is a middle-class clientele. In exchange for payment, such clients receive counselling on how to better cope with psychological tensions, work pressures, and personal troubles.

Private practitioners also obtain lucrative work from government agencies that, for example, contract out family assessments to be used in juvenile court. When social workers carry out such contracts for a state agency, they come back full circle in collaborating with the state. True, they have won a measure of independence in their day-to-day work; they are no longer civil servants. But when they receive government contracts, they are expected to carry out work that does not question the constraints on the extent or type of service allowed under these contracts.

Moreover, while exceptions exist, most social workers in private practice become more and more profit-oriented. This promotes not only certain attitudes, but also certain forms of relationships with clients and government that parallel those inherent in business enterprises. Furthermore, if these private practitioners find they can manage their businesses and make a living at it, the lesson is that capitalism does work — it has for them. In this way, they not only affirm conservative ideology but also act in ways that perpetuate its structures. This ideology also becomes reflected by mainstream social services, which are starting to call social service clients "customers."

Despite some controversy over private practice, social workers who have opened private offices have been openly welcomed by professional social work organizations. Such acceptance among social work's official organizations has paved the way for a much larger expansion of private enterprise into the social services. There is a definite trend, much of it imported from the United States, of having private corporations organize large-scale services in child care, hospitals, nursing homes, children's group homes, long-term care, and other social services. These private chains may charge their customers directly or receive a flat rate from the government, getting, for example, so many dollars per bed.

Since the primary objective is to maximize profits, their emphasis is on a mass service with a strong incentive to cut costs. Ernie Lightman, economist at University of Toronto, states, "There is a growing array of data to suggest that higher profits are most likely to be achieved through the lowering of service delivery standards."[20] Despite telling evidence that private nursing homes have frequently failed to provide humane patient care, even periodic public scandals have failed to stem the tide of essential social services being provided on the basis of private profit. Any semblance of public discussion about social needs, about how best to deliver quality service, and about prevention, is then reduced to financial decisions by shareholders within these private companies.

Another feature of this development of social service for profit is the development of a hierarchy of service from deluxe to inadequate. Of course, services then become equated with hefty price differentials. All of this is rationalized as getting what you pay for. Just as you have choices in buying cars, why shouldn't you also have choices in purchasing social services? In a twist of irony, the very social services that were supposed to modify the inequalities produced by the system end up by being sold to those most able to afford them.

With the growing push to privatize various branches of the public sector comes a striking similarity between what is happening in the social services and in the universities.[21] During the phase of "pushing to privatize," both social services and universities have experienced major cuts in public sector funding, causing a deterioration in the quality of service delivered. Both are experiencing more centralization of power within administration, modelled after private sector structures. Like social service clients, university students are finding a more impersonal institution, with less mentoring, higher expectations and weaker institutional supports, and more pressure on them to speed up their exit time. Professors, like social service providers, are also experiencing the downloading of administrative tasks (such as fundraising) while teaching more students. Both within universities and social services, participants are encouraged to launch themselves into orbits of private enterprise as the best security for their future.

The push to privatize Canadian social services gets an added boost whenever right-wing conservative governments are elected. For instance, under Ontario's Harris government in the 1990s the provincial welfare authorities, as part of their workfare project, invited a private-sector broker to take people on welfare and place them in jobs within the temporary-help industry. After offering short-term training, the private-sector broker saw to it that welfare clients registered with temporary-help agencies in the private sector. The initial training consisted of a total of three hours in which instructors extolled the virtues of temporary work, patronized clients about the importance of proper grooming and being punctual, and then offered tips on how to sell themselves to potential employers. The welfare clients were told in no uncertain terms that if they refused the work offered by the temporary-help companies, they would be cut off welfare.

Leah Vosko, a McMaster University researcher who studied this case, found that the broker had delivered a clear message to the clients: "They have no choice but to accept their location at the bottom of the labour market: low waged, casual light industrial work and de-skilled clerical work are among the few *suitable* employment alternatives currently available to social assistance recipients." The job referrals, Vosko notes, had an overt gender bias: "As a general rule, men were encouraged to dress in casual clothes since they would most likely be placed in light industrial work and women were to 'dress for the office,' mirroring the internal sex-segregation common to the temporary help industry."[22]

Vosko documents a client's response to the coercion: "They don't tell you anything. You just get this little thing in the mail telling you that you have to report on such and such a day to such and such a place and that's it . . . I mean, it's really threatening. It tells that you either do it or you don't get any money."[23]

But aside from shifting the welfare poor into the pool of the working poor within the precarious temporary-help industry, this social service is integrated with the corporate model in another way. Since the program is geared to reducing the number of people on welfare, it is seen as "saving" money for government. The amount "saved" via shoving people off welfare is then used to calculate the fee paid to the private-sector broker. In this case the fee could be 10 per cent or more of the amount "saved" by a government that no longer has to pay welfare to the clients.[24] Therefore, the greater the speed and number of people "processed off welfare," the greater the financial reward to the broker.

In the United States this way of rewarding private consultants and corporations for getting people off welfare has become a big business.[25] No wonder the executives in some of these businesses are eyeing Canada as more than just a nice place to visit. The pickings won't only be in government services. Non-profit social agencies operating outside of government but funded by government have seen the rules change in some parts of the country. Instead of an agency's funding being based on the government conducting rigorous reviews of the agency's budget, these non-profit agencies are now being forced into competitive bidding against private corporations that have discovered there are profits to be made in providing social services.

While social agencies have always been restricted by insufficient financing of their programs, there used to be more of a non-profit climate in which service providers could put more emphasis on client well-being. Today the new emphasis in most social agencies is on the "bottom line." Before the advent of short-term, contracting-out of social services, service providers had more continuity and flexibility with clients, as well as greater job security.

That is now changing, for example, in Ontario's long-term care. Instead of being institutionalized, people with disabilities and older people have long been enabled to live at home because of voluntary services such as Meals on Wheels, house cleaning, personal care, and friendly visiting. Where home-care services are funded through competitive bidding, the non-profit agencies are at a real disadvantage. For-profit corporations can promise to deliver the same service at less cost, because salaries for home-care workers within non-profit agencies are generally higher (though still not great) than are paid by private corporations.[26] For many non-profit social agencies, if they lose only once in this bidding war they will be forced to close their doors because they have no other source of income. Governments that favour a private-market approach will not be particularly disturbed by the collapse of the non-profit sector. An administrator of a non-profit long-term care agency comments on the effects of this privatization:

"For the client, there's no choice. A hospital will tell them, 'You go home NOW: we'll give you home care at the level we decide.' Clients come out quicker and sicker from hospitals, which increases the responsibilities of home-care workers. And by metering out maximum levels of service, staff is pressured, for example — when giving a bath to a client, to be in and out of the client's home in half an hour, little time for talk, little sense of humanity — off they rush to the next client. That, plus the government's efforts to compress wages, leads to less job satisfaction, and will over time lead to bigger job turnover — with less continuity of service for clients. While all this is happening we see non-acute clients being squeezed out of services they used to receive, and having to rely on the private market."

Is it too far-fetched, then, to predict that as social work attempts to expand its professional credibility it will continue to embrace the corporate model and turn its back on the have-nots?

To succeed in such a scenario, the profession would have to cover up its behaviour by carefully conveying a double message. By issuing periodic public statements, social work professional associations would declare their commitment to social justice, to helping the poor, the powerless, and the unemployed. Meanwhile social services would also earn a reputation among decision-makers of having tough-minded managers capable of keeping their staff and budgets in line and their clients in their place. If social work supervisors were able to convince front-line professionals that the best way to help clients is to accept the agency's constraints, the next step would be for front-line workers to pass this message on to their clients. From the vantage point of many clients, that future is already here.

6 UNEMPLOYMENT TO WELFARE TO POVERTY:
CLIENTS SPEAK OUT

As I saw it, the line was firmly drawn. It was them — Social Services, representing the provincial government — against me, someone who happened to be unemployed and out of choices. After my initial interview, I felt rage, anger, depression, bitterness, and a sense of hopelessness. I was ashamed that I had to apply for welfare, ashamed that I didn't have a job, and ashamed of being poor. Because welfare did not give me enough to live on, I felt that I did not deserve any better. The lack of healthy food led to depression and the downward spiral continued.

> — forty-one-year-old woman on welfare,
> from *Our Neighbours' Voices*

POLITICIANS NEVER SAY "forget full employment." On the contrary, they all promise "jobs, jobs, jobs." Why is it then, that so many people are jobless?

In her book *Cult of Impotence*, writer Linda McQuaig examines government's levers for controlling the economy. She particularly focuses on how economists have framed the choices: It is either bring down inflation or bring down unemployment. While most of us would surely prefer to bring unemployment down to somewhere near zero, McQuaig notes that the wealthiest people in Canada prefer to make inflation their target, keeping it as low as possible. Predictably, Ottawa's consistent choice is to keep inflation in check.

McQuaig probes this government strategy and discovers the elegant mathematical formula used by economists to hide the political nature of the process. According to the formula, creating more unemployment — after economists coldly calculate its "natural level" —

becomes a key mechanism used to achieve inflation control. Referring to the math, McQuaig notes: "It sounded awesome in its specificity, certainly not something that could be challenged on the grounds of being unfair. It wasn't a question of fairness or unfairness. What was involved here was science."[1]

Who benefits from this particular "science"? It would not be the individuals who lose their jobs as a result of government decisions to deliberately boost unemployment. But the rich do benefit from higher unemployment, because when there are far more people than jobs, workers tend to compete against each other to get or to keep jobs, which in turn keeps wages — and, coincidentally, unions — in check. Lower wages keep employers smiling, because that increases their profits.

Apparently these gains are still not enough for the affluent. In order to bring their expenses down further, business leaders succeeded in pressuring the federal government to reduce coverage provided by Unemployment Insurance (UI), now called Employment Insurance. According to Armine Yalnizyan, "In 1990, 87% of all unemployed Canadians received UI benefits. This proportion dropped to 42% by 1997 and is still falling." By 1998 in Ontario, Yalnizyan found, less than 30 per cent of the unemployed were receiving benefits."[2]

Although unemployment means there are more people than there are available jobs, the official rates don't indicate the true magnitude of the problem. When you add people who have given up looking altogether because there are not enough jobs to go around, plus people who are involuntarily working part-time because they can't find decent full-time jobs, plus others experiencing significant underemployment, the actual unemployment rate nationally is much higher than the official version. In 1999 the estimated real number of unemployed people in Canada was over three million people, with a real unemployment rate of over 20 per cent of the workforce.[3] Then there are those many people who have had to accept jobs at minimum or poverty wages — simply because employers are allowed to get away with it.

Excluded from these figures are women who are carers in the home (but might prefer to work outside the home if they could find jobs), whose work is not considered productive because they toil within the reproductive side of our economy. As Dorothy O'Connell puts it, "Raising wheat is work, driving a garbage truck is work, raising children is nothing."[4] Margrit Eichler adds:

> Until very recently most people were unaware of the fact that unpaid household work is in fact work. Why on earth is this a new insight at a

theoretical level? Women have known it all along. However, if you look at economic theories and at the way, for instance, economists, sociologists or other people who write about these issues deal with them, it is a totally new and revolutionary insight.[5]

High unemployment erodes the gains made by women for access to jobs and to independent incomes. Their weak bargaining position makes them probable candidates to be first to lose their jobs or to settle for lower wages. Aboriginal peoples and new immigrants are also likely to experience limited choices and to settle for low-paying, non-union, unsteady, and unreliable jobs. Curiously, this reinforces attitudes portraying them as unsteady and unreliable individuals.

With limited access to decent jobs, crime can appeal as a career, which in turn closes more doors. A young black Maritimer gave a graphic account of the impact of racism and a "clouded" personal history when a job referral agency sent him out for an interview:

"So I called and made an appointment. When I went up to the office, there were two women sitting in the waiting room. I sat down and waited too. This fella comes out of the office and calls out my name. I said 'Yes, I'm here' and I stand up. The fella looks up from his file, sees my face and freezes. Why he practically pushed me down on the chair! I knew I had no chance at a job there.

"And anyhow, whenever I apply for a job right on the application form there's a section that says, do you have a criminal record? When you put down 'yes,' that finishes your chance for a job."

High unemployment not only hurts the most vulnerable in the workforce — women, people of colour, and youth — but also undermines the labour movement's victories from an earlier era, victories that promised secure income to anyone willing to become employed. When unemployment insurance benefits run out, or if an applicant does not qualify, the source of support shifts away from the federal government to provincial and municipal public assistance (or welfare) programs. There is a direct, and well-documented, link between higher unemployment and higher welfare caseloads.[6]

Social workers have known for a long time that unemployment and the pressures of irregular employment produce enormous social and personal stress. Aside from the well-known effects of frustration and demoralization, unemployment can also cause personal depression and other mental health problems. The health-care costs alone from increased illness due to unemployment in Canada come to an estimated $1 billion each year.[7] As Neil Tudiver puts it, "With such widespread unemployment, fear of being without work has become pervasive. Considerable stress is the result, which can impair performance, even as people strive to work harder and longer in order to forestall layoff."[8]

Meanwhile business leaders continue to lobby for their own solution. In this process, valuable work becomes more and more equated with employment within business corporations. The value of child care in or out of the home becomes further marginalized. Public services are seen as causing deficits and as being havens for incompetents, which allows business leaders to sound completely reasonable as they urge cuts in social programs. We are told not to worry and that "the answer for job creation" is to make it as easy as possible for corporations to maximize their profits, to attract new investments, to create new jobs.

Researcher Gordon Ternowetsky of the University of Northern British Columbia, reporting on the employment records of eleven profitable companies, found that the corporations had "downsized" themselves by a total of seventeen thousand employees at the same time as their profits soared — to a lofty \$3.7 billion.[9] Yet our political leaders are still stuck in the misguided hope that job creation will be led by the private sector. Meanwhile business leaders and their mass media blame the public sector and its social programs for government deficits. Indeed, deficits and lower taxes have been rallying cries for a quick fix to an ailing economy.

Government and business leaders regularly trot out their economists to prescribe the solution: Chop social programs. It seems not to matter that unemployment insurance and all welfare programs together have contributed to less than 6 per cent of the federal debt.[10] Besides self-interest and a slavish devotion to the needs of the affluent, the economists have surprisingly little basis to justify their position. Instead, the hard economic evidence suggests a different conclusion: "Canada's fiscal crisis is *not* the result of an unaffordable system of social programs. Canada has neither over-provided nor over-spent on social programs. Rather, Canada has under-collected relative to both the capacity of its citizens and corporations to contribute to the social security of Canadians."[11]

One study, for instance, revealed that thousands of profitable corporations in Canada were paying no tax on their profits. Another study, by Ternowetsky, similarly found that during a recent ten-year period over \$140 billion in corporate profits were not taxed. Marvyn Novick, an advocate for the Child Poverty Action Group, calls such corporate behaviour "economic dumping" via "corporate shedding," with the corporations ridding themselves of taxes and labour costs and thereby fuelling the breakdown of the economy.[12] This economic dumping by the rich is so extensive that poverty could be eliminated in Canada simply by reducing tax breaks for business and high-income earners.[13] But that would take a brand of political courage that is rare among current politicians.

At the same time as they are on the warpath against social programs, corporate leaders eagerly seek government handouts for themselves. To its credit, *Time* magazine researched government handouts to U.S. companies and found, "The rationale is that subsidies and tax breaks granted to companies create jobs. That rationale is a myth."[14] *Time* also found that the largest companies had "erased more jobs" than they had created in the 1990s, "and yet they are the biggest beneficiaries of corporate welfare." To achieve these results a vast army of corporate bureaucrats from eleven thousand organizations was busily lobbying all levels of government. In addition, these corporate bodies "conduct seminars, conferences and training sessions. They have their own trade associations. They publish their own journals and newsletters. They create attractive websites on the Internet. And they never call it 'welfare.' They call it 'economic incentive.' "[15]

Canada's corporate bureaucrats, while fewer in number, have been just as effective. Our elected leaders receive a constant stream of "objective" messages from the business media, as well as being the object of direct lobbying for law, policies, and rules favourable to business interests. The Alliance of Manufacturers and Exporters of Canada (AMEC), the Business Council on National Issues (BCNI), the Fraser Institute, and the C.D. Howe Institute are a sampling of business think tanks and lobbying groups that have hefty budgets to pay economists and others to sway both public opinion and public officials.[16] The response has been public policies that continue to favour the rich, combined with decades of cuts to social programs, such as cuts to services for homeless youth and cuts to women's shelters, added to cuts to employment insurance and welfare.

The growing number of food banks attests to the country's growing hunger as well as the unravelling of the social security safety net.[17] Food banks, virtually unknown prior to 1980, serve mainly welfare clients, but are also used by recipients of unemployment insurance who find that the government cheques are too small to cover all their basic needs. Researcher Graham Riches notes that food banks create the illusion that the problem of hunger is being solved:

They allow us to believe that the problem is being met and they deflect attention away from government and its legislated responsibilities. They serve to undermine social and economic rights. In this sense they play a key role in the depoliticization of hunger as a public issue, particularly when they enlist the services of the media to support them in food drives. In this way the media come to portray hunger and the work of food banks as just another charitable cause.[18]

As Riches points out, food, much like health care, is too important to be left to the vagaries of the private market. He reminds us that the United Nations International Covenant on Economic, Social and Cultural Rights recognizes the right of people "to an adequate standard of living . . . including adequate food, clothing and housing."[19]

Meanwhile, as Sally Rutherford of the Canadian Federation of Agriculture (among many others) argues, there is more than enough food to go around in this world. "The farmers of the world have produced enough food to satisfy the world's population. . . . The problem isn't too little food, but rather too little political will to see that food is distributed in an equitable manner."[20]

Professor David Hulchanski of the University of Toronto, who specializes in the study of housing, offers another illustration: *"Just as the private market has failed in the area of food, it's the same with housing. The private market cannot house low-income people. It never could. Poor people are pushed out by the real estate market. That's why in the Netherlands, for instance, the housing for the city of Amsterdam is 60 per cent non-profit."*

But in Canada, where food chains and real estate corporations claim the capacity to serve everyone, homelessness and hunger grow. Rather than looking at the root cause, namely the fundamental flaws of the private-market system, the prevailing approach is to shift the blame onto the men, women, and children who are poor. Meanwhile social services that were originally intended to soften the failures of the market system are running dry and, as a result, the gap between the haves and have-nots continues to widen. Another result is that while wealth continues to concentrate into the hands of the most affluent, the middle class is shrinking. In the view of researchers Mike Burke and John Shields, "The middle is being hollowed out and an *hour glass labour market* created . . . that is, a workforce in which one part of the population is materially well off and secure and the larger portion is economically insecure."[21] The motor of this regressive change is the increasing power of corporations, both at home and on the international level.

GLOBALIZATION AND SOCIAL PROGRAMS

The international arena is a contested location. One form of globalization that has intensified in recent decades has been the push by transnational corporations to monopolize business across increasingly large segments of the planet. Maude Barlow and Tony Clarke point out how far matters had gone by the late 1990s: "Fifty-one of the world's top one hundred economies are individual corporations. Mitsubishi is richer than Indonesia, the fourth most populous country on Earth. General Motors has more money than Denmark. Ford trumps South Africa. Toyota is bigger than Norway. K-Mart is actually larger than 161 countries."[22]

The International Forum on Globalization, a non-profit international watchdog, examined the effects of this corporate-led globalization. Meeting in Siena, Italy, the Forum found that severe human suffering was being caused by volatile global financial markets due to current global trade and investment patterns:

> This volatility is bringing massive economic breakdown in some nations, insecurity in all nations, unprecedented hardships for millions of people, growing unemployment and dislocation in all regions, direct assaults on environmental and labour conditions, loss of wilderness and biodiversity, massive population shifts, increased racial and ethnic tensions, and other disastrous results. Such dire outcomes are now manifest throughout the world, and are increasing daily.[23]

These market patterns and their harmful consequences, the International Forum noted, are the result of rules made by a series of international bodies:

> These rules have been created and enforced by the World Trade Organization (WTO), the International Monetary Fund (IMF), the General Agreement on Tariffs and Trade (GATT), the North American Free Trade Agreement (NAFTA), the Maastricht Agreement, the World Bank, and other global bureaucracies that currently discipline governments in the area of trade and financial investment.[24]

One of the ways in which these global financial institutions have disciplined poor nations is by imposing Structural Adjustment Programs. This means that in exchange for receiving investments, credits, and loans, Third World nations have first to agree to a series of conditions that include substantial cuts in government spending for health, education, and social assistance. Similar demands from business leaders continue to urge Canada and other industrialized nations to cut their social programs — making all the clearer the meaning of global corporate control.

At the same time, another version of globalization is also taking form — a ground-up version, one challenging corporate power. The work of the International Forum on Globalization, for instance, is calling for new ways of bringing together citizen organizations, communities, and nation-states to "place human, social and ecological values *above* economic values (and corporate profit)."[25] This ground-up version of globalization is about reinvigorating democratic accountability and placing priority on social equity. But while this international opposition is gathering momentum, the prevailing trend is still heavily tilted towards the global expansion of corporate power. Canada is conforming to this trend, with mounting social casualties.

According to an unemployed Maritimer: "It's been so hard for so long that after a while it destroys you inside, piece by piece. After a while you start going numb."[26]

If finding a decent job is next to impossible for so many people, what do they find and experience when they turn to Canada's welfare system for help?

ENTERING THE WELFARE SYSTEM

It has become commonplace for people in need to desperately try to avoid getting into the welfare system in the first place. Part of this is a matter of personal pride and hopes alongside a prevailing sense of the work ethic, a belief that the individual has to look after her or himself and not go to the state for handouts. This is a basic tenet of the status quo — the belief that each individual has both the responsibility and the opportunity to "make it." The ideology avoids any serious consideration of community or collective responsibility for poverty and for social improvement.

When the uncertain status of being on welfare is added to the fact of colour the barriers become formidable, and not just in cases of employment:

"With six children I had a terrible time finding a place to live. When they found out I was on welfare, lots of places wouldn't rent to me. The fact I was a single parent made it worse and it didn't matter to them the fact I was widowed. Most people don't like to admit that there are people who have to live on welfare, so they push that idea aside. I've had doors slammed in my face!

"The fact that I'm an Indian woman makes it even worse. One place I

called, the woman said 'Yes, I have a place available' and so I went there. As soon as she sees I'm brown she says, 'Sorry we don't rent to Native people.'"

There is most often a debilitating sense of dehumanization in being on welfare. Given that their child-care work is constantly being devalued as non-work, a feeling of desperation often haunts women with low incomes. Dorothy O'Connell writes: "That is why some women will shoplift before they go on welfare, will bounce cheques, will almost starve themselves and their children before taking that last step."[27]

For many women, taking that last step leads to other problems: *"I did a favour to this neighbour, she was going into hospital to have a baby, so I offered to babysit her two children. Fine? Her husband comes to my place and you know what he wants? He wants to go to bed with me! I refuse and he says, 'You'll be sorry.' He figures I'm on welfare, I'm a single parent — I'm fair game. I told him where to go."*

A welfare client from another part of the country reported that her landlord told her that if she had sex with him he would take $150 a month off her rent. "He used the master key to walk in our place any time and said it's his tax dollars that were paying for me so he could do it!"[28]

One woman on welfare said that it is not much different from being married — either way you get *"put down all the time — that's pretty hard for the head to take!"* She adds:

"My rent just went up $125. Welfare tells me to find somewhere cheaper. I tell them I've been looking and even got a letter from the housing registry that says I should stay where I am because I'm paying the going rate and there are so few vacancies in Vancouver. But welfare won't pay for the increase . . . you get to feel that they're blaming me for the fact my husband took off."

Another welfare client put it this way: *"As a single parent on welfare, you feel so vulnerable, so unprotected. You're game for the weirdos on the streets. I've got a double lock on my door, but that doesn't stop the strain — the strain is financial and emotional and it can get to your health too."*

When this strain is assessed by professional helpers — the social workers — it is often diagnosed, especially in the case of women, as the client's own psychological or psychiatric problems; as Helen Levine states:

Men's stress and distress are generally linked with occupational hazards — too much pressure or responsibility on the job or unemployment — or absence of adequate nurturance and support at home. For women, stress and distress are typically defined as mental health problems. Our turmoil is not linked to the occupational hazards of child-care and domestic labour, to poverty, unemployment or the double work-load, to the misogyny that assaults us daily at multiple levels. We are not expected even to claim a support system at home — we are supposed to provide it. Women's distress is said to be primarily "in the head."[29]

Social work counselling has equated women's unhappiness with "sickness" when the sources of that unhappiness have been the profound oppression of women in and beyond the family, in the paid and unpaid workplace. When social workers define human struggles as being mainly in the head, they help to further immobilize women, to add another load, another stigma, onto the burdens women are expected to carry.

The idea of women in social distress being somehow "sick" is connected in part to the witchcraft trials of the sixteenth century, where "witches" were often poor elderly women beggars and the accusations of witchcraft were in part an attempt by rich men to get them out of the way, to avoid the guilt they might otherwise feel by seeing them huddling outside their doors every day, begging.[30] Levine observes:

> Contemporary women are no longer called witches and burned as in the Middle Ages, but are instead helped to self-destruct. This self-destruct training is an insidious tool used to contain women's rage and despair, to invalidate our experience of the world. It produces guilt, anxiety and depression — a sense of impotence that keeps us docile and fearful, unable to act on our own behalf. The helping professions, in practice as in theory, collude with and reinforce the self-destruct mechanism in women.[31]

SOCIAL SERVICES: A MAJOR DISENCHANTMENT

Some three decades ago the Special Senate Committee on Poverty provided the public with a glimpse into what it saw as a highly unsatisfactory situation. It commented critically on the approach then used by welfare offices: "It repels both the people who depend on the handouts and those who administer them. Alienation on the part of welfare recipients and disenchantment on the part of welfare administrators were evident in much of the testimony."[32]

In 1997 Senator Erminie Joy Cohen presented her report *Sounding the Alarm: Poverty in Canada,* in which she concludes: "The government of Canada has made many promises to the international community to protect the lives and livelihoods of its most vulnerable citizens. Yet to date, it has made no progress in this area."[33] Shedding light as to why governments in Canada have made so little progress, Hugh Shewell, policy analyst at York University, concludes that a statement by the Canadian Conference of Catholic Bishops in 1985 still has as much relevance today: "The basic contradiction of our times rests in the structural domination of capital . . . over people, over labour, over communities."[34]

As a result, users of social services frequently face a dehumanizing experience in which human need is given short shrift — a situation confirmed by studies coast to coast.[35] Clients are subtly reminded again and again that they come from a class, gender, or race, or have a sexual orientation, disability, or other identity, that is deemed inferior. One client remarked on how she felt treated inside an agency: *"The way they look at the dollars — it's like they just ring up their figures on a cash register. You're worth so much for this, so much for that — they make you feel like an animal."*

Outside the agencies there are also problems:

"At a grocery store once, when I had a voucher * *— it's on a piece of blue paper, they have to fill it in, then you have to sign it — I had spent fifty cents less than the amount of the voucher. One cashier shouts over to the next cashier, 'Hey, here's someone with a voucher, can I give her change?' The other one answers, 'No, you're not supposed to give them any money.' I felt like they were talking about somebody who wasn't a person. I just wanted to tell them to forget about it, keep the damn change! Instead they were shouting and the whole store knew I was on welfare."*

Such events month after month demoralize clients. Because the amount that welfare departments allow for rent is typically much lower than the actual rent charged, the recipient has to make up the difference from the food budget. In some provinces clients are allowed to receive a financial supplement to buy food, but this is only a loan. As one person on welfare said: *"They'll subtract this amount from your next cheque, so you're short next month and you always end up being short. Always behind. You get the feeling that's the way they want it."*

The dynamics lead to clients feeling trapped. Even when, as happens occasionally, the rates are raised, the trap remains. *"Sometimes*

---

* Food vouchers are certificates that can be used in place of cash at certain grocery stores, and are sometimes granted if a family runs short before the end of the month.

welfare gives us a raise — at last. We won't be eating macaroni. But nothing changes. Because then the rent goes up and wipes out the raise."

The irony here is that this woman was living in public housing: The rent was raised by the public housing authority. So what one branch of government was "giving" with one hand, another branch was taking away with another.

Continual demoralization often leads to further personal crises, shattering the welfare recipient's sense of self — what remains is a shadow of the person, which is then duly imprinted by social workers onto the official files of the state: *"Of course you never see the files that welfare keeps on you. If you're in the office and the worker gets called out, she'll take your file with her. Yet it's our life! So they have us by the strings. We're their puppets. And you better dance!"*

Most social workers do not consciously enjoy controlling "their" clients. Indeed, most of them would be annoyed at the suggestion that they manipulate clients to keep them in their place. There are no job descriptions calling for the manipulation of clients. The imposition of social controls is often subtle and confusing because officially clients are not presented as people to be subjugated. On the contrary, modern social work literature presents the client in a positive light: "The client has rights — the right to service, the right to participate, the right to fail. . . . The client has strengths, modes of adaptation, and ways of coping. The client brings a particular set of motivations, capacities and opportunities."[36]

While this is the theory, in practice most clients find that the rights and strengths do not shine through the bureaucratic haze. Perhaps the most extreme — and therefore revealing — case of alienation of client from worker comes in the restrictive institutional settings of prisons or mental hospitals. In prisons, social workers and other helping professionals, such as chaplains and psychologists, are hired as part of programs defined as "opportunities for social, emotional, physical, personal, and spiritual development." According to the Solicitor General's Office, "Each offender's program is monitored by professional staff who also counsel the offender and assess his or her program."[37] It is all in the name of "rehabilitation."

"Rehabilitation? I get a laugh when a judge says he's giving you a jail sentence so you can get "rehabilitated." What rehabilitation? It's a big farce. There's only rehabilitation in the imagination of the judge. When you get sent to prison, there's a piece of paper and it tells them to take you from point A to point B. Point B is prison. The prison gets the piece of paper and the only thing they do, they try to keep you there."

The major irony is the belief that rehabilitation can happen at all in a cell block or in the wards of a mental institution, where behaviour is monitored and severely restricted and the main requirement is to conform to behavioural norms established by administrators and professionals.

There have been numerous accounts of women's experiences inside psychiatric institutions. Phyllis Chesler, in *Women and Madness,* documents how most of the twenty-four women she interviewed had been put into these institutions "wholly against their will, through brutal physical force, trickery, or in a state of coma following unsuccessful suicide attempts."[38] In another account a woman recalls the missed opportunities for sharing concerns with other women patients in a psychiatric institution:

> Patients said almost nothing at the ward meetings except for announcement of activities. And then it ended. I had been intrigued by the idea of this group, its possibilities. I know there have been all kinds of complaints and concerns and so afterwards asked G. why there were no comments, no grievances aired. The reply — fear, *FEAR,* **FEAR.** Patients are worried about the grapevine from most of the nurses to the doctors, their "dossier," the repercussions that might arise if real problems were aired. So everyone keeps mum. It's power politics and the women are clear re who holds the power.[39]

The revolving door syndrome common within prisons and mental-health services illustrates that social workers fail in their rehabilitation efforts more often than not — and it is the punitive nature of the institutions that prevails: *"You get hardened. So if I'm walking down a cell block and someone is stabbed, I keep walking. I don't see nothin' and I don't say nothin'. You keep your mouth shut for your own good."*

Such accounts from people in prisons and mental hospitals led Bonnie Burstow and Don Weitz to note, "The hospital, alas, turns out to be as much a prison as the prison is a madhouse." In *Shrink Resistant,* which contains vivid accounts by "inmates" of their lives in mental institutions, Burstow and Weitz conclude: "Once locked up . . . you are more likely to be abused if you are Black, Native, female, gay, poor or old."[40]

Prisons and other institutions are more than locks and high walls. The pressure to submit to the dominant view of class, gender, cultural background, and sexuality is everywhere. Invisible walls accompany our social relations whenever we interact with others. These walls stretch on throughout our lives, and the toll is high not only in locked institutions. A study of lesbian, gay, and bisexual youth who were or had recently been residents in group homes, treatment centres, and shelters in the Toronto area revealed, most disturbingly, "that these youths, particularly gay males, were not assured physical safety within residential settings. They painfully recounted stories of physical threats if they were open about their sexuality. Young lesbian women told us that their sexuality was undermined, silenced and pathologized by frontline workers in residential settings."[41]

WORKERS AND CLIENTS: CONSTRAINTS AND CONTRACTS

In theory, contracts between workers and clients recognize the goal of self-determination, which means that workers are supposed to avoid imposing solutions on clients. The idea of self-determination holds that social work is effective only when clients make their own choices and decisions (with exceptions, such as when clients decide to break the law or harm others). Built upon the value of client self-determination, a social work contract is ostensibly a mutual agreement between worker and client about the goals of the service and the general method of reaching these goals. It is seen as a means of "involving" a client in making choices about what is to be done.

According to one text, the contract encourages the client "to use his or her skills and resources in the work on problem resolution."[42] A contract, then, implies equal power between social worker and client. Yet in reality there is no such equality. Most social work relationships are not one of a willing buyer and a willing seller. Most clients arrive at social agencies with little if any choice. Most often, their real choice would be not to be there at all.

All too often, social workers behave as if clients have many more choices than really exist. Many workers subscribe to the myth that everyone in the society, including clients, can exercise a full range of choices on the basis of equal opportunity. Blaming the victim is the end result of such a perspective. A probation officer in the Maritimes offers one version of this approach:

"My approach to helping inmates when they get out is clear: Don't ask me to do anything more for you than you're doing yourself. I tell them you're in the driver seat and you got your foot on the pedal. Just remember I've got a foot I can put on the brake. I don't hide my authority and I'm honest about it. . . . You let the parolee know it's easy for you to send him back to prison. I'm trying to keep you on the street. They know you've got a task and sometimes it's not pleasant, but I tell them: They're the

ones who decide. If they choose to do something, it's up to them. All I can do is try the best I can."

With few jobs available, with inadequate welfare payments, with the pressures of a competitive society, the relationship between client and worker reveals clearly where the social control lies. In the end it is the social worker who makes the critical decisions.

Disabled people have consistently experienced sharp barriers, resulting in higher levels of unemployment than the general population: "As a result, currently disabled people are more likely to be out of work than non-disabled people, they are out of work longer than other unemployed workers, and when they do find work it is more often than not low-paid, low-status work with poor working conditions."[43]

But when disabled people receive help, as one of them says, "We have to be very tolerant of non-disabled people's behaviour towards us, either because we need their help or because we can't afford to provoke their hostility and anger. When we do, we feel guilty."[44]

Given the stigma attached to welfare and its meagre levels of assistance, it is understandable that clients develop negative feelings about agencies and their workers. The client experience of relative powerlessness inevitably widens the gulf between client and worker. One woman, for instance, arranged with the welfare office to get a homemaker who would come into the household and help with child care and other domestic chores.

"Once I got called to the welfare office — this was after I'd had a homemaker. Welfare wanted to know — how come I didn't have enough sheets on the bed? How come there weren't enough clothes? When I came home with a few friends, I could tell the homemaker thought we were all going to be drinking. It so happens I don't drink! But they still wanted me to explain. They even asked me, how come I didn't have any coffee or tea? I was furious. I told them I go without what I like so my kids can have what they need, but I guess they couldn't understand that. Before I could even have this homemaker, they wanted to know where I was going, what I was going to do, everything. Even why couldn't I get a babysitter?"

Fear is another major factor that enters into the worker-client relationship. A client in the Maritimes said: *"When I applied for welfare, I even knew the amount I was entitled to. It was higher than what my social worker said — but I was afraid to push for it. I was reluctant because of fear — I might lose all of it. I can now see how you become too dependent on the worker. How women's passive roles are reinforced by welfare."*

THE PUSH TO WORKFARE

Workfare programs are blunt. Clients are told that if they refuse to accept an assigned job or training or are not planning to find a job, they will immediately be cut off welfare. "Encouraging" welfare clients to get a job is not new. Workfare is just the latest scheme for "helping" the poor to improve their conditions.

The Canada Assistance Plan, which no longer exists, had blocked workfare. The federal government had prevented provinces from forcing welfare clients to work for their welfare checks. Under the Canada Assistance Plan the federal government could specify conditions that provinces had to meet if they wanted to receive federal funds for social assistance programs. One of those conditions was that hunger and poverty could not be used to coerce the disadvantaged into becoming employed.

When business leaders implicitly urged governments to abandon the disadvantaged in the 1980s and 1990s, Ottawa repealed the Canada Assistance Plan and thereby destroyed the very minimal national standards that had existed for social assistance, such as the right of welfare applicants to appeal to an independent tribunal if they were refused assistance. At the same time as it dismantled such standards, the federal government shifted to a system of giving provinces block grants for health care, postsecondary education, and social assistance. This new arrangement is called the Canada Health and Social Transfer (CHST).

This arrangement allows provinces to put the squeeze on social services. The National Anti-Poverty Organization (NAPO) warns, "Provincial governments could choose not to fund social assistance at all, and use the funding for the more politically palatable health care and postsecondary education."[45]

Why has workfare become so popular? In recent years, talk-radio and other forms of media, as well as business and government leaders, have been unrelenting in promoting prejudices against the poor. "Welfare recipients," NAPO says, "are barraged with images and slogans blaming them for being poor, targeting them as the cause of high debts and deficits, reinforcing notions that they are 'lazy' and 'worthless.'"[46]

The promotion of prejudices against the poor — known as *poor bashing* — causes the poor to feel humiliated and despised. "Poor bashing has infected Canadian society," concludes a government survey of poverty in Canada.[47] Because it is so pervasive, poor bashing has given further impetus to the spread of workfare programs. An overview of "welfare-to-work" programs found: "In Alberta, single parents with a five-month-old baby are notified that they need to think about preparing for work. When the child is six months old, the program worker will meet with the mother to formulate an employment plan. It is possible for a single parent to lose their welfare benefits if they refuse to begin planning their exit from social assistance."[48]

So much for choices, family values, and giving value to the work of being a full-time parent. NAPO's study found that the working conditions of workfare left more than a little to be desired:

> In most provinces workfare recipients are not protected under employment standards legislation; do not have the right to join or organize trade unions; and do not receive the same benefits or wages as their non-workfare colleagues. . . . Without even basic employment protection, recipients are vulnerable to unscrupulous employers who may threaten or coerce them, leaving them without basic financial supports or recourse to appeal.[49]

The advocates of workfare argue that the program will "get people off welfare and into jobs." In making that claim, the advocates make a curious leap of faith that after completing workfare "training" welfare clients will have no trouble graduating into one of the many decent-paying jobs that are supposedly "out there." Yet social research documents that more and more jobs today are low-paying, part-time, and non-unionized, with no vacation benefits or supplementary dental or pension coverage.[50] Continuing high unemployment suggests there are not even enough of these poor jobs to go around. There are countless examples of how people with little money experience these conditions. For instance:

> Fasting one day a week, walking thirty blocks to apply for a job to save the bus fare, then walking back. Getting turned down for that dishwasher job. Finally getting your high school diploma and then finding out it makes no difference.[51]

> I've had four years in university, I've got two degrees, $35,000 in debts, and no more closer to getting a job than four years ago. . . . If something doesn't change, people are going to commit suicide. I've lost 75 pounds averaging a meal a day for a year and a half.[52]

As for its promise of moving clients into jobs, Eric Shragge, professor at McGill University who researched the workfare experience in different regions of North America, concludes: "Workfare measures have not been effective in getting people back to work, particularly in the long-term."[53]

If workfare does not substantially benefit the poor, why then has there been this big push to set the programs in place? People who are not poor gain at least two benefits from a government's implementation of workfare programs. First, people who for whatever reason need to feel superior to the poor gain a psychological affirmation. After all, they can now tell themselves that government is "kicking ass" to force "those inferiors" into shaping up.

The second benefit is economic. Evidence shows that workfare provides financial benefits to business corporations, which under workfare can hire a cheaper workforce subsidized by taxpayers.[54] The cheaper cost of labour puts a downward spin on wages as more and more people compete for low-paying jobs. While the official line is that social services are for the benefit of the needy, it is the business sector than ends up pocketing the gains for itself. When political and business leaders team up, as they have done historically, to further undermine labour unions through legislation or repression, this can serve to push labour costs down even more, causing employers to smile all the way to the bank.

BROKEN PROMISES . . . AND THEIR CONSEQUENCES

The net effect of the public assistance morass is to undermine the stated objectives of most welfare legislation. Provincial public assistance laws usually claim to "assist the disadvantaged" or to "provide relief to the destitute" or generally help the poor, marginal, or dislocated get back on their feet. Yet social service workers experience these promises being broken on a daily basis by the myriad ways in which they are prevented from providing adequate help to the over 2.5 million Canadians on welfare.[55]

Clients are aware that at least some social workers find the working conditions intolerable. The good social workers either "quit or go bizarre," reported one client. The rest "become stinking bureaucrats." One person, a member of a client advocacy group, told me about getting a call from a social worker who didn't even want to give her name: *"She told me how she'd tried and tried to help a client, but she said 'the system wouldn't let me.' She burst out crying over the phone."*

Barbara Blouin, a researcher in Nova Scotia, found that almost all municipalities in that province demand that people on welfare who are deemed to be "employable" must actively look for work before they can receive payments, even if the area in question has high unemployment. She also found that the "employable unemployed" are treated especially badly: If you are in that group and if you are single or have no dependents, you are not considered eligible for welfare in about one-third of the province's municipalities.[56]

The stress everywhere now, it seems, is on job training. Jean Swanson, of the Vancouver organization End Legislated Poverty, observes that the emphasis on training perpetuates the myth that the main reason people are poor is because they are untrained, unskilled, or don't work: "There are plenty of trained and skilled people doing work our society would die without. Waitresses, child-care workers, cleaners, fruit pickers, seamstresses are all important and skilled people. . . . They live in poverty because their wages are so low. We need to provide more money, not training for these people."[57]

Where should the money come from? One approach suggests that the government should somehow subsidize low-waged workers. Swanson disagrees. She advocates that corporations, not taxpayers, should be paying these wages. Swanson argues that the provinces should pass laws for a hefty increase in the minimum wage, which would cost taxpayers nothing but place the onus on employers.[58] This change would undoubtedly be opposed by the corporate sector. Today most politicians would choose to back the conservative approach: cutting social programs, stigmatizing the poor, and keeping minimum wages at substandard levels. A former welfare client who is a single mother describes the consequences:

"By November of last year I went off welfare. I was holding down two jobs, one with the Y, the other with a day care, but the salaries were terribly low. I was bringing in $100 less than when I was on welfare. So I got a third job, at another day care. All these jobs were for different times of the day, different days of the week, but it ended up I was working from 8:30 a.m. till 6 p.m. for five days a week, juggling these three jobs. It was hard but I just never wanted to go back to welfare. I felt I was better than dirt."

The welfare department's authority to terminate payments creates profound fear and anxiety among male as well as female welfare clients. At first glance the policies appear to make sense. Social workers, representing the state and its proverbial taxpayers, don't want to pay out good money to people who don't need it. The department wants to know about any extra income on the part of the clients. Consequently, what usually is considered private information — gifts or inheritances or the wages of part-time employment — ceases to be private. The information becomes a matter of vital interest to the social worker, and a matter of eligibility for the recipient.

If a single mother on welfare has a male friend, does he give her any money? If so, she is expected to declare the amount, which is then deducted from her next welfare cheque. Or the welfare office could decide that the woman is no longer in need of financial help and stop the cheques. Social workers and other employees of welfare offices are expected to make sure that all extra client income is declared. Again, it is a key example of a double standard of morality regarding women and men on welfare: No one asks a man whom he's sleeping with. If there is a "man in the house," that is, if he is not just visiting but is co-habiting with the woman, she could be charged with fraud if she has not reported it. Officially the welfare department is not supposed to interfere with a woman's right to have a housemate. But in practice welfare officials will investigate to satisfy themselves whether a woman is "just sleeping with" someone else or actually co-habiting with another person.[59] There is an expectation that women exchange sexual, domestic, and child-care services in return for private support.

The tension this creates for women on welfare can be intolerable. As one Aboriginal woman told me, *"I had a boyfriend and they kept asking him these questions. After a while, they just bothered him too much and he left. So they even get between you and a boyfriend."*

Such client experiences give rise to accusations about social workers being snoopy and prying into what should be private business. In fact, most provinces have *fraud squads* as part of their welfare departments, and the job of these squads is to catch welfare applicants who lie about their income. Yet, according to Ian Morrison of the Clinic Resource Office of Ontario Legal Aid, a current comprehensive study of welfare fraud does not exist. Morrison notes that because there is a good amount of discretion within the administration of welfare programs it is easier to search out tax fraud than welfare fraud. Some studies have suggested that welfare fraud ranges from 3 to 5 per cent of total cases. Metro Toronto's "hot line," established to receive tips about suspected fraud, found that about half of the people snitched on were not on welfare at all. Of those who were on welfare and suspected of cheating, only 1 per cent were found guilty of fraud.[60]

The Quebec government's claims that its welfare cops were saving a lot of money were found to be grossly exaggerated by researchers from the Université de Montréal, who concluded that these inspectors cost three times more in salary and benefits than what they recovered in fraud and errors.[61] Yet the considerably greater attention that politicians and the media pay to cheating on welfare as compared to cheating on taxes illustrates a class prejudice against the poor, who are seen as fair game for blame, whereas the rich are protected by assumptions of respectability.

Consequently, clients on welfare must put up with harassment from investigators. One client was still fuming at her experience:

"This friend of mine had no job, had no place to go. I agreed to help him out. I admitted him to my place. He wasn't living with me, he wasn't giving me money. I was just trying to help him out. This causes welfare to investigate me. Now they tell me I have to report all overnight guests. Then they tell me I had to come to the welfare office. I went with an advocate from a community group. I get down there and this inspector tells us: 'All people on welfare are public property!' Can you believe it!? We're now 'public property'!! I got so mad!! I told him why not put me and my children in a zoo?! Can you believe it? I was lucky I had witnesses who heard him. This just gives you some idea what we have to put up with."

In this instance the client was part of a client group whose members gave each other moral support and realized when the agency was overstepping even its normally punitive boundaries. But most clients are not so fortunate. More often than not such conduct by the agency would proceed unreported and uncontested because most clients — women especially — are verbally beaten down, socially isolated, and worn out just surviving. Clients don't necessarily see any difference between social workers and fraud investigators. Many social workers have an implicit social policing function so that in the client's eyes, workers and investigators are all lumped together as "them."

IN THE INTERESTS OF THE YOUNG . . . AND OLD

The gulf between clients and social agencies is not confined to public assistance. Child welfare agencies frequently blame mothers in the name of serving and protecting children. Helping mothers establish and claim a decent life for themselves is seen to have little relation to safeguarding the "best interests of the child."

Until recently professional theory has tended to blame wife and mother in situations of sexual abuse that are typically cases of fathers abusing daughters:

> When incest occurs, professional theory and practice routinely point to the mother as having been guilty of a form of desertion within the family

— having withdrawn passively or actively from vital aspects of her role, sexually and otherwise. The implication is that "normal" mothers subordinate their own needs, preferences and wishes to those of husband and children. In dealing with the sexual assault committed by husband and father, it is common practice among helping professionals to concentrate on the "inadequate" performance of wife and mother. . . . And if daughters were not inappropriately seductive, fathers would not "fall prey" to sexual assault.[62]

Such assumptions lead to a destructive relationship between social worker and client. An Alberta woman, for instance, became involved with social services after her husband had been found abusing her daughter:

"Then social service made a stinking mistake. They told us my husband could come home if he took Antabuse.* Him coming back put pressure on me and pressure on my daughter, who tried suicide after that. At the time I was in stinking shape. Who knows what you're feeling when there's incest and as to social services — they knew absolutely zilch!"

Meanwhile the public gets a different version of what social workers are expected to do:

> The Department must look on each child and family as a unique situation and make available the appropriate service from a wide range of resources. . . . The Department has the responsibility to provide a high quality of service to children in care, keeping in mind the child's short and long term needs in respect to *his* family, *his* community and *his* healthy functioning as a productive individual.[63]

These seemingly "lofty" goals are contradicted by client experience. A young teenage girl's experience of social work in Alberta caused frustration and anger:

"After they found out about the incest, after they knew what happened, the social worker came over to the house. And the social worker talked to everyone else. She talked to my father, she talked to my mother, but she never talked to me. I want to know why? — why the social worker didn't take into consideration what the victim feels like? It's like you're the one that did something wrong! You're the bad egg! And meanwhile my father gets to stay in the house and I get sent away!"

Many of the children serviced by social workers, however, are not victims of sexual or physical abuse — their main "problem" is that they happen to be poor. Most social workers would agree that welfare pay-

---

* Antabuse is a drug to curb alcoholism.

ments don't cover the financial costs of single parenting. But at the same time as they have this special inside knowledge, social workers are not allowed to authorize the required extra funds. This puts welfare mothers in a bind. One of them remarked: *"Welfare comes to your home and they say 'your children look undernourished' and they blame the parents. But they're the ones who don't give enough money."*

Clients and social workers know that lack of adequate income contributes to child welfare problems, and there are studies that confirm it. According to the National Council of Welfare: "Not only are low-income children much more likely to be removed from their families, but their experience in care also tends to be more difficult. Poor kids face a greater likelihood of remaining in care for a lengthy period and . . . are twice as likely as children from non-poor families to come into care more than once."[64]

Marilyn Callahan's research into child welfare leads her to conclude: "One of the most troubling aspects of child welfare is this separation between poverty and child care. The relationship between these two factors is so self-evident it seems amazing that child welfare services do not make it front and centre in their business. But they do not."[65]

Being young and Aboriginal as well as poor creates special problems. Indeed, these conditions represent a quantum leap into hardship because of the long-term effects of colonialism. The House of Commons report on Indian Self-Government in Canada observed:

> Throughout the hearings, Indian witnesses condemned the policies of provincial welfare authorities for removing Indian children from reserves in cases where, in the opinion of the authorities, they were not being properly cared for by their parents. Witnesses criticized provincial authorities for judging situations by non-Indian standards, which are culturally different.[66]

Most social workers who go to Indian reserves tend to apply the dominant society's definition of what "child neglect" means. Consequently these social workers can end up removing an Indian child from the reserve, when according to Aboriginal culture the child is not being neglected.

> In one Indian community, a ten year old boy had been left alone for a few days, and the itinerant non-Native social worker was considering apprehension [removing the child from his home]. A community leader, concerned about the situation, asked to accompany the social worker to

the home of the child. On arrival, he asked the boy to make breakfast. The boy did so, using food left for him in the refrigerator by neighbours. When asked whether he was concerned about being alone during the absence of his grandfather, the boy indicated he had easy access to neighbours, who checked up on him periodically to ensure that all was well.[67]

In this instance, the boy was not "apprehended."

But all too often social workers from outside Aboriginal communities will make decisions based on inadequate knowledge about First Nations cultures. This problem, combined with the dominant society's racism, has left a bitter harvest: "All of our lives we've been controlled by the larger society. Institutions, governments, organizations — they tell us how to live, how to raise our children, etc. Eventually, if someone does it for you all the time, you lose enthusiasm, motivation and individuality. For Native people, this has been termed as cultural genocide."[68]

From any child's point of view, it is a frightening and bewildering experience to be separated from parents. Social workers, emergency shelters, courts, police, foster parents, group homes, and other institutions: It becomes a maze that adds to anxiety rather than relieves it. In the case of a twelve-year-old girl in Alberta who had been sexually abused by her father, both she and her younger sister were removed from their home to be placed in a foster home. A social worker took the girl and her sister to see a doctor and later a police detective. The twelve-year-old recalled what happened after meeting with the police:

"The social worker took me and my sister and we drove for a long time in the dark — I didn't know where I was going. I didn't know whether to jump out of the car and run or what. My sister didn't understand what was happening. She didn't understand what was going on or where we were going. She was getting pretty upset figuring that we were going to be taken away from home forever and everything. When we got to the foster home, the social worker told me that nobody here knows anything about what happened. She told me not to tell anybody — she said just keep everything to yourself. Nobody's supposed to know. At first I felt kind of relieved, like thinking that nobody would know. It would be a secret, but when I got there I kind of needed somebody to talk to. But there was nobody to talk to, because I was afraid if I told them I might get into trouble with the social worker."

While the social work professional has an adult view of how it all fits together, the experience is usually one of powerlessness and confusion for the child. One child said his experience was like being a pin-ball-machine ball, with the buttons being pushed by the welfare system and the child bouncing from one hard place to another: "You get all these pent-up feelings towards the system because . . . you don't under-stand why you were taken away because then you want to see your parents but they won't let you, why are you in the place? You get all these pent-up things and you've got to take them out on someone, eh."[69]

This anger can intensify as these young girls and boys learn that the best jobs and biggest cars are reserved for other people who lead lives pointedly different than theirs. Despite a few exceptions, most of these youths won't be able to attend universities, earn high salaries, or inherit large fortunes. Yet our culture tells them "You're equal to every-one else." No wonder they become confused. Blocked by high youth unemployment, there is pressure and temptation to "turn to crime" as a way out.

Not that all such youth end up violating the law. But some do, which can result in police arrests and imprisonment in youth detention centres. Often hired by these institutions, social workers find the agen-cies are often modelled upon adult prisons. A youth in Alberta reported: "This one guy said to me, 'If I had my way, I'd lock up every single juvenile delinquent and throw away the key.' So I don't think it's a question of helping us. I don't think they give a shit."[70]

Some of these youths will rebel against being slotted into an infe-rior social class. They will rebel against a system that they see as hav-ing the best things reserved for others. Yet bit by bit their spirits are broken by institutions of which social workers are a part.

Social activists try to inform elected officials about the negative impacts of poverty, and sometimes the message is heard. Canada's prime minister has gone so far as to admit, "The fact is, we pay a heavy price for having children in our society grow up in poverty."[71] His state-ment is consistent with a House of Commons resolution that passed unanimously in 1989 and stated: "This House . . . seeks to achieve the goal of eliminating poverty among Canadian children by the year 2000."[72]

Nice words — but in the decade after the federal government passed that resolution, child poverty increased by 49 per cent.[73] Clearly these politicians are not walking their talk. Worse, the federal govern-ment has withdrawn dollars from programs ranging from postsec-ondary education to social housing to health care. For that reason

Campaign 2000, a non-partisan coalition of over seventy organizations from across the country, conducts ongoing political education to alert the public about what needs to be done to reduce systemic inequalities.

Of course, not only children feel the impact of these inequalities. Institutions for the elderly also provide a shock for people who have believed in the myth that our society and its institutions take care to provide for our essential well-being. For instance, an eighty-year-old man who began shopping around for social and medical services to help his ailing wife visited several nursing homes:

"I found nursing homes are like institutions for people who have committed some crime. A few seemed good but in others staff were inadequate or indifferent and I felt they didn't know how to look after old people. Those places I saw had very few nurses, though they're calling them 'nursing' homes. One place I went to — it was a three-storey house and I walked all over the place before I could find a staff person and she had come up from the basement. The whole place was very shabby, wallpaper peeling off the walls; people who were residents, none of them were talking, they just looked at you in a dumb sort of way."

Imagine, as well, the shock his wife was in for, as patient. This example shows, once again, the sexual dichotomy prevailing in social services. There is *his* old age and then there is *hers*. The huge majority of inmates in such nursing homes are women.

THE FIRST NATIONS: NO USE FOR WELFARE WORKERS?

Although Aboriginal peoples constitute about 2 per cent of the Canadian population, they averaged about 10 per cent of prisoners in federal penitentiaries in the late 1980s. The Royal Commission on Aboriginal Peoples notes that the overrepresentation of Aboriginal people in Canadian prisons "is getting worse, not better."[74] According to sociologist Marianne Nielsen, "Considering that 80% of Native young people drop out of school before completion, this means that a young Native boy has a much better chance of being arrested before he turns 18 than he does of graduating from high school."[75]

Not that Aboriginal girls have it easy, either. For example, in Alberta 49 per cent of the girls in young offender institutions were Aboriginal.[76] Clearly, the justice system is failing Aboriginal peoples.

Although the provinces employ many social workers who work with First Nations communities, the federal government has also hired professionals though its Department of Indian and Northern Affairs. That, however, is not necessarily an improvement, as I discovered several years ago when I was part of an inquiry into the federal government's services to Aboriginal people in Northern Alberta. The Chief and Council of the Edmonton-Hobbema District indicated: *"There is no two-way communication with the Department. They come here with their programs and expect us to take them."*

In my experience there are a few white social workers who are the exceptions, who have developed a sensitivity to intercultural communication and acquired extensive knowledge and appreciation for Aboriginal cultures. But more typical are these examples from Edmonton-Hobbema:

"I don't know anything about Indian people but I volunteered to work on the reserve when no other staff member would."

"My skin colour is different. I don't feel I should be working on the reserve and I'm so consciously aware that I'm different."

Not surprisingly, this leads to the following reaction by an Indian client: *"I have no use for welfare workers because I never see them."*

Non-clients are also affected by the social relations shaped by the dominant society. This pits one First Nations group against another. An Aboriginal person living on a reserve says: *"Welfare stinks — people should get off their asses and work."*

Also divisive are the attitudes taught to Aboriginal students as part of their professional training. Yvonne Howse, from the Cree nation, says that schools of social work "present a one-sided view based on western philosophy" and only "limited information regarding the perspective of a tribal person." Howse, a social work educator in Saskatchewan, adds: "The other hindrance I see is tribal people themselves because of the indoctrinations, brainwashing of our own classes, and attitudes we have ourselves."[77]

More specifically, some First Nations leaders worry about what graduates from university bring back with them when they return to work on Indian reserves as employees of band councils:

[They] come back believing that because they have a degree they have a title now. They must be treated like an elite and behave like an elite. . . . Now the privileged class are the fulltime employees of the band. . . . They are the ones who decide which changes have to take place. I really get concerned about that. They don't consult with their own members. They've decided that because they're there and they have the position and they have the training they know what the answer is. We no longer need government agents to perpetuate the colonial system. We have it within many of our own communities.[78]

media will often present such movements in an unfavourable light, thereby influencing many others to disparage them as well.

Many countries today are home to a series of separate social movements comprising indigenous peoples, environmentalists, women, anti-poverty groups, labour, anti-racist and human rights activists, lesbians, gay men, and bisexuals, older people, disabled men and women — and others. These movements are growing in Canada as well. Each of them is more or less radical, insofar as it is working away at clearing out the fundamental roots of oppression/exploitation harming the well-being and growth of its members and others. Sometimes these separate movements have overlapping memberships, and sometimes they work together in coalitions. Separately and together they challenge the direction of a society driven by global corporate elites made up mainly of privileged, rich males.

For social workers who engage in *anti-oppression practice*, there is a strong connection between, on the one hand, providing individual assistance to people belonging to disempowered groups, and, on the other hand, working with social movements connected to these disempowered groups. By linking these two ways of working, social service providers are challenging social services from the ground up. We are reframing "private" problems as public issues. That is, concerns about matters such as money, sexuality, disability, illness, age, religion, and skin colour cease to be purely private matters and become understood also as political issues related to the well-being of countless people.

In short, we are breaking out from the invisible walls that mould our thoughts and actions to perpetuate unequal social relations. By breaking out from conventional practice, such social work moves away from the central position of implicit power over clients towards encouraging clients to take matters into their own hands by forming personal and political support groups. Through these support groups individual clients learn they are not alone in their struggles and not to blame for structural problems. The groups reduce personal isolation and make possible a degree of mutual support.

Changing attitudes in social work have been profoundly influenced by the women's movement, which has contributed basic principles of counselling that go counter to traditional ways of providing service. Helen Levine highlights some of the basic differences in feminist counselling: "It has to do with an approach, a feminist way of defining women's struggles and facilitating change. It is no mysterious, professional technique. The focus is on women helping women in a non-hierarchical, reciprocal and supportive way. . . . It rests on a critical analysis of the sexism embedded in the theory and practice of the helping professions."[1]

Feminist analysis also emphasizes the centrality of joining the private and public dimensions of women's lives. For example, the gendered and unequal division of paid and unpaid labour in and beyond the home, with its negative impact on women's health, income, and status, is defined as exploitation that impacts personally and politically on all women.

By emphasizing both the personal and political dimension of social problems, feminist social workers are helping to debunk the mistaken view that social work with individuals and families necessarily means supporting the status quo. Feminists have demonstrated that an empowering approach can and must include working with individuals and families — but within a politics of transforming patriarchal structures and patterns. Such an integration of personal and political dimensions is a far cry from conventional counselling (including the ecological approach), which often reduces social problems to individual pathologies and defective communication. Social work professor Maurice Moreau once stated: "Social problems are not caused by deficits in communication between individuals and systems as both ecology and systems theory posit. Differential access to power and conflict between systems are the problem and not a lack of mutual fit, reciprocity, interdependence and balance between individuals and systems."[2]

Moreau pioneered a structural approach to social work practice, built upon a critical analysis of the various exploitative social divisions in society: "It is an analysis which places alongside each other the divisions of class, gender, race, age, ability/disability and sexuality as the most significant social relations of advanced patriarchal capitalism."[3] Rather than prescribing a hierarchy of these major yet different social relations, Moreau would agree with the approach of anti-racist educator George Sefa Dei, who suggested:

> The pedagogy of the anti-racist educator is to discuss the issues of race, class, gender, sexuality and other forms of power relations simultaneously and in a manner that does not attempt to hierarchize the varied oppressions in society. Students should be made to understand the dialectical relationship of race, class, gender and sexuality and how these issues are experienced as interlocking systems of oppression.[4]

This interlocking has implications for social work's approach to social change. Basic change for the better becomes possible only when many individuals develop a shared consciousness of the numerous layers of oppression that together serve to subordinate the majority of people in society — and when we can better appreciate how these various oppressions have a multiple impact on our own lives.

But as we become more acutely aware of injustices and how the multiple layers of oppressions interact to reinforce each other, we can also feel overwhelmed. We can feel the loss of the faith we once had in the ability of government or other institutions to set things right. Typical reactions include going into denial or feeling helpless and acquiescing to the system and its power-holders. But there is another and better path. Instead of giving implicit consent to these multiple and various top-down, oppressive relations, we can consciously choose to withdraw consent: that is something that *can* be done by an individual. To become empowered (and to help empower others) it is also important to seek mutual support by participating in networks and social movements committed to the transformation of our social relations. In doing this we can begin to develop a liberation practice, working upward to change and democratize the system.

At times, it does seem hopeless. Yet historian and human rights activist Howard Zinn reminds us that people are often surprised by the sudden emergence of a popular movement that overthrows a tyranny:

> We are surprised because we have not taken notice of the quiet simmerings of indignation, of the first faint sounds of protest, of the scattered signs of resistance that, in the midst of our despair, portend the excitement of change. The isolated acts begin to join, the individual thrusts blend into organized actions, and one day, often when the situation seems most hopeless, there bursts onto the scene a movement.[5]

RECONSTRUCTING SOCIAL WORKER-CLIENT RELATIONSHIPS

The multiple and overlapping oppressions of our system and their interwoven social relations have resulted in violence, humiliation, and totally inadequate resources for the First Nations, people of colour, lesbians and gay men, the unemployed, the disabled, the elderly, the mentally ill, and others — with women forming the greatest number in all these groupings. While numerous radical social workers point out that primary attention must be given to providing short-term and long-term resources, Moreau suggested that social workers must also be sensitive to the "ideas, feelings and behaviour of clients which contribute to the client's own oppression or contribute to the oppression of others."[6]

Such a focus on client ideas, feelings, and behaviour is quite different from fixing blame onto clients for their situations. On the contrary, such a focus recognizes that when various forms of discrimination against oppressed populations become internalized, women, children, and men who use social services tend to believe they are incompetents or failures. Radical social work also recognizes that prolonged oppressive relations can have severe destructive consequences for the personalities of people we serve.

Rather than a social worker deciding which of a client's ideas, feelings, and behaviour require changing, the process becomes a mutual, shared one. In rejecting the top-down approach that sets the worker apart, Levine writes, "I like the notion of shared work, shared learning, shared perspectives on the part of both provider and consumer. Each brings her own knowledge, skills, experience and tasks — and a recognition of the human fallibility of both — in working towards change."[7] This kind of process can reduce the power gaps between workers and clients while sharply increasing the possibilities for an egalitarian client-worker relationship.

As part of this shift from conventional practice, York University researcher Karen Swift offers suggestions based on her critique of social service responses to child neglect. She suggests we step back from our everyday practice to "see the invisible." She analyses how oppressed women have been socially constructed as "bad mothers." She suggests, instead, that if we apply a critical consciousness we can reframe "the problem":

> The "immature" mother may then be seen . . . as a person shouldering a share of labour out of keeping with available resources; as a woman struggling to fit fragments of traditional culture into an isolating urban environment; as someone facing racial discrimination on a daily basis; as a victim of violence herself; as a person whose problems and resource deficits are shared by many others.[8]

In the 1990s Marilyn Callahan, a researcher at University of Victoria, documented efforts to reconstruct child welfare services in British Columbia. Parents reported for allegedly neglecting or abusing their children were given the option of working together in a group. Later they would meet as a larger group with their front-line workers, who had meanwhile been getting together as a staff group. The purpose of this larger meeting was to brainstorm how to meet community standards for parenting and how to overcome obstacles to that goal. This model represented a change from the emphasis on case-by-case investigations conducted by child welfare workers.

Participation was voluntary. The parents who volunteered were all women. Although the process was difficult at times, mothers and workers all shared a strong commitment to the well-being of children. Mothers benefited from this reconstructed service in several ways: "Most women had not thought of their contribution as work and had not been encouraged to do so. Indeed they were categorized as 'unemployable' or 'unemployed' by their welfare workers. Yet as they talked about their daily lives and the barriers set up by agency policies, they realized that they carried out complex tasks and overcame substantial adversities."[9]

Other positive results were a series of self-help efforts, including a community garden, a clothing exchange, the start of a small business, and child-care co-operatives — these to alleviate immediate financial needs. Workers and clients banded together to advocate for better policies and services, based on their direct experience. Most workers enjoyed this new approach to practice, which gave them renewed energy. Parents reported improved self-confidence and an improved capacity to parent. They felt better about themselves and less isolated.[10] Through such reconstructed social services, our social work practice changes. In responding to people seeking help, we become co-investigators with them into the unequal social relations that have an impact on their lives, and we work with them on how to best counteract this oppression.

Such explorations with severely oppressed individuals can be fraught with the pain of discovering deep personal and emotional commitments rooted in promises that the system never meant to keep. Further, such help can also discover lost, hidden, or suppressed strengths that are capable of renewal and growth. A former client who experienced this more mutual form of social work explains the implications for empowerment:

"For me empowerment begins with the individual's self-esteem. As you increase it, you feel better about yourself, about your children, about others. It's a process where you start small, then go on to the bigger picture. That's how I was helped. I came out of my marriage tortured, my bones broken, weighing eighty pounds. He ended up in jail for it. I was alive but weak. My social worker built on my motivation, on my spark. She encouraged me to become more involved in our locally run

community programs, first as a volunteer, then as staff. After a few years of working in my community, where there's a lot of poverty, my confidence grew. I noticed police officers didn't respond well to calls about wife assault, so a group of us arranged community meetings with the police. That didn't work because we felt dumped upon. We knew police attitudes had to change and we worked on that. To make a long story short, I was invited to do five training sessions for the police department. During those sessions I heard some amazing attitudes from some of the officers. I asked myself what the hell were they doing? I almost gave up but I realized it takes time, especially for the old-timers. Now we're planning to set up a new group of women who have experienced abusive men."

When social workers become case critical — that is, critical of conventional social work and its trappings — we are able to draw upon Paulo Freire's approach to adult education and help people name rather than suppress the oppressive relations that have so strong an impact on their thoughts, feelings, and behaviour.[11]

Consequently, for professor Joyce West Stevens, social work means helping clients to learn "to resist social devaluation and victimization."[12] How do we do this? Akua Benjamin, a Black woman activist who teaches social work, offers suggestions:

"Applying an anti-oppression approach in social work means that you begin with a critical understanding of the "social." That means focusing on the client's social location and social identity within social structures and systems. This helps the worker to be more effective, including assessments, problem-solving, offering supports, and helping clients to address personal situations or negotiating barriers within larger systems.

"Speaking of barriers, these will be found within policies and procedures that impact on our clients. For instance, a new immigrant from an extended family background and now residing in public housing may be unaware of the policy concerning the length of time that a member of her family is allowed to visit at her home — usually three months. The immigrant may also be unaware of the consequences of non-compliance with such a policy and the nuances in the policy that allow some flexibility in its application. As the worker to this new immigrant, you become a cultural interpreter and ally as you expose both the strengths and the flaws in policies and in systems."

Instead of providing empathy focused narrowly on an individual client, social work becomes reconstructed as service providers contribute towards a *social empathy*, which both values the experiences and struggles of clients as individuals and makes linkages personally and politically with others in similar circumstances.[13] Such linkages open the way for the people we work with to consider actions that are less dependent on individualistic remedies and that move through an exploration of solutions that benefit themselves as well as others in similar situations.

Because social workers often work with individuals on a case-by-case basis, we need to take care to differentiate "individuality" from "individualism."[14] As effective helpers, we respect the uniqueness of each person (*individuality*). At the same time we reject *individualism* because it focuses on the individual as the exclusive source and solution of problems; we reject it because of individualism's tendency to zero in on intrapsychic pathology while denying structural inequalities, a tendency that invites a justification for self-centred and greedy behaviour.

By contrast, Moreau's approach was to build respect for each client's individuality, and he offered guidelines to social workers who were looking to help set the stage for client empowerment. He suggested that client power and choices increase as a result of greater access to material resources. Client power and choices also gain ground when there is greater freedom in the client-worker relationship, greater awareness about systemic sources of oppression, and greater consciousness about others similarly oppressed. Client power and choices also increase as a result of an enhanced incentive to join the activism of social movements, and from a greater ability to change personal behaviour that is harmful to oneself or to others.[15]

Such a multiple approach to empowerment is applicable to all social work specializations, from casework to group work, from family work to research, from administration to community work. For example, this ground-up approach has been applied to social work research via participatory research, a method that grew out of popular education movements in Asia, Africa, and Latin America. This method "argues for the articulation of points of view by the dominated or subordinated, whether from gender, race, ethnicity, or other structures of subordination."[16]

Peter Park, co-author of a book on *participatory research*, sees this method as providing "space for the oppressed to use their intellectual power to be critical and innovative in order to fashion a world free from domination and exploitation."[17] Yet even this major breakthrough is being challenged to take a further step forward. U.S. feminist and activist Patricia Maguire comments on the participatory literature up to the early 1980s:

The voices and observations of women participants were largely unheard. Women were often invisible, submerged, or hidden in case study reports or theoretical discussion. Gender was usually rendered indistinguishable by terms such as the "*people*," the "campesinos," the "villagers," or simply, the "oppressed". . . . Participatory and feminist research agrees that knowledge, which is socially constructed, is power, and both are committed to empowering oppressed people. Participatory research has highlighted the centrality of power in the social construction of knowledge, yet it has largely ignored the centrality of male power in that construction.[18]

We have to be aware, then, that useful theories do evolve, challenging previously hidden inequalities, in order to create better theory that takes in a wider range of emancipatory needs.

In feminist social work with women, a worker's skill of self-disclosure "can demonstrate a common history of oppression and indicate a vulnerability to many of the same stresses and conflicts that clients experience," as Mary Russell, a feminist social worker in British Columbia, notes.[19] According to Russell, this approach is intended to foster a more egalitarian client-worker relationship.

The time to use self-disclosure depends on the circumstances. Feminist Donna Baines reflects on her social work with severely oppressed women:

In my experience, self-disclosure increased rather than decreased the distance between me and the client. It highlighted the difference between us and the greater ease with which I could live my live and resolve personal and social problems. Rather than normalize a client's experience, self-disclosure may revictimize poor women and women of color by reemphasizing an unattainable, oppressive, hegemonic, White middle class standard.[20]

Pockets of reconstructed social work are emerging within mainstream social services. Callahan suggests that this is more likely to happen when workers are able to develop alliances with sympathetic policy-makers and managers. She also notes the value "of developing alliances between those within the bureaucracy and those in their policy communities: namely social movement members, union members and academics."[21]

In a somewhat different way, Yvonne Howse and Harvey Stalwick also emphasize dialogue as a key in social work relationships with Aboriginal peoples:

It allows Natives to express their long hidden feelings and, in a very direct way, opens the eyes of social workers to the fact that much of the

past and previous social work practice with Native families is bad practice and cannot be allowed to continue. With the best of intent it has
destroyed families. Indeed dialogue is one way of empowering Natives. It
allows them to name their oppressors, to expose conditions and [to] take
this necessary first step in freeing people to face and resolve problems.[22]

Dialogue becomes potent when Aboriginal people are helped by
Aboriginal people relying on traditional First Nations healing approaches.
Ann Charter, an educator with the University of Manitoba's School of
Social Work, documents an example of a group process to help twelve
men, all of them Aboriginal and under court order to obtain treatment
for their violence against women.[23] These men were in denial of their
abuse, and Charter describes how the First Nations Medicine Wheel
helped each of them to overcome the denial and take full responsibility
for their actions. She explains how the teachings of the Medicine Wheel
provides a "focus on the need for respect in acknowledging all forms of
life and accepting that where there is balance there may also be unbal-
ance. It is understood that the lack of balance or harmony is the point
where sickness or the need for healing begins." Charter locates these
teachings within the context of First Nations culture: "Cultural impera-
tives such as non-interference, sharing, non-competitiveness, acceptance
of responsibility for one's actions, distancing of problems, and acknowledgement of the experiences and wisdom of everyone are expressed
through the Medicine Wheel teachings."[24]

The writings of Kathy Absolon and a number of other First Nations
people document a rich spiritual legacy through which Aboriginal peoples approach the healing process within their own communities and
beyond. Cultures indigenous not only to North America but also to
Africa place immense value on spirituality. This value is being endorsed
today by leaders from these cultures, not in order to withdraw from
this world but to equip people, such as social workers, with the capacity to act to transform social services in the direction of equality.

Jerome Schiele of the State University of New York at Stony Brook
notes that the defamation and colonization of Africa and of people of
African descent were the result of a Eurocentric approach emphasizing
fragmentation, conflict, and domination.[25] He argues that this Eurocentric approach has perpetuated inequality in North America, thereby sti-
fling social work. Schiele adds: "Central to the Afrocentric world view
is the emphasis on interdependence, collectivity and spirituality. . . .
Spirituality is taken here to mean the nonmaterial or invisible substance that connects all elements of the universe. Whether animate or

inanimate, all elements are assumed to have a spiritual base and to
have emanated from a similar universal source."[26] This common source
incorporates the values of human interconnectedness and morality,
which welcome equality:

> The focus on morality in the Afrocentric paradigm also encourages the
> belief that human beings have a proclivity towards goodness and con-
> struction rather than evil and destruction. Too often in western philoso-
> phy and western social science the norm of human behaviour is thought
> to be that of evil and destruction. A corollary of the perpetuation of this
> belief is that people begin to use it to justify decadent behaviour and the
> practice of inequality.[27]

Schiele joins writers from First Nations cultures who suggest that we
can all benefit from a reassessment of our Eurocultural practices and
from the adoption within our own practice of egalitarian insights from
other cultures.

For George Sefa Dei, the reassessment of Eurocentric practice is
essential to the dismantling of racism:

> The starting point for anti-racist work in Canadian schools is for the edu-
> cator to problematize Eurocentric, white male privilege and supremacy,
> and the consequent social inequalities in our pluralistic society. Anti-
> racist education, therefore, is a discourse about the social inequality
> experienced by all non-white people of various class backgrounds and
> sexual orientations.[28]

It is not unusual for a person to be oppressed in more than one
way. For example, part of the identities of gay men, lesbians, and bisexuals may be racialized. That is why social work educator Brian O'Neill
wants to see social services develop an organizational climate that "is
safe for open discussion of differences of race, culture and sexual orientation. In order to achieve this goal, agencies should officially recognize that same-sex sexual orientation is a legitimate aspect of human
diversity and that heterosexism is as unacceptable as racism, ethnocen-
trism and other forms of oppression."[29]

These various ways of reconstructing client-worker relationships
serve to widen the scope of mainstream social services. Such reconstructed relationships represent significant steps forward on the social
work continuum between conventional (or status quo) practice and liberation practice. Further forward steps are taken as social service
providers participate in or support collective action through alternative
social services.

ALTERNATIVE SOCIAL SERVICES

Alternative services attempt to institutionalize new forms of social relations: establishing a shelter for battered women, a crisis phone line, a
drop-in and information centre, or a community centre controlled by
Aboriginal people. This is what the authors of *In and Against the State*
refer to as making new social relations.[30]

Alternative services usually spring from the work of a specific
oppressed community or movement: First Nations people, ethnic and
visible minorities, lesbians, bisexuals, and gay men, local tenants'
groups, the disabled, or ex-psychiatric patients, with women being
worse off in each of these groups, which is why women are the majority users of social services. Alternative services emphasize the principle
of consumer control over professional services.

The women's movement has been especially influential in developing non-hierarchical approaches to organizing and delivering feminist
services. Many of the newer services are organized as co-ops or collectives so that staff co-operatively make major decisions, often with
essential input from the users of the service. Staff and sometimes users
— not only management — have a major say in hiring. The services
are often staffed and co-ordinated by people rooted in the particular
community being served, people who are personally committed to the
reduction or elimination of structural inequalities. Despite the
inevitable differences and diversity, they tend to have a shared analysis
of basic causes of problems and what creates the need for their services.

Callahan observes that innovations by feminist shelters include the
practice "that those who have to implement the decisions should be
those who make them." This means that shelters sometimes have
"house meetings" in which "residents and staff sort out the logistics of
their day-to-day living" and other meetings in which staff, volunteers,
and resident representatives get together to develop programs."[31] Feminist counselling supports this approach, and to maximize egalitarian
values it extends a non-hierarchical approach into the helping relationship itself.

When Michèle Kérisit and Nérée St-Amand conducted a study of
over one hundred alternative community services across the country,
they found that, as key ingredients, the services provided a welcoming
atmosphere and a sense of belonging that evolved through informal
interpersonal relationships among participants: "For disadvantaged
families, having one's own space where people can get to know each

other better, where they can share with others, if only to talk to other parents who are having the same problem, is vital. An open place is preferred where one feels at home and can reweave social bonds that have been broken and destabilized by poverty."[32]

The Single Mother's Housing Network, a Vancouver project designed to alleviate the high risks of poverty, isolation, emotional stress, and exhaustion experienced by single-mother families, provides an example of a feminist alternative service. Single mothers who register for this service get the opportunity to match themselves with other people on the list to find shared housing accommodation. Authors Kathryn McCannell, Colleen Lumb, and Paule McNicoll describe the service:

> After an interview with the social worker, who is familiar with other registrants, several names may be provided to the woman, who can then make contact and arrange to meet to explore possibilities. If the social worker feels home-sharing may be complicated by particular factors in the woman's situation, for example, an obviously unresolved separation, or an expressed rigidity around lifestyle, she raises these issues with the woman. The choice, however, of whether to proceed, remains the woman's. Time is spent exploring children's needs and coping styles, to ensure care and consideration is given to their participation in the match. . . . The matches vary in length, from several months to a period of years. The women involved represent a variety of ages, incomes, and cultural backgrounds. The advantages most often mentioned concern support — financial and emotional.[33]

Through this alternative network, the participants experience co-operative living. They meet new friends and, in a sense, contribute to social action through their collaboration with others in need of support. McCannell, Lumb, and McNicoll note that women coming to the network are not viewed as "cases" that "present problems," but rather as experts on their own situation, people who have much to offer one another and share a common task of seeking alternative living arrangements.[34]

In another area of social work, Jennifer Ann Pritchard, a graduate of Ryerson's School of Social Work, contrasts her eight years of experience working in bureaucratic group homes with her student experience of working for an organization run by people with disabilities:

"Group homes give services which are highly individualized, so people with disabilities are kept separate from each other; there's no such thing as meetings, just among people with disabilities. But in self-help groups

there's more of a collective sense of potential, hope, possibility, and risk-taking . . . and I found that people with disabilities had a type of camaraderie and humour with each other that's rare in group homes. In the group home system there's a tendency to deny the disability, to render the person with disability as much like a non-disabled person as possible. By contrast, in self-help groups people embrace their disability, saying, 'This is who I am, dammit. I am as valuable as anyone.' There's a strong sense of validating each other's experience with disability. In this way, people with disabilities are turning the tables on the conventional perception of disabilities as being ugly, not valuable, and a lesser form of life."

A disabled woman puts it this way: "I do not want to have to try to emulate what a non-disabled woman looks like in order to assert positive things about myself. I want to be able to celebrate my difference, not hide from it."[35]

Similarly, social workers involved with efforts of Aboriginal peoples to protect their cultures and restore their autonomy find that they too are connecting the personal with the political. As part of the political mobilization for self-government, the transfer of social services to Aboriginal communities across the country is underway, but how it is happening raises questions. As Sid Fiddler puts it, "In theory a policy of transferring responsibility for administering programs to Indian people as delegated powers should improve the delivery of services; instead present funding arrangements have the opposite effect." Noting the absence of authentic Aboriginal control over transferred services, Fiddler concludes: "In the transfer of program and service responsibilities in education, health and social services to Indian people, budgetary allocations do not reflect the real costs of inflation or increased costs due to larger numbers of Indian people requiring or eligible for services."[36]

Aside from the absence of commitment by federal and provincial governments for adequate funding of social services, the challenge also becomes one of implementing alternatives that genuinely reflect Aboriginal cultural traditions and aspirations rather than merely reproducing Eurocentric social service hierarchies run by Aboriginal people. Even given the severe constraints, this challenge is being met by some services such as the Ma Mawi Wi Chi Itata Centre in Winnipeg, where group training programs for Aboriginal youth incorporate Aboriginal talking circles and traditional healing.[37]

Alternative services can also yield political insights. Urban Calling Last, an Indian active in alternative services to Aboriginal people in Calgary, recalls:

"When I became an activist, I wouldn't say my dignity improved. I always had my dignity; because of my grandfather I was raised in a traditional Indian way. My credibility with my people definitely increased; they had confidence in what I was saying. There's learning from books but I was talking from experience. Another thing I noticed after I became an activist, the police stopped harassing me; they still harassed other Indians. So we don't have equality before the law. The law treats one group one way and another group another way."

On an international level, Jim Albert, a social work educator at Carleton University with extensive experience in Central America, documents the personal involvement and the politics of shared decision-making in Esteli, a small city in Nicaragua. He writes about how the extensive networks of grassroots organizations at the block and neighbourhood levels blossomed when the government became supportive of sharing its power with popular organizations focused on health and social services. Albert points to a lesson for social work: "We need to be clear about our own attitudes concerning the inherent capacity of people to act spontaneously on their own behalf. If we have faith in the people then our role will be to learn from and support their efforts. This challenges the traditional practice of community development which has tended to take a more directive role."[38]

Within social work education, professors Maureen Wilson and André Jacob, with extensive experience in Latin America, advocate the adoption of an economic model based on sustainability that "depends not on growth in economic output, but on progress toward equity and security against deprivation." To illustrate the numerous examples in which grassroots initiatives created co-operative organization, Wilson and Jacob describe Villa El Salvador in Peru, where for twenty years people living in poverty had developed viable organizations based on neighbourhoods that organized activities around housing, health, collective kitchens, sports, education, culture, and economic production. By the early 1990s this co-op network involved about three hundred thousand people. These kinds of efforts in Latin America can pose severe threats to the local privileged elites, at times leading to violent repression by the country's military and police forces. Nevertheless, Wilson and Jacob see these grassroots co-ops as the best hope for ending despair, because there could be "no sustainable development without control by the communities involved in defining their own issues and finding their own solutions."[39]

Action to build structures of greater equality and shared power has special relevance to social work, traditionally viewed as a woman's profession with mostly women as front-line practitioners and clients. "Women have always served others and have been told that their glory and fulfillment is to be found in the denial of themselves," Angela Miles states. Caring has been used against women to keep them trapped and silenced. But caring can have a liberating potential. In Miles's view:

> Women's service has not been only forced service to their masters, it has been also the caring and nurturing of each other and our children. It has been the building and maintenance of the social connections and commitment that embody what is human in our society. It extends far beyond what is forced from women as subordinates to become in many cases freely chosen expressions of love and support which are not the self-denial but the expression of women's selves in the world. At the same time as it has oiled the wheels of an oppressive system and eased the lot of our rulers, women's service has kept alive an alternative, and in part subversive, set of values and ways of life.[40]

This form of service — based not on self-denial but on feminism's alternative vision — inspires alternative services. The method rejects mainstream ideology, reinforced by conventional social agencies, which first defines clients as inadequate and/or pathological "cases" and then puts forth professional "expertise" to rehabilitate, to "normalize" individuals and families into conformity with prevailing patterns.

By contrast, social movements offer a different view of personal problems, seeing unequal power relations and unequal material resources as the source of the problem. Alternative services also have to be flexible, as Callahan illustrates by reference to transition houses for abused women and children: "In rural British Columbia the concept of a transition house makes little sense. Women are too widely scattered to use it easily and it would be impossible to conceal the identity of such a house in a small town. Instead, safe houses, a network of individual homes where residents volunteer to shelter women and children, have been developed."[41]

Social movements and their alternative services are indeed subversive. They are in conflict with the services and objectives of conventional social agencies. But most important, instead of helping to legitimate society's undemocratic structures and institutions they are committed to exposing and fundamentally changing them.

ALTERNATIVE SOCIAL SERVICES: ISSUES AND PITFALLS

Just as the dominant society's version of conventional social services has become an instrument for the perpetuation of inequality, when social services become part of oppressed and potentially transformative communities they become oppositional and the workers become part of the struggle for liberation. That same struggle includes outreach and consciousness-raising activities.

Jillian Ridington notes the changed political climate and the more sophisticated analysis used by feminists, based on years of trying to change things on shoestring budgets and realizing the changes were only band-aids. She writes:

> There is a chasm now between the women we have become and the women who need feminist services. They come from a perspective that was once our own, but which our vision now tells us is obscured — we can no longer see the world as non-feminists still see it. Their needs are those of our more innocent selves: support, a chance to exchange experiences with other women; information, which may lead to insights and autonomy.[42]

This recognition can serve as a caution against the trap of arrogance. Having developed a critical awareness, we sometimes become self-righteous and forget the importance of listening to, learning from, and sharing with the very groups we see as most oppressed. Helen Levine points out:

> It was no accident that consciousness-raising in small groups sparked the widespread beginnings of the contemporary women's movement. It offered safe space for women to tell the real "stories" of our lives, to listen to one another without judgement and blame, to grasp the commonalities among us. It was a woman-centred base, grounded in internal and external realities, that led to opening up, sharing, analysis and action. I see this as a continuous and essential base in any social change movement.[43]

When some alternative services become viable, grow, and gain credibility, they face a new challenge. They want to hire more staff, possibly including social workers, but that requires money. So they draw up proposals and submit them to various branches of government or to an agency such as the United Way, asking for funding and taking the risk of co-optation. Cindy Player describes the dilemma with reference to abused women and their children: "We desperately need funding in order to provide necessary support and shelter for women and children. But far too often, the strings attached to that funding run counter to our feminist philosophy."[44]

When governments find they can't control the alternative services, funds are eventually cut or eliminated. For example, when funds are taken away from women's shelters, the users either go without support or have to resort to the traditional services such as the Salvation Army and the welfare department. Nevertheless, despite such setbacks, the number of shelters and transition houses for abused women has grown steadily across Canada, from just a handful in the 1970s to 450 in 1998.[45] Furthermore, women's shelters have begun to widen their response to answer the needs of women who are oppressed because of colour, ethnic background, or disability, as well as gender.[46]

Given the enormous difficulties in working either within traditional agencies or within alternative services, some social workers have opted for a form of private practice that rejects the corporate and hierarchical models. These social workers offer their services on the assumption that the selling of a service is not in and of itself exploitative. Food co-ops, after all, sell food and publishing collectives sell books without necessarily becoming capitalist or sexist. It depends on the kinds of social relations generated by the effort. Some social workers in private practice ideally commit themselves to an egalitarian and democratic approach, which they apply to their relationships with others, including their interaction with clients. In addition they get essential social nourishment and new ideas from their personal and political roots in one or more of the grassroots movements.

Such practitioners, however, don't have it easy because of the inevitable shortages of funds. They find themselves face to face with major contradictions, around developing egalitarian and accessible relations with service users, while working as professional entrepreneurs. It becomes tempting to slip back into the more conventional model that divides the user from the service provider, or to become more interested in money and profits than user well-being.

Bob Mullaly cautions:

> Social workers must be careful not to romanticize alternative organizations. Anyone who has ever been associated with such an organization will know how difficult it is to work collectively and cooperatively and to share all decision-making when we, as North Americans, have been socialized into working and living in social institutions where hierarchy, specialization, and an over-reliance on rules prevails.[47]

While co-operative, egalitarian alternatives face strong resistance, nevertheless they can (even with their flaws) allow us to meet needs in more humane and more effective ways. The vision of alternatives can generate a more widespread challenge, namely, to democratize not just social services but all public services, ranging from health to transportation. The meeting of this challenge requires community participation and control over the direction of the services. But alternative institutions go beyond public services and extend to commercial enterprises via the development of alternative business structures. These enterprises are often small, underfinanced, and constrained by governments wanting to reshape co-operative community initiatives into private enterprise.

Greg MacLeod, a professor at University College of Cape Breton, has examined the workings of Canadian community-controlled enterprises. One of those projects, New Dawn, has been providing affordable housing in Cape Breton for some twenty-five years. MacLeod's research was inspired by the successful cluster of community-controlled enterprises known as Mondragon in the Basque region of Spain. Created over fifty years ago, and now employing over thirty thousand workers, Mondragon includes a variety of enterprises, such as financial services, furniture and food stores, and manufacturing for export trade. Surpluses are returned to the community via its health, education, and social programs. The difference between the highest and lowest paid workers is capped at a ratio of six to one, a figure decided by the community. According to MacLeod, Mondragon's enterprises "are examples of powerful corporate systems being intentionally directed for the good of local communities rather than to the profit of anonymous and distant shareholders."[48]

As we gain experience from the growth of alternative institutions we will need to widen our focus on democratization: from government departments to large, private business corporations.[49] That such a goal is rarely mentioned nowadays only shows how much business elites have succeeded in insulating their corporate affairs and goals from fundamental critiques — in "rolling back the boundaries of politics."[50] Yet if we restrict our own projects and goals to the realm of social services and community economic development, we grant corporate leaders immunity from accountability to the larger society. Most of the social injustices documented in this book can be traced to government actions that have been substantially influenced by business leaders. Yet those leaders are primarily accountable to their shareholders. That must change. It is time to make business leaders fully accountable for the economic, social, and political damage inflicted upon communities due to their actions. We must generate public pressure on private corporations to require them to establish democratic representation and procedures.

Despite the gap between this larger vision of transformation and the smallness of today's alternative social services, these alternatives do make an essential contribution. They illustrate through direct, everyday experience that radically different kinds of services are feasible, practical, and more personally satisfying than practice within conventional institutions. They become prototypes for the liberated institutions of the future, providing us with positive, hopeful glimpses of what might be and practical lessons on how to get there.

SOCIAL ACTION GROUPS

If alternative services point the way to new forms of accountable institutions, social action channels political pressure upon individuals and established institutions to change their practices. Social action usually involves the mobilization of significant numbers of people to carry out non-violent protests and demonstrations. Such mass mobilization seemed to peak in North America with the civil rights and other movements in the 1960s and early 1970s. Then for a while it bloomed in Eastern Europe, and later shifted to other continents. It returned in force with Ontario's Days of Actions during the mid-1990s, followed by the "Battle of Seattle" surrounding the World Trade Organization meetings in late 1999.

Across Canada social action has persisted as a strategy used by various disempowered groups to press their claims for justice. Whether it is Aboriginal peoples blockading a timber road to protect their land, lesbian and gay pride parades that witness support for spousal benefits for same-sex couples, or pensioners protesting against policies that erode their standard of living, various social action tactics continue to be evident throughout the country.

The shift from a passive acceptance of conditions to activism takes many forms. A sole-support mother experienced in surviving on a low income says: "Before I started learning about changing our society, I pretty much felt that I was always at the mercy of something: job schedules, or lack of money, or my ex-husband, or exhaustion. But thinking politically helps you become a doer. You start changing things yourself, and don't spend so much energy adapting to situations that others create."[51]

Social action groups vary in size and organization. One small yet effective group included mothers who, as clients of child welfare services, formed a self-help group. Some of these women had faced intimidation and violence by men and had knowledge about self-protection. One of them complained about an ex-partner who, after receiving a court order not to enter her premises, had parked his truck in her driveway.

> The empty truck served as a reminder of his continuing presence, although the police said they could not intervene unless he actually entered her home or harmed her in some way. The group of women/ mothers decided to take action, writing a letter to the man informing him that they were aware of his activities and watching over their friend. The truck disappeared.[52]

Welfare rights groups have also re-emerged to raise public awareness about the oppressive conditions experienced by people on social assistance. In Montreal some welfare clients developed a number of such groups, encouraged by social workers employed mainly by community centres and settlement houses in low-income areas of the city. The social workers, including myself, were active members of these groups, but it was understood that our role would be limited to acting as advisors or resource people — an arrangement promoted by both clients and social workers. The clients accepted us partly because we listened carefully. As Uma Narayan points out: "Members of an oppressed group have a more immediate, subtle and critical knowledge about the nature of their oppression than people who are non-members of the oppressed group. . . . They know first-hand the detailed and concrete ways in which oppression affects the major and minor details of their social and psychic lives."[53]

We were careful not to usurp their leadership. Rather, we encouraged and supported theirs. Maritime activist and popular educator Anne Bishop cautions: "Try to avoid the trap of 'knowing what is good for them.' Do not take leadership. They are the only ones who can figure out what is good for them, and developing their own leadership strengthens their organizations. It is fine to add thoughts or resources to the process by asking questions of the individuals with whom you have already built up some trust and equality."[54]

We held informal meetings with an agenda decided by the clients, and their appraisals of their various hardships turned out to be quite different than the usual professional assessments. They told about how teachers showed obvious discrimination against their children, how landlords refused to repair broken heaters, and how in all cases there didn't seem to be anything they could do about it. The clients saw these kinds of relationships as "the problem" — as opposed to feeling that there was something inherently wrong with themselves. As the meetings went on, our relations with clients became more personal, mutual, and voluntary than the usual worker-client relationship.

By the time new clients found out that some people in the group were social workers, they had also witnessed our willingness to listen, to learn, and to be critical of social agencies. Typically, they were surprised, and more than one of them told us, "You're not like the others." In fact, we were acting in ways that were different from conventional social workers. Yes, we were indeed professionally on the job and we cared about the people we worked with. But we were interested, they could see, in doing more than nod our heads at their stories and make notes on bureaucratic forms.

For a short period of time a number of these groups developed, drawing in clients from different neighbourhoods. Group members began to advocate for each other at welfare offices and in the process we discovered our collective strength, which was in opposition to the individual stigma experienced by welfare recipients. One very practical result was that clients found they could increase their welfare cheques by arguing for their legal entitlements.

We carried out at least one action that was both serious and fun. It came about after the groups had requested permission to set up information booths in the waiting rooms of the welfare offices. The welfare department said no. So one bright morning, three welfare activists walked up one flight of stairs into a welfare office, carrying a portable cardtable, a pitcher of hot coffee, paper cups, and a stack of information booklets. They set up the table in the waiting area and proceeded to offer coffee and information to other clients waiting for appointments.

A well-dressed administrator soon popped out of an office cubicle and asked the three "outsiders" to leave and take their things with them. They said they'd rather stay, and continued to offer coffee and information. In a huff the administrator retreated into his cubicle and presumably phoned the welfare director, who presumably called the police.

I was with a second group of people waiting in a parked car, motor running, across the street from the welfare office. In the car we had a radio set-up that kept us in continuous contact with our three people inside. Those of us in the car were to serve as lookouts for the police.

Sure enough, half an hour after our people had first gone into the welfare office, we heard sirens and saw a number of rather large, white-helmeted policemen riding into view on their motorcycles. We felt like comedians in a movie, waiting to tip off a casino about an imminent raid.

We contacted our friends inside and told them the police were on their way. Our inside people closed up their portable table, took their coffee pitcher, said goodbye to the other clients, and started down the stairs towards the street. The police were by that time making their way up the stairs, where they met three courteous, neatly dressed, harmless-looking people coming down. The three gave greetings to the police, who smiled back and kept climbing the stairs. The last officer patiently held the door open to help our friends exit onto the street. Now all the police were inside and our friends outside. They came across the street, hopped into our car, and off we went to another welfare office for a repeat performance.

SOCIAL ACTION GROUPS AS BUILDING BLOCKS

Although client groups have rocked the boat, does this approach offer promise for fundamental social change? Gary Cameron, a social worker active with community groups in Montreal, offers a sobering observation: "Most social action organizations do not survive. Their average lifespan is probably about five years. Those that do survive are barely recognizable as social action organizations. A multi-issue, mass-based organization has proved to be exceedingly difficult to maintain."[55]

In addition to a possibly limited life-span, social action groups face a new dilemma when they do succeed in producing reforms. Feminist writer and activist Charlotte Bunch refers to this problem in the context of the women's liberation movement: "Unless we are determined to prevent it, reforms most often enhance the privilege of a few at the expense of the many. Unless good political education accompanies work on a reform, success can lead to the conclusion that the system works or failure can lead to cynicism about women's ability to bring about change."[56]

It is true that once client groups are organized, many of their demands — for example, more government funding for a community centre, or changes to specific social legislation — can, after considerable struggle, be accommodated by the state and social agencies. Such accommodation does not alter the basic relations of power, a fact frequently obscured by the minor concessions that are granted.

Roxanna Ng, Gillian Walker, and Jacob Muller, analysing the processes of social change in Canada, point out that community initiatives for improved social conditions are often subverted by decisions that channel community activities into conformity with the status quo: "The commonly held notions of the state as standing over and above individuals in civil society, and the community as representing the good and benevolent sphere of social life, are inadequate to account for how 'ruling' takes place and has consequences for people's lives."[57] These writers, along with others, suggest that communities, like the state, be viewed as contested areas, recognizing that while opposition to oppressive social relations may sometimes erupt into anger and organized action, the prevailing pattern within many communities continues to favour upper-class, white, male, heterosexual, able-bodied individuals.

Where does that leave client groups that opt for social action? Are social workers who support such groups inevitably limited to working for superficial changes? When client groups develop their personal and political interests in a direction that leads to social action, many clients and professionals stumble onto a discovery. We realize, perhaps for the first time, that there are many others in similar positions who are also angry with receiving the short end of the stick. We discover that as a group we can break the silence, name our experiences, take action, and become empowered.

Very frequently such group actions are diametrically opposed to the "normal" flow of power within the welfare state. When social workers join client groups involved in social action there are implications for their practice. As Gary Cameron puts it, "The social action perspective insists that as social workers confront the inevitable shortages of resources, they put pressure upwards on the system rather than downwards on clients to accept their fate."[58] Such power reversals in isolated instances won't by themselves produce social transformation, just as radical counselling and alternative social services won't by themselves transform the welfare state. Nevertheless, social action groups form essential building blocks to support personal and political liberation.

As feminist activist Diana Ralph reminds us, social action can be limited when it targets the wrong groups. In light of the power of international financial markets to impose conditions on governments, including our own, Ralph concludes that trying to bring about change through influencing politicians will no longer work: "Postcard campaigns and marches on Parliament Hill, no matter how large, will be ignored, because the focus of power no longer resides there (if it ever did). . . .

What we need to do is rebuild and mobilize our popular bases to take on the corporations and banks directly, through militant actions such as general strikes, boycotts, and creation of our own counter-institutions."[59]

LABOUR UNIONS AND SOCIAL WORK

Most social service providers belong to unions, because most of us are employed at workplaces that have been unionized. The advantage of being part of a larger union is that member social workers benefit from the strength of the larger group and the collective agreements it achieves. Unionization, especially in the public sector, has raised salaries for social service workers, although the government sometimes rolls back these gains through contracting-out or demanding wage concessions. For example, the federal government offered to pay the John Howard Society (a non-profit, voluntary agency) to carry out parole work that would otherwise be done by the better paid federal parole service. While such moves are ostensibly to save money, they effectively undermine the job security and improved working conditions that federal parole officers have won through collective agreements.

It is well known that, historically, labour unions have struggled for better working conditions and pay. Perhaps less well known are the efforts by the labour movement to urge governments to develop social programs such as old age pensions, unemployment insurance, and medicare. These social programs would not have been established if labour had not pressed for them through the political arena. During periods when these programs come under attack it is, again, the labour movement, along with others, that organizes opposition to the cutbacks.

Although unions strive to be among the most democratic of our institutions — with rank and file participation a visible priority on convention floors or in meeting halls — people of colour and feminists have criticized them for being not only white, male-dominated organizations, but also preoccupied with product rather than process, and for avoiding the needs of women and people from diverse cultural/ethnic backgrounds. Pressure from unionized people of colour has led to the development of human rights programs within unions, stressing the message that racism weakens the union movement. Similarly, feminist activists are making unions more responsive to gender equality. As Denise Kouri states, "Fighting for women's issues inevitably means fighting for rank and file control of unions, because that is where women are, and rank and file control is what is needed to change trade union policies."[60]

Confronted — directly and indirectly — by the women's move-ment, the union movement has become much more involved in the struggle for equal pay for work of equal value, child care, maternity leave, pensions for older women, paid child-care leave, sexual harass-ment, and other issues initiated by women. Sandy Fox argues, "That linking of broader issues to the more traditional economic concerns of union conventions was the result of a lot of hard work by union activists with the help and support of feminists outside the union movement."[61]

Yet the reality is that for many front-line social workers, women as well as men, union involvement means one more meeting, on our own time, on top of an already overloaded schedule. For the majority of front-line workers, who are women, the obstacles are even steeper because many are burdened with the double workload of employment and child care. At the same time, for those workers who do become active with their unions the benefits are clear. According to social worker and union leader Karen McNama: *"Unions are important for front-line social workers because they serve as a protection against abuses by managers. By 'abuses' I mean the long hours we are made to work; the heaviness of the caseload and I don't just mean numbers. Unions allow us an opportunity to have a voice, to disagree with management without get-ting hit with 'insubordination.'"*[62]

When McNama led her union in a strike at Toronto's Children's Aid Society, it was not for salary hikes but to oppose cuts to social ser-vices. *"Before we'd return to work we insisted that we obtain a letter from the Board [of directors] stating there would be no layoffs and no cuts in services for the duration of this collective agreement. Only after we received this letter did we settle and return to work."*

Unions within social agencies can also foster the type of peer sup-port so important for an emancipatory form of social work. In addition unions have at times helped to augment the resources needed by clients. Social work activist Pam Chapman tells about her work at an emergency shelter in a dilapidated, stuffy building that was under-staffed and overcrowded — full of babies crying and mothers yelling. Staff had been continuously asking management to address the build-ing's conditions, but nothing had changed:

"Fortunately the union did make a difference. The union steward got all the staff together and asked us to fill out question sheets, so we could list the problems and our suggestions for combatting these problems. Besides the problems associated with the overcrowding issue, we had been

pushing for a children's program in the shelter. The union called a meeting with the shelter's management and at that meeting the union demanded action. Soon after, the children's program was established and other conditions improved as well."[63]

While unions provide opportunities for empowerment, Leo Panitch and Donald Swartz argue that unions have been co-opted by turning their organizations into bureaucracies preoccupied with technocratic procedures at the expense of mass mobilization. They argue, "Ideologically, the labour movement is still largely enveloped in an understanding which tends to reduce the state to the government of the day, and fails to see the state as a constituent element of capitalist domination."[64] At the same time some unionists are working hard to lead the labour movement in more radical directions. So it is that conflicts and contradictions operate not only at the larger societal levels but also within the labour movement itself, just as they do within social work.

Unions have proved to be excellent field placements for social work students. For example, over the years I have acted as a field work consultant to over eighty Ryerson students placed at the Toronto Labour Council and other labour settings. Student projects have included working with immigrant workers laid off due to plant closures, with resident councils in labour-sponsored co-op housing projects, and with union counselling programs.*

Despite some positive links to labour unions, most social workers prefer to view themselves as professionals aspiring to managerial positions, and this view is reflected in their practice. Deena Ladd, a social work graduate from Ryerson and labour organizer in Toronto, observes:

"Most social workers see the people they work with as 'clients' rather than as workers, or as unemployed. They don't see clients in relation to the economic system and so tend not to ask, 'Are you experiencing problems with your supervisor, or at work generally?' A client may have worked somewhere for five years without any wage increase, or may be exhausted due to an unhealthy work environment, but instead social workers zero in on family problems."

In her work Ladd helped to unionize a number of community-based agencies that provide social services to new immigrants. She also took up what is called a "community unionism" approach. In commu-

---

* Union counsellors are volunteers within local unions who offer peer counselling, referrals, and follow-up.

nity unionism, according to Andy Banks, associate editor of *Labour Research Review,* "Instead of being organizations representing workers at particular facilities of particular employees, unions are transformed into a community-wide movement that organizes around workplace related issues of economic justice and worker abuse."[65] By combining the union movement's focus on corporate structures with a community organizing focus on diverse community leadership and mobilization, Ladd's work addressed the plight of garment workers, mainly immigrant women who spoke little English and sewed in their own homes for subcontractors that supplied retail outlets:

"We began organizing the homeworkers campaign for fair wages. We held conferences, rallies, and demonstrations. We went outside the union to form coalitions with diverse women's groups, including anti-racist, feminist, and lesbian activists, progressive church, labour, and grassroots leaders. At one rally, to make linkages with women facing similar struggles internationally, we had representation of labour/community leaders from Mexico and Nicaragua as our guest speakers. Through our educational campaign, we were able to identify terrible working conditions in Canada, such as homeworkers being paid far below minimum wage, sometimes not being paid at all, and constantly being at the mercy of the retailers' subcontractors. For a garment that may retail at $300, a homeworker might get $3, working long hours in her basement — of course with no UI, no CPP, no Workers' Compensation. So who's making the profit? At whose expense? When the wider public heard these things were happening here in Canada and not some far-off place, people were outraged — that supported our efforts. One of my most fulfilling experiences was to help in the formation of a strong Homeworkers' Association and to see the homeworkers taking control over their organization as an important stage in this struggle."

For students, educators, and workers, the labour movement's emphasis on solidarity and collective action in general casts the role of social workers into a broader emancipatory context. It encourages both reflection and analysis of wider issues and the formation of important links with other movements, with other workers, and with alternative services.

COALITIONS AND SOCIAL CHANGE MOVEMENTS

Radical counselling and union activism are anti-oppression forms of work inside mainstream social services. A strategy typically from outside these agencies is social action; another is the building up of alternative services, which can in turn offer an additional home for progressive social work, social action, and union activism. All of these anti-oppression strategies contribute, each in its own way, to empowerment. This is why coalitions that strengthen social movements are so important. Due to their independent, grassroots responses to undemocratic institutions, social movements are able to translate an individual's desire for change into collective action.

Social movements, like community networks, contain subgroups reflecting, in part, different political currents. These currents range in outlook from wanting to change only some of the social system's unfair practices to seeking a total dismantling of all oppressive structures and relations.[66] Patricia Daenzer, social work educator and Director of Women's Studies at McMaster University, examines why some subgroups need space to be separate. Referring to Black women in Canada Daenzer states, "In order to join forces with other movements such as feminism, we must first stand apart and reclaim our social and political sense."[67] Self-emancipation, in contrast to previous integration approaches, "involves liberation from the alien ideas and imposed culture of the oppressor," she notes. "As women we are burdened with the additional challenges of liberating ourselves from White male patriarchy, White oppression, and Black male subordination."[68]

As social service workers learn to participate in coalitions and social movements, our role provides a sharp contrast to the perspectives and actions encouraged by the managers of the welfare state. This in turn provides other social workers with alternative models of practice. Eric Shragge observes, "Posters, newspapers, announcements of meetings, and worker initiated speakers from outside groups can help build solidarity between workers, clients and social movements."[69]

A further step is for social workers to place the question of client well-being high on the agendas of their unions and agencies. Although agency managers tend to resist initiatives that empower workers or clients, management responses are worth testing on a case-by-case basis. Managers also experience the system's contradictions, and at times we can persuade them to be supportive, even though the normal expectations of their positions might point in an opposite direction.

Social workers also at times join various social movements in campaigning for election candidates for political office — understandably so, since different fates can await social services depending on which political party forms the government at provincial or federal levels. While promises made by Liberal/Conservative/Reform/Social

Credit parties sound slightly different, all of these parties are heavily financed by the business sector, with its agenda of cutting back on government, which in turn means reducing the costs of social services and privatization. By comparison, the New Democratic Party (NDP), with financial support from organized labour, has been more sympathetic to social services. But once in power (which has only happened at the provincial level), the NDP too falls under the immense pressures of big business, and it finds little room for expanding or improving social services.[70]

Decades ago the social democrats seemed to have more courage to stand up to established power. As a result, they legalized medicare over the strenuous objections of the medical establishment, and they also championed social housing and more generous pensions and unemployment insurance, along with numerous other social programs.

Today there is a consensus among the social activists I work with that the most effective political priority is to put energy into helping to organize strong grassroots social justice movements and to encourage coalitions among these movements. Without the effective extraparliamentary presence of those social movements, no matter which political party is elected the field is left open to corporate lobbyists. One of the ways that coalitions of social movements flex their muscle is through rallies, protests, and demonstrations. Reverend Susan Eagle links such events to social progress: "I like marches. They remind me that we are a people on the move, that history is moving forward, that nothing stands still. Even the battles we have fought and won are not stationary. If we don't fight to keep them, they slide away from us."[71]

Our collective strength grows when various social movements join together in co-ordinated alternative institutions and mass action. Yet in the end, who is this "mass" — except you and me and many others who oppose undemocratic institutions?

It is not easy to struggle, either inside or outside the system or in some combination, and to work in directions opposed by the system's power-holders. It is not easy partly because it involves a lot of unlearning. As feminists point out, it involves breaking out from a version of social change in which men take over leadership roles, expecting women to make meals, look after the children, or do the housework. Change includes not only altering our daily lives, including our practice of politics, but also building our awareness that politics is not simply confined to the public sphere. As Joan Gilroy of the Maritime School of Social Work points out, "Politics occurs in the kitchen, the bedroom, the classroom and the social work interview as well as in the legislature, law court and boardroom."[72]

Our collusion with privilege presents an obstacle to the building of coalitions that could work towards a more egalitarian society. Part of the problem is that privilege has been made invisible. In analysing her own sense of privilege, U.S. feminist Peggy McIntosh says the key lesson was what she was taught *not* to see: "As a white person, I realized I had been taught about racism as something which puts others at a disadvantage, but I had been taught not to see one of its corollary aspects, white privilege, which puts me at an advantage." She says, for example, "I can be sure that if I need legal or medical help, my race will not work against me," and "I am never asked to speak for all the people of my racial group." In her view, "Whites are carefully taught not to recognize white privilege, as males are taught not to recognize male privilege."[73]

Hidden privilege, McIntosh argues, results not just from racism but also from other interconnected oppressions such as those based on sexual orientation, abilities/disabilities, gender, social class, and religion. This complex of oppressions means that privilege is widely dispersed throughout the population. At the same time it is spread out in extremely unequal ways. Among the many people who benefit from some privilege there are enormous variations of power, with the greatest privilege accruing to those with the greatest power.

Janet Sawyer uses the term *internalized dominance* to indicate that dominant power is generally invisible to the privileged who exercise it. Sawyer explains this power is not noticed because it is seen as "normal," and because "That which is seen as 'normal' is defined that way by those who have power in society."[74]

Dianne de Champlain and Rosalie Goldstein include the term "internalized dominance" as part of their education of social work students at the University of Victoria. De Champlain and Goldstein focus on the part that each of us plays in the construction of structural barriers that perpetuate oppression: "The idea of working to expose the barriers that we have created is a crucial aspect of anti-oppression. . . . Our personal beliefs and attitudes that are oppressive must also be identified."[75]

As social workers we see the suffering both within individuals and within entire groups and communities. While trying to reduce the pain, social services usually fail to address its flip side: privilege. Lilla Watson, an Australian Aboriginal elder, hints at this failure: "If you are

here to help me, I'm not interested. If you are here because your liberation is wrapped up in mine, then let us work together."[76]

In probing how our various liberations are intertwined, Julie
Salverson, a theatre animator and popular educator, asks: "What happens when we deny, in fact don't even remember, our own experience
of being violated and try to combat our unnamed oppressors by joining
some other oppressed group's battle?" This is often the case when
activists, both within and outside social work, make alliances with a
variety of disempowered groups. Salverson suggests: "Our task is to
break not only societal patterns but also our individual ones, so as not
to reproduce the violence and crippling 'cops' we carry within us. . . . If
we as activists are constantly involved in situations that are about conflict, about power imbalances, we had better do our best to become
conscious of what these outer situations echo inside us."[77]

Most of us have experienced a mixture of privilege and the pain of
oppression. The nature of the balance between pain and privilege
varies, depending on our personal histories and our gender, racial,
class, and other characteristics. This diversity of experience may pre-
clude a single explanation or a single theory of transformation. Each
social movement, ranging from First Nations to labour unions, has its
own distinct experience supplemented by its members' experiences,
which are both diverse and constantly changing. As a result each
movement's own understanding of its specific oppression tends to be
fluid, evolving as conditions change. Barbara Findlay, author of *With
All of Who We Are,* suggests: "Perhaps we will find that truth is information prismed through different experiences and locations in the world,
and that we are mistaken to be striving after one unitary theory."[78]

POSTMODERNISM

Postmodernism is influencing social work education. Postmodern writers view the modern era as a historical period now over. This past era
— or "modernity" — was a time when people had faith in stable, universal truths, such as the certainty that science and rationality would
create progress for everyone to enjoy. Yet, the postmodern critique
would say, science has been used to inflict violence on a bloody, huge
scale and to create out-of-control environmental poisons, including
potential disasters from nuclear wastes and fallout. Postmodernism
reflected a radical questioning of the "grand theories" and ideologies of
the modern era, but particularly, in the arts, architecture, and criticism,
suggested a revolt against authority.

Modernity, a number of scholars would argue, is an experiment that failed, and "our present historical condition" is better explained through the concept of postmodernism.[79] That new approach challenges us to recognize that conventional rules seemingly guiding our actions are not inevitable and that we can create alternatives.[80]

The influential French philosopher Michel Foucault investigated how the questionable "truths" revered by society are subtly imposed on us to create our personal, subjective understanding of reality. In interpreting Foucault's view of power, social work educator Frank Wang explains: "Power operates through constructing our subjectivities, shaping our identities, regulating our views of the world. . . . What power can do is induce us to participate."[81] But what we participate in, according to postmodernism, is our own self-colonization for the benefit of others. Foucault himself suggests: "As soon as there is a power relation, there is a possibility of resistance."[82]

Postmodernism's view of change was influenced by the expansion of diverse social movements in Western industrialized societies from the 1960s onward. This diversity suggested that both oppression and resistance have multiple sources within society. Postmodernists see these sources as being located within local arenas in which individuals interact with one another and where, for example, the diversity of identities is expressed by participants through specific interactions. Bob Mullaly points out that postmodernism has helped us clarify the importance of not brushing differences under the carpet.[83]

Identity politics, for instance, addresses inequalities reproduced by the larger system on the basis of our different identities. To say we are "all the same" not only denies the very differences that should be recognized and celebrated, but can also deny structural inequalities. If the person in question is gay, lesbian, or bisexual, the denials of difference can be a subtle invitation for that person to go back into the closet. When people firmly implanted in mainstream culture say to First Nations peoples, "We are all the same," the statement disrespects the distinctive culture that many Aboriginal people want not just to keep alive but to celebrate. Similarly, to say to people whose skin colour is not white "We are all the same" is an odd denial of obvious differences grounded not just in colour but in historical and present-day realities.

Of course, someone might say "We are all the same" with all the best intentions in the world, perhaps as an attempt to move beyond negative stereotypes. But the attempt backfires every time. The acceptance of others cannot come about through a denial of differences. On the contrary, acceptance requires an open recognition of, and respect for, difference.

At the same time, critics have suggested that people can go overboard in emphasizing differences. An overemphasis on difference can play into the divide-and-rule tactics exercised by society's most privileged. Mullaly puts it this way:

> While post-modernists have argued for otherness, difference, localism, and fragmentation, capitalism has taken another course — globalization of capital accumulation that is being used to subjugate the very groups and localities for whom post-modernism expresses its concern. By denying the existence of universal phenomena and by fragmenting people under the banner of localism, is post-modernism not aiding and abetting this subjugation?[84]

A postmodern approach known as narrative therapy has become popular among social workers. This therapy strives to legitimize the deep meaning that clients give to their own stories (their narratives). While recognizing that no one ever becomes the full author of their own story, due to circumstances beyond their control, narrative therapy helps clients to reclaim and revision their own stories in order to become more effective authors of their own lives.[85] But this approach has its limitations, as feminist researchers Shari Brotman and Shoshana Pollack warn: "The main principles of postmodernism that this approach [narrative therapy] adopts are the subjective self as knowledge source, diversity and difference, uncertainty, and multiple viewpoints."[86]

Although narrative therapy may help social workers understand the client's reality better than they would using conventional social work approaches, Brotman and Pollack caution that postmodern theory — applied, for instance, via narrative therapy — fails to provide a comprehensive analysis of power and therefore undermines liberatory social movements.[87] As well, some conservative scholars are interpreting and using Foucault's work in ways that ignore his radical critique, which only adds to the controversy surrounding postmodernism.

Still, a portion of postmodern theory can be helpful in removing a severe stumbling block in the path of social justice movements. Activists and radical social workers know the great difficulties faced by diverse social movements in working to build and sustain effective coalitions. Unfortunately, social movements often tend to compete with each other, each pushing its own particular analysis forward as *the* best answer to achieve social or political goals. This approach is understandable, because we are all influenced by constant messages from the mainstream: "There is only *one* way that's best, and it's *my* way." As we tune into, for example, talk shows on radio or television, we hear the intensity of conviction that accompanies claims such as: "Government can't do anything right," or "The poor deserve what they get." When these "truths" are promoted with typical missionary fervour, such expressions of mainstream beliefs become as dogmatic as those of religious fundamentalism. Applying Foucault's approach to "unsettle" such externally imposed "truths," we can work to "unsettle" the widespread subjective submission to dogmatism, whether of the religious or secular variety.[88]

But fanaticism about the superiority of particular beliefs does not exist in isolation. When we add the particular "truths" that prop up global corporate control, we end up with a toxic combination. More specifically, global corporate expansion rests upon the so-called "truths" that human beings are essentially about hierarchy, competition, and greed. The heavy corporate influence over culture has inserted these values into the subjective attitudes of many individuals. This celebration of patriarchal capitalism is being carried out with the zeal of fundamentalist fanatics, even while it is muted by a veneer of smiles, moderation, and slick images via massive, worldwide, electronic communications systems.

The result is a lethal mixture of extreme intolerance, reflected often in a casual dismissal of differences, including different opinions. Predictably, there will continue to be countless examples of a dogmatic mainstream backlash dismissing social justice movements. At the same time, when our social movements try to work together we have ourselves not been immune to pervasive patterns of intolerance.

Our challenge, therefore, is to recognize that the nature of our intolerance is socially constructed. It is vital for us to let go of the negative subjectivities. We must resist our subjective submission to dogmatism, competition, hierarchy, and greed — and unearth the roots of these deeply implanted values, which have served to excuse cruel and inhuman behaviour. Fortunately, other, more human options do allow our humanity, rather than our perversity, to blossom.

From my own experience, I have seen that activists who have worked on their own attitudes and have succeeded in ejecting this internalized dogmatism find that they are better able to relate to the various approaches of diverse community, grassroots, and social movements. As we discover the similarities and differences of our lived subjugation, we can honour the differences while at the same time forging personal and political alliances around our commonalities. Those commonalities are rooted in the plurality of mistreatment, regardless of the different sources of oppression and exploitation. Here we need to join postmodern theory with social and political action.

BRIDGING THE PERSONAL AND THE POLITICAL

As agents of emancipation, all of us need to work to dismantle sources of exploitation and oppression. We act on these goals by developing alliances based on mutual respect for differences, and by working to create common positions, common statements, and common priorities. Our process of liberation will depend on organizing unified actions reflecting an inclusive approach to social justice. The aim may not be to build one big movement, but to reach consensus on how today's different movements can co-operate effectively to dismantle the system's unjust and undemocratic structures. Different historical moments and locations will suggest differing strategies for our liberation process.

Today many activists are involved with either single-issue organizations or with a single social movement. This anti-oppression work is extremely valuable as a springboard for *liberation practice*, which is evolving both within and outside of social work. In Canada liberation practice in social work now means helping to strengthen interpersonal alliances with diversely oppressed individuals. It also means helping to connect a single-issue or a single social movement to the task of forming coalitions among diverse social movements working to dismantle systemic oppression and exploitation.

Such coalitions of social movements become liberation practice when: (1) they show an understanding of and respect for the diverse identities of their members, and (2) they harness grassroots power using a variety of strategies to work at substantially reducing the gap between the haves and the have-nots. Until such liberation practices become strong, the powers-that-be will continue their divide-and-rule tactics — reforming this or that law, releasing some funds here or there, opening the gates of corporate promotion to this or that group — while doing nothing to democratize the economic/political structures responsible for the growing gap between the rich and poor. As we strengthen our own liberation practice, we are challenged to widen our political involvement while at the same time deepening our personal healing.

In probing the link between the personal and political, Anne

Bishop writes: "Unhealed childhood pain seems to be a key mechanism for learning how we behave as oppressors and oppressed. Childhood scars leave a deep distrust of the possibility of safety and equality, and many of us as adults react by using and accepting 'power-over,' by creating hierarchies wherever we go."[89] To undo this damage, Bishop notes: "Because of my observation that people who approach other oppressed people as allies are those who are involved in their own process of liberation from oppression, I also believe that one must be in the process of liberation from one's own oppression to become an ally in another's liberation."[90]

Her words fit my own efforts at becoming an ally. For example, when I have been invited by a women's caucus or by First Nations groups to join their strategy meetings, it has been important for me to recognize that my being white, male, and middle class makes me part of the oppression. As Bishop puts it:

> Remember that everyone in the oppressor group is part of the oppression. It is ridiculous to claim you are not sexist if you are a man, or not racist if you are white, and so on. No matter how much work you have done on that area yourself, there is more to be done. All members of this society grow up surrounded by oppressive attitudes; we are marinated in it. It runs in our veins; it is as invisible to us as the air we breathe. I do not believe anyone raised in western society can ever claim to have finished ridding themselves completely of their oppressive attitudes. It is an ongoing task, like keeping the dishes clean.[91]

Blunt, honest talk will be part of that effort. For example: "Aboriginal Peoples are not 'sick' peoples in need of 'therapy' and 'healing': we are wronged peoples in need of justice. Those who cannot appreciate this distinction have no right to consider themselves advocates for or friends to Aboriginal Peoples."[92] Akua Benjamin recalled a recent event:

"When I was having a conversation with a dear friend who is Aboriginal, she turned to me and asked: 'Did I realize I was part of the oppression of her people?' I was shocked; totally speechless. Me? An oppressor? My ancestors were forced as slaves to come from Africa. We were forced onto ships which brought us to the Americas — to labour in horribly cruel conditions. While First Nations were being exterminated, we were slaves — so how could I be an oppressor? Then I stopped myself and reflected. I listened again to what she had said, but this time I heard her as an ally, as if by a second ear. It was a rude awakening. I'm in Canada now — and benefiting from what the Europeans had done. Now I'm making my life

*here without any acknowledgement that this was indeed the First Nations'
home, not just their land. This is the unsightliness of privilege. We must
meet it through a double consciousness. By double I mean for us to develop a critical awareness of — our past and present realities of our oppression — and simultaneously of our power and privilege. I should add, as a
matter of historical record, many slaves survived as a result of the assistance of First Nations peoples."*

In my case, my own privilege includes knowing I won't be hassled
by police because of my skin colour, knowing that when I made a complaint at our daughter's school my gender increased the odds of being
taken seriously, knowing that our household income can buy more
than bare necessities, and the list goes on.

As part of my own liberation, I also need to name my own childhood pain, to remove it from the realm of a long, uncomfortable
silence, and to address the loss of my own parents who — because they
were Jews — were killed by Nazis. Although the Holocaust happened
over fifty years ago, it was decades before I could talk about it, and
only recently have I been learning to write about it. In 1942 during the
Nazi occupation of Belgium, my parents along with many others were
forcibly transported to the Auschwitz concentration camp in Poland.
My father was killed en route. My mother was killed in Auschwitz in
1944. I survived by being hidden by non-Jews in Belgium.

I have reflected on those events for a long time — and my journey
of healing has been multilayered, partly within my Jewish community
and partly outside of it. When I remember those childhood years — I
last saw my parents when I was five years old — I still have flashbacks
of the fear and the loss; but through fragments of memory I also feel
their love. At other times I am incensed at the sheer stupidity of
labelling any community, any nation, or any "race" as subhuman.

Yet I also believe we *can* learn from Nazi history, especially
because its menacing echoes are alive today. In a way smoother yet
similar to the scapegoating done under fascist regimes, Canadians
today sense a greater intolerance against Aboriginal peoples, the
unemployed, women, new immigrants from Southern countries, Quebec or other regions, lesbians, gay men, bisexuals, people with disabilities, and others including those who are poor or near poor.

But the danger does not lurk among the handful of Nazi crackpots
strutting about on our streets with their swastikas on display. Rather,
the real danger stems from those in positions of influence who blame
politically weak groups for the failure of the economy. This tactic of

blaming victims and survivors and blaming the social services has fun-
nelled immense public resentment onto various oppressed groups. As a
result, a cancerous smokescreen has vaulted upward, producing those
thick, poisonous, yet invisible walls to hide and cover up the enormous
privileges accumulated by the most powerful elites. These are the walls
that confound us. As if to elicit our consent, crumbs of privilege are
then tossed our way so that in our gratitude we will keep the unequal
patterns intact.

My experience and my reflection lead me to the conclusion,
shared by many others, that these processes of scapegoating are being
driven by none other than Canada's elites. More specifically, I mean big
business leaders, their squabbling politicians, their arid economists,
their self-serving "news" shapers, their enforcers, their "me-first" enter-
tainers, and their various hangers-on. There is no need for a conspiracy. It is enough that these elites share common values: hierarchy, individualism, and private greed.

The result is the illusion of democracy. More precisely, the most
powerful elites within the upper class — consisting mainly of white,
heterosexual, able-bodied, rich males — are calling the shots. Fuelled
by their international business investments, they are steering social
change on the road that leads to more and more inequality. These are
therefore the people to be challenged, along with the competitive
greed spawned by their private corporations and their top-down control. These are the structures and the social relations that must be thor-
oughly democratized and transformed into processes of decency.

Granted this is uphill work. Since most of the mainstream media
consistently distort the goals, events, and other efforts of social movements, there is a growing consensus among activists about the urgent
need to strengthen our own media and to create new outlets to challenge the messages of commercial television, radio, and print media.
The challenge for our emergent media will be to engage in dialogues to
help create the knowledge necessary to meet the challenges of our personal and global liberation. Activist and scholar Janet Conway suggests
that the site of production for this knowledge is within progressive
social movements. She identifies the features of such knowledge-pro-
duction as including "its embeddedness in day-to-day social movement
struggles; its accountability to a broad, democratic and organized
base." Conway views the creation of such knowledge as dynamic and
evolving "in recognition of the dialogical relationship between activist
educators and a popular 'base.'"[93]

As we push for change, the backlash from established power groups will be fierce. As Linda Torney, president of the Toronto Labour Council, says, we cannot hope to match the dollars of the rich and powerful: "But we can match and outrun them with our numbers, our commitment, our brains and our time — if we work together."[94]

To the extent that social work supports and strengthens this process, our efforts will be motivated by altruism of a different stripe than the altruism that pervades elitist professionalism. Genuine caring about others necessarily includes action based on a personal and political awareness of the root causes of social inequalities. This action works to reclaim the meaning of human dignity and human equality by shattering the top-down conformity prescribed by managers of the social service bureaucracies.

As we recognize the invisible walls for what they are, we gain an appreciation of the diversity of people blocked from power and decision-making regarding the direction of our society. When all these blocked segments of the population are added together, the sum becomes an overwhelming majority of the public.

Ultimately we represent the majority not only because our numbers add up. We are the majority because everyone suffers when decisions by a privileged minority poison our air, water, and soil. So too all of us are harmed when we allow our interdependence to be ruptured by institutions that promote greed and treat people as objects to be manipulated. Therefore when we engage in significant change for the better, we not only help others, but also begin to liberate ourselves, politically and personally.

As an adult, I found that my personal journey into liberation had come up against a formidable obstacle. I noticed that Judaism was functioning like much of Christianity, in having made peace with systemic inequalities. Yet because my family had helped me develop a positive Jewish identity, I was able to discover that within Judaism there were small but vibrant forms of resistance to injustice.

Rabbi Michael Lerner points out that a hopeful message from the biblical texts comprising the Torah is that we can liberate ourselves from entrenched habits of inherited cruelty that have been passed on from generation to generation. While the Torah's authors expressed a quantum leap in spiritual evolution, liberation for religious Jews means letting go of long-standing oppressions and prejudices that became part of the Torah.[95] Such a letting go on my part — while simultaneously connecting with the spirituality of sacred Jewish texts — has strengthened my own commitment to liberation practice. The Jewish magazine *Tikkun* calls this approach the politics of meaning:

> We seek to link that spiritual nourishment to social movements that will heal the distortions in our economic, political and social institutions. Our politics of meaning is an attempt to create a "new bottom line," in which ethical, spiritual and ecological values will replace the materialism, selfishness, and cynicism of contemporary American life.[96]

At the same time as I receive spiritual strength from Jewish sources, I am also grateful for the insights shared by caring friends and allies within Aboriginal communities. The pathways to Jewish and Aboriginal spirituality have helped me to recognize the hidden strengths that have fuelled people's struggles for emancipation over the long haul. I am encouraged when I see that others from various faith communities quite different from mine are able to build on their spirituality to inspire their social justice activism.[97]

As part of my activism, I enjoy learning from friends and allies. During a conversation with Barbara Riley, one of my First Nations mentors, I used the phrase "dominant elites." Barbara just smiled. We sat quietly for a while, then she said:

"I don't use the term 'dominant' any more. Makes it seem like they have all the power. They don't. If we say 'they're dominant' it's like saying we're powerless. We're not. You're not powerless, Ben — unless you give up your power to them. I say 'mainstream' when talking about white elites. I find it makes it easier for me to act on our power, so we can build our communities and make changes to stop being oppressed."

Contributing to our power is the transformative energy generated by our human caring, which flows from our basic interdependence. Writer bell hooks recalls the civil rights struggles to end segregation based on colour of skin. She refers to the black and white activists who worked together to win racial justice. Hooks believes that "the small circles of love we have managed to form in our individual lives" serve as practical reminders that a community without racism is not just a dream:

> It already exists for those of us who have done the work of educating ourselves for critical consciousness in ways that enabled a letting go of white supremacist assumptions and values. The process of decolonization (unlearning white supremacy by divesting of white privilege if we were white or vestiges of internalized racism if we were black) transformed our minds and our habits of being.[98]

That kind of transformation enables us to develop a liberation practice that transcends differences even while honouring them.

These personal and political changes are important, because when we challenge privilege we are choosing a side; we do resist and we do mobilize power. But that power is different than power-over. It is power oriented to the reconstruction of social relations themselves. This effort is undoubtedly a tall order — yet it is essential for achieving authentic liberation from the multiple oppressions imprisoning our daily lives.

That is the vision of participatory democracy. Social and economic justice demands a transformation of power, including a basic redistribution of wealth — so that the practice of democracy comes within the reach of everyone, rather than being manipulated by those who now dominate the heights of our political and social structures. That, then, is the challenge — for you, for me — not just for social workers, but for everyone.

NOTES

CHAPTER 1: SOCIAL WORK AND THE PUBLIC CONSCIENCE

1 Estimates provided by Michael Shapcott, National Housing and Homeless Network, Toronto, Nov. 26, 1999.

2 Shawn McCarthy, "RCMP Officers Pepper-Spray Demonstrators," *The Globe and Mail*, Nov. 18, 1999, p.A4.

3 The mayors who endorsed this *State of Emergency Declaration* are from Vancouver, Surry, Edmonton, Calgary, Saskatoon, Regina, Winnipeg, Windsor, London, Kitchener, Hamilton, Mississauga, Toronto, Ottawa, Montreal, Lavalle, Quebec, Halifax, and St. John's. The *State of Emergency Declaration* was drafted by the Toronto Disaster Relief Committee and also endorsed by the Federation of Canadian Municipalities at its annual meeting in June 1999. This information was provided to me by Peter Zimmerman, executive assistant to Councillor Jack Layton, Toronto, Aug. 10, 1999.

4 Brian Lee Crowley, "The Budget Speech We Wish He'd Give," *The Globe and Mail*, Feb. 13, 1999, pp.D1-2. "Mr. Finance Minister, with great humility, we suggest you throw away the 1999 budget speech you plan to table on Tuesday. Brian Lee Crowley, one of the stalwart members of our editorial board, has designed a better, braver course of fiscal action for the year. Herewith, the text of his speech for you."

5 Libby Davies, MP, *Homelessness: An Un-natural Disaster — A Time to Act*, Parliament of Canada, Ottawa, 1999, p.4. This brief report and its recommendations resulted from her visit to nine communities in five provinces from coast to coast, when she met with anti-poverty activists, service providers, volunteers, homeless men and women, and elected representatives. One of her recommendations calls on the federal government to commit an additional 1 per cent of its budget to meet basic housing needs in Canada.

6 Cathy Crowe, "In the Calculation of Real Disasters Homelessness Has Easily Won Its Place," *The Toronto Star*, Oct. 30, 1998, p.A21. Briefing sessions on homelessness and community responses were provided to me by Kira Heineck, Cathy Crowe, Michael Shapcott, and David Hulchanski of the Toronto Disaster Relief Committee, August 1999.

7 Marjorie Bencz, "Harsh Cuts to Alberta Social Assistance," *NAPO News* (Ottawa: National Anti-Poverty Organization), no.42 (Spring 1994), p.3.

8 Marilyn Callahan, Barbara Field, Carol Hubberstey, and Brian Wharf, *Best Practices in Child Welfare: Perspectives from Parents, Social Workers and Community Partners*, Family and Community Research Program, School of Social Work, University of Victoria, June 1998, p.58. The study was funded by the B.C. Ministry for Children and Families.

9 Jennifer Dale and Peggy Foster, *Feminists and State Welfare* (London: Routledge & Kegan Paul, 1986), p.96.

10 See, for example, *The Canadian Encyclopedia* (Edmonton: Hurtig, 1985), "The Welfare State," p.1930.

11 Ian Gough, *The Political Economy of the Welfare State* (London: Macmillan, 1979), p.12.

12 Armine Yalnizyan, *The Growing Gap: A Report on Growing Inequality between the Rich and Poor in Canada* (Toronto: Centre for Social Justice, 1998), pp.13-14. See also, for analysis of the concentration of wealth among the few, Jim Stanford, *Paper Boom: Why Real Prosperity Requires a New Approach to Canada's Economy* (Ottawa: Canadian Centre for Policy Alternatives and James Lorimer, 1999).

13 Jillian Oderkirk, "Disabilities Among Children," *Canadian Social Trends* (Ottawa: Statistics Canada), no.31 (Winter 1993), p.25. See also Centre for International Statistics on Economic and Social Welfare, Countdown 93, *Campaign 2000 Child Poverty Indicator Report*, Canadian Council on Social Development, Ottawa, November 1993, pp.12-15. For inequalities in health and socio-economic status, see National Council of Welfare, *Health, Health Care and Medicare* (Ottawa, 1990), p.15; and Irving Rootman, "Inequities in Health: Sources and Solutions," *Health Promotion*, Winter 1988, pp.1-8. For linkages between income and mental health in children, see Dr. Dan Offord's study, reported by Debra Black, "A Tough Time in Childhood," *The Toronto Star*, Jan. 28, 1989, p.H1.

14 Margaret Philp, "UN Committee Lambastes Canada on Human Rights," *The Globe and Mail*, Dec. 5, 1998, p.A7. See also United Nations Committee on Economic, Social and Cultural Rights, *Consideration of Reports Submitted by States Parties under Articles 16 and 17 of the Covenant: Concluding Observations of the Committee on Economic, Social and Cultural Rights — Canada*, unedited version, E/C.12/2/add.31, New York, Dec. 4, 1998.

15 John Porter, *The Vertical Mosaic: An Analysis of Social Class and Power in Canada* (Toronto: University of Toronto Press, 1965), p.264.

16 Jane Ursel, "The State and the Maintenance of Patriarchy: A Case Study of Family, Labour and Welfare Legislation in Canada," in *Family, Economy and the State: The Social Reproduction Process under Capitalism*, ed. James Dickinson and Bob Russell (Toronto: Garamond Press, 1986), p.150.

17 Dorothy E. Smith, "Women, Class and Family," in Varda Burstyn and Dorothy Smith, *Women, Class, Family and the State* (Toronto: Garamond Press, 1985), p.2.

18 Margrit Eichler, "The Connection Between Paid and Unpaid Labour," in *Women's Paid and Unpaid Work: Historical and Contemporary Perspectives*, ed. Paula Bourne (Toronto: New Hogtown Press, 1985), p.63. Women's average annual wage remains below that of men. In 1990 women's real average annual wage was 60 per cent of men's, an increase from 53 per cent in 1980. Abdul Rashid, "Changes in Real Wages," *Canadian Social Trends*, no.32 (Spring 1994), p.17.

19 United Nations, *The United Nations and the Advancement of Women: 1945-1996*, revised edition, vol. 6, Blue Books Series (New York: United Nations Department of Public Information, 1996), p.654, item 16. See also Naomi Neft and Ann D. Levine, *Where Women Stand: An International Report on the Status of Women in 140 Countries, 1997-1998* (New York: Random House, 1997).

20 Based on a random sample of 420 women, 54 per cent of the women had experienced an unwanted or intrusive sexual experience before reaching the age of sixteen. *Final Report of the Canadian Panel on Violence Against Women, Changing the Landscape, Ending Violence — Achieving Equality* (Ottawa: Minister of Supply and Services Canada, 1993), p.9. See also Karen Rodgers, "Wife Assault in Canada," *Canadian Social Trends*, Autumn 1994, pp.3-8.

21 Wallace Clement, *The Canadian Corporate Elite: An Analysis of Economic Power* (Toronto: McClelland and Stewart, 1975), p.2.

22 Mary O'Brien, "Feminist Praxis," in *Feminism in Canada: From Pressure to Politics*, ed. Angela R. Miles and Geraldine Finn (Montreal: Black Rose, 1982), pp.265-66.

23 Ibid., p.254.

24 Todd Gitlin, *The Whole World Is Watching: Mass Media in the Making and Unmaking of the New Left* (Berkeley: University of California Press, 1980), p.9.

25 Ibid., p.10.

26 Bob Mullaly, *Structural Social Work: Ideology, Theory, and Practice*, 2nd ed. (Toronto: Oxford University Press, 1997), p.151. The manipulative role played by the news media in shaping our attitudes is examined in the documentary film *Manufacturing Consent*, directed by Mark Achbar, Peter Wintonick, and Adam Symansky, two parts, VHS, co-produced by Necessary Illusions and National Film Board, Montreal, 1992.

27 Canadian Association of Social Workers, *Social Work Code of Ethics*, Ottawa, 1994, pp.10, 24.

28 Bank for International Settlements, Central Bank Survey of Foreign Exchange and Derivatives, Market Activity 1998, *Press Release*, CH-4002, Basle, Switzerland, May 10, 1999 <www.bis.org>.

29 Howard Zinn, *You Can't Be Neutral on a Moving Train: A Personal History of Our Times* (Boston: Beacon Press, 1994), p.208.

30 Yalnizyan, *Growing Gap*, p.71.

31 Canada, *Looking Forward, Looking Back: Report of the Royal Commission on Aboriginal Peoples*, vol. 1 (Ottawa: Minister of Supply and Services Canada), p.7.

32 Tim Schouls, John Olthuis, and Diane Engelstad, "The Basic Dilemma: Sovereignty or Assimilation," in *Nation to Nation: Aboriginal Sovereignty and the Future of Canada*, ed. Diane Engelstad and John Bird (Concord, Ont.: Anansi, 1992), p.14.

33 Jean Leonard Elliott and Augie Fleras, *Unequal Relations: An Introduction to Race and Ethnic Dynamics in Canada* (Scarborough, Ont.: Prentice-Hall, 1992), p.52.

34 Frances Henry, Carol Tator, Winston Mattis, and Tim Rees, *The Colour of Democracy: Racism in Canadian Society* (Toronto: Harcourt Brace, 1995), p.328.

35 Elliott and Fleras, *Unequal Relations*, p.64.

36 Ibid., p.55.

37 bell hooks, *Killing Rage: Ending Racism* (New York: Henry Holt, 1995), p.254.

38 B. Singh Bolaria and Peter Li, *Racial Oppression in Canada* (Toronto: Garamond Press, 1985), p.181. See also the Africville Genealogy Society, ed., *The Spirit of Africville* (Halifax: Formac, 1992), and its review by Dorothy E. Moore, *Canadian Journal of Mental Health*, vol.12, no.2 (Fall 1992), pp.128-31.

39 "Refugees on the Line . . . ," *The Moment* (Toronto: Jesuit Centre), vol.3, no.1 (Spring 1989). The hostility continues against poorer immigrants, but if you are a rich immigrant with $100,000 to $350,000 to invest in Canada, you can buy your way into this country. See Tim Harper and David Vienneau, "Clampdown on Immigration," *The Toronto Star*, Oct. 29, 1994, pp.A1, A24; also, *Refugee Update* (Jesuit Centre for Social Faith and Justice), no.24 (Winter 1995).

40 James T. Sears, "Thinking Critically/Intervening Effectively about Homophobia and Heterosexism," in *Overcoming Heterosexism and Homophobia: Strategies That Work*, ed. James T. Sears and Walter L. Williams (New York: Columbia University Press, 1997), p.16.

41 Ibid.

42 Bonnie Burstow, *Radical Feminist Therapy: Working in the Context of Violence* (London: Sage Publications, 1992), p.67.

43 Kathleen Bennett, "Feminist Bisexuality: A Both/And Option for an Either/Or World," in *Close to Home: Bisexuality and Feminism*, ed. Elizabeth Reba Weise (Seattle, Wash.: Seal, 1992), pp.209-11.

44 "Bisexual Issues in Community Services," flyer, prepared by Bisexual Women of Toronto, 1999, p.1.

45 Jenny Morris, *Pride against Prejudice: Transforming Attitudes to Disability* (Philadelphia: New Society Publishers, 1991), p.115.
46 James I. Charlton, *Nothing About Us Without Us: Disability Oppression and Empowerment* (Berkeley: University of California Press, 1998), p.8.
47 Lynda Aitken and Gabriele Griffin, *Gender Issues in Elder Abuse* (London: Sage, 1996), p.7.
48 Ibid.
49 Nancy Adamson, Linda Briskin, and Margaret McPhail, *Feminist Organizing for Change: The Contemporary Women's Movement in Canada* (Toronto: Oxford University Press, 1988), pp.98-99.
50 Ibid., p.99.
51 Donna Baines, "Everyday Practices of Race, Class and Gender: Struggles, Skills, and Radical Social Work," *Journal of Progressive Human Services*, forthcoming, typescript p.7. See also Steven Wineman, *The Politics of Human Services: Radical Alternatives to the Welfare State* (Montreal: Black Rose Books, 1984); Donna Baines, "Feminist Social Work in the Inner City: Challenges of Race, Class and Gender," *Affilia: Journal of Social Work and Women*, vol.12, no.3 (1997), pp.297-317.
52 Neil Thompson, *Anti-Discriminatory Practice*, 2nd ed. (London: Macmillan, 1997), p.12.
53 Yvonne Howse and Harvey Stalwick, "Social Work and the First Nation Movement: 'Our Children, Our Culture,'" in *Social Work and Social Change in Canada*, ed. Brian Wharf (Toronto: McClelland and Stewart, 1990), pp.80, 87. Howse and Stalwick were focusing on transformed social services to Aboriginal people, but their approach can be applied to other oppressed populations as well.
54 Mullaly, *Structural Social Work*, pp.138-39.
55 Ibid., p.139.
56 Ibid., p.168.
57 Callahan et al., *Best Practices in Child Welfare*, p.18.
58 Kirk Makin, "Gay Couples Win Rights: They're Entitled to the Same Spousal Support as Common-Law Couples, Top Court Rules," *The Globe and Mail*, May 21, 1999, pp.A1, A8; in this case, the Supreme Court of Canada decided that Ontario must change its Family Law Act to cease discriminating against same-sex couples with reference to support payments when common-law relationships break down. For mainstream responses to Gay Pride Day, see also John Barber, "Gay Pride Parade Gains Mainstream Acceptance," *The Globe and Mail*, June 16, 1999, p.A6.
59 Yalnizyan, *Growing Gap*, p.62.
60 Ibid., p.45. See also, for the growing concentration of financial wealth in the United States, Edward N. Wolff, *Top Heavy: A Study of the Increasing Inequality of Wealth in America* (New York: Twentieth Century Fund, 1995), p.11.
61 Callahan et al., *Best Practices in Child Welfare*, p.55.

CHAPTER 2: THE ROOTS OF SOCIAL WORK: EARLY ATTITUDES

1 Statute cited by Karl de Schweinitz, *England's Road to Social Security* (New York: Barnes, 1943), pp.21-22.
2 Mary Daly, *Gyn/Ecology: The Metaethics of Radical Feminism* (Boston: Beacon Press, 1978), p.180.
3 Ibid., pp.178-222.
4 Quoted in de Schweinitz, *England's Road*, p.26. See also W. Friedlander and R. Apte, *Introduction to Social Welfare* (Englewood Cliffs, N.J.: Prentice-Hall, 1980), pp.9-18.

5 Mimi Abramovitz, *Regulating the Lives of Women: Social Welfare Policy from Colonial Times to the Present* (Boston: South End Press, 1988), p.40.

6 Don Bellamy, "Social Welfare in Canada," in *Encyclopedia of Social Work* (New York: National Association of Social Workers, 1965), p.37.

7 Ibid.

8 Allan Irving, " 'The Master Principle of Administering Relief': Jeremy Bentham, Sir Francis Bond Head and the Establishment of the Principle of Less Eligibility in Upper Canada," *Canadian Review of Social Policy,* no.23 (May 1989), p.17.

9 Dennis Guest, *The Emergence of Social Security in Canada* (Vancouver: University of British Columbia, 1980), p.12.

10 Report of the Aboriginal Committee, Community Panel, *Liberating Our Children, Liberating Our Nations,* Family and Children's Services Legislation Review in British Columbia, Victoria, 1992, p.14.

11 Ibid., pp.18-19. See also Ronald Wright, *Stolen Continents: The New World Through Indian Eyes Since 1492* (Toronto: Penguin, 1992); Vic Satzewich and Terry Wotherspoon, *First Nations: Race, Class and Gender Relations* (Scarborough, Ont.: Nelson, 1993); Frank James Tester and Peter Kulchyski, *Tammarniit (Mistakes): Inuit Relocation in the Eastern Arctic 1939-63* (Vancouver: University of British Columbia Press, 1994); Jim Albert, "500 Years of Indigenous Survival and Struggle," *Canadian Review of Social Policy,* no.28 (1991), pp.109-13; Hugh Shewell, "Origins of Contemporary Indian Social Welfare in the Canadian Liberal State: A Historical Case Study in Social Policy, 1873-1965," Ph.D. thesis, Faculty of Social Work, University of Toronto, 1995.

12 Pat Thane, "Women and the Poor Law in Victorian and Edwardian England," *History Workshop,* no.6 (Autumn 1978), p.31.

13 David Macarov, *The Design of Social Welfare* (New York: Holt, Rinehart & Winston, 1978), pp.191-200. See also Ashley Montagu, *On Being Human* (New York: Hawthorn, 1966).

14 S. Marcus, "Their Brothers' Keepers," in Willard Gaylin et al., *Doing Good: The Limits of Benevolence* (New York: Pantheon, 1978), p.51.

15 Ibid.

16 Philip Corrigan and Val Corrigan, "State Formation and Social Policy until 1871," in Noel Parry, Michael Rustin, and Carol Satyamurti, *Social Work, Welfare and the State* (Beverly Hills, Cal.: Sage, 1980), p.14.

17 Jennifer Dale and Peggy Foster, *Feminists and State Welfare* (London: Routledge & Kegan Paul, 1986), p.34.

18 By 1882 there were ninety-two social agencies in the United States modelled after the British C.O.S. These were the forerunners of the Family Service Associations now found in many U.S. and Canadian locations. See P. Popple, "Contexts of Practice," in *Handbook of Clinical Social Work,* ed. A. Rosenblatt and D. Waldvogel (San Francisco: Jossey-Bass, 1983), p.75. See also Bernard Lappin, "Stages in the Development of Community Organization Work as a Social Work Method," Ph.D. dissertation, School of Social Work, University of Toronto, 1965, p.64. Lappin's thesis provides an overview of the C.O.S. and early Settlement House movements. Another useful source focusing on the history of social welfare is Friedlander and Apte, *Introduction to Social Welfare,* chs.2, 3.

19 Quoted in Roy Lubove, *Professional Altruist* (Boston: Harvard, 1965), p.13.

20 For a study of the linkages between churches, women's reform groups, and the early formation of the social work profession, see Carol Baines, *Women's Reform Organizations in Canada 1870-1930: A Historical Perspective,* Working Papers on Social Welfare in Canada, Faculty of Social Work, University of Toronto, 1988.

21 Lappin, "Stages," p.64.

22 Carol T. Baines, "Women's Professions and an Ethic of Care," in *Women's Caring: Fem-*

inist Perspectives on Social Welfare, 2nd ed., ed. Carol T. Baines, Patricia M. Evans, and Sheila M. Neysmith (Toronto: Oxford University Press, 1998), p.30.

23 Ibid., pp.59-60.

24 Dale and Foster, *Feminists and State Welfare,* p.38.

25 Quoted in Guest, *Emergence of Social Security,* p.80.

26 Terry Copp, *The Anatomy of Poverty: The Condition of the Working Class in Montreal 1907-1929* (Toronto: McClelland and Stewart, 1974), p.106.

27 Quoted in ibid., p.115.

28 Quoted in Guest, *Emergence of Social Security,* p.57. Charlotte Whitton also opposed family allowances, which were nevertheless introduced in 1944. See Brigitte Kitchen, "Wartime Social Reform: The Introduction of Family Allowances," *Canadian Journal of Social Work Education,* vol.7, no.1 (1981), pp.29-54.

29 Quoted in *Social Welfare,* vol. 14, no. 6 (March 1932), pp.117, 119.

30 Copp, *Anatomy of Poverty,* p.127. On the growth of the welfare state, see also Allan Irving, "Canadian Fabians: The Work and Thought of Harry Cassidy and Leonard Marsh, 1930-1945," *Canadian Journal of Social Work Education,* vol.7, no.1 (1981), pp.7-28; James Struthers, *No Fault of Their Own: Unemployment and the Canadian Welfare State, 1914-1941* (Toronto: University of Toronto Press, 1983); and a special issue on "Leonard Marsh, Social Welfare Pioneer," in *Journal of Canadian Studies,* vol.21, no.2 (Summer 1986), especially Allan Moscovitch, "The Welfare State Since 1975," for more recent developments.

31 Canada, House of Commons, *Minutes of the Proceedings of the Special Committee on Indian Self-Government,* no.40, Oct. 12, 1983, Oct. 20, 1983.

32 Quoted in Alvin Finkel, "Origins of the Welfare State in Canada," in *The Canadian State: Political Economy and Political Power,* ed. Leo Panitch (Toronto: University of Toronto Press, 1977), p.349. See also Bill Lee, "Colonization and Community: Implications for First Nations Development," *Community Development Journal,* vol.27, no.3 (1992), pp.211-19.

33 Quoted in Peter Findlay, "The 'Welfare State' and the State of Welfare in Canada," paper presented at Annual Conference of Canadian Association of Schools of Social Work, Ottawa, 1982, p.9.

34 Dennis Guest, "Social Security," in *Canadian Encyclopedia* (Edmonton: Hurtig, 1985), p.1723.

35 Bertha Capen Reynolds, *Social Work and Social Living: Explorations in Philosophy and Practice* [1951], Classics Series (Silver Spring, Md.: National Association of Social Workers, 1975, 1987), p.165.

36 Bridget Moran, *A Little Rebellion* (Vancouver: Arsenal Pulp Press, 1992), pp.69-70.

37 Joanne C. Turner and Francis J. Turner, eds., *Canadian Social Welfare* (Toronto: Collier Macmillan, 1981), p.3.

38 Wanda Bernard, Lydia Lucas-White, and Dorothy Moore, "Two Hands Tied Behind Her Back: The Dual Negative Status of 'Minority Group' Women," paper presented to CASSW Annual Conference, Dalhousie University, Halifax, June 1981, p.17.

39 Ibid.

40 Saul D. Alinsky, *Reveille for Radicals* (Chicago: University of Chicago, 1946), p.82, quoted in Bryan M. Knight, "Poverty in Canada," in *Canada and Social Change,* ed. Dimitrios L. Roussopoulos (Montreal: Black Rose, 1973), p.23.

41 Copp, *Anatomy of Poverty,* p.127.

CHAPTER 3: SCHOOLS OF ALTRUISM

1 Naomi Klein, "Political Correctness and Apathy: All the Bickering about Universities Ignores a Small Fact — Students are Starving," *This Magazine,* vol.25, no.8 (May 1992), pp.11-14; Canadian Federation of Students, "Students Demand Action on Student Debt, Tuition Fees," Press Release, Jan. 20, 1998 <http://www.cfs-fcee>.

2 Joanne Darlaston, "On the Fringe: Experiences of Marginalization" in *Planet Social Work* (University of Toronto Social Work Student Publication, ed. Rob Eves), vol.1, no.1 (1992), p.10.

3 Joan Turner, "There Comes a Time," in *Perspectives on Women in the 1980s,* ed. Joan Turner and Lois Emery (Winnipeg: University of Manitoba, 1983), p.8.

4 Ibid.

5 Colleen Lundy and Gillian Walker, "The Status of Women in Social Work Education Revisited: Some Preliminary Findings," School of Social Work, Carleton University, Ottawa, 1989, p.11.

6 See Ashley Montagu, *On Being Human* (New York: Hawthorn, 1966), pp.27-46.

7 Eric Fromm, *The Art of Loving* (New York: Bantam, 1956), pp.50, 19.

8 That pattern was set a number of years ago. See, for instance, John A. Crane, "Employment of Social Service Graduates in Canada," a study carried out by the Canadian Association of Schools of Social Work, Ottawa, 1974, p.89.

9 Brenda DuBois and Karia Krogsrud Miley, *Social Work: An Empowering Profession* (Boston: Allyn and Bacon, 1999), pp.54-55.

10 Richard Cloward and Frances Fox Piven, "Notes Toward a Radical Social Work," in *Radical Social Work,* ed. R. Bailey and M. Drake (New York: Pantheon, 1976), p.xv.

11 Allen Pincus and Anne Minahan, *Social Work Practice: Model and Method* (Itasca, Ill.: Peacock, 1973), p.8.

12 For a discussion of "difference" and commonalities among various oppressions, see Tim Stainton and Karen Swift, " 'Difference' and Social Work Curriculum," *Canadian Social Work Review*, vol.13, no.1 (Winter 1996), pp.75-87.

13 Helen Levine, "The Personal Is Political: Feminism and the Helping Professions," in *Feminism in Canada: From Pressure to Politics,* ed. Angela R. Miles and Geraldine Finn (Montreal: Black Rose, 1982), p.200.

14 Sharon Taylor, "Gender in Development: A Feminist Process for Transforming University and Society," in *Oval Works: Feminist Social Work Scholarship,* Social Work Discussion Papers, School of Social Work, Memorial University of Newfoundland, St. John's, 1992, p.35.

15 Ibid., pp.31, 32.

16 Joan Gilroy, "Social Work and the Women's Movement," in *Social Work and Social Change in Canada,* ed. Brian Wharf (Toronto: McClelland and Stewart, 1990), pp.72, 73.

17 Correspondence with Dorothy Moore, Halifax, August 1994; Dorothy E. Moore, "Recruitment and Admission of Minority Students to Schools of Social Work," *Canadian Social Work Review,* vol.8, no.2 (Summer 1991), p.199.

18 Lena Dominelli, *Anti-Racist Social Work: A Challenge for White Practitioners and Educators,* 2nd ed. (London: Macmillan, 1997), pp.42, 66.

19 Doman Lum, *Social Work Practice and People of Color: A Process-Stage Approach*, 3rd ed. (Pacific Grove, Cal.: Brooks/Cole, 1996), p.36.

20 Gale Wills and Roy Hanes, "Report Workshop on Persons with Disabilities and Social Work Education in Canada," Persons with Disabilities Caucus, Canadian Association of Schools of Social Work, Ottawa, 1993, p.8.

21 Brian J. O'Neill, "Institutional Ethnography: Studying Institutions from the Margins," *Journal of Sociology and Social Welfare,* vol.25, no.4 (December 1998), p.134. See

also Brian J. O'Neill, "Canadian Social Work Education and Same Sex Sexual Orientation," *Canadian Social Work Review,* vol.12, no.2 (Summer 1995), pp.159-74.

22 Jill Abramczyk, "Why Schools of Social Work Must Challenge Heterosexism," student paper, submitted to Challenging Heterosexism course, Faculty of Graduate Studies and Research, School of Social Work, Carleton University, March 1994, p.18.

23 Roopchand Seebaran, "Social Work Education: An Empowerment Approach," Vancouver: University of British Columbia, School of Social Work, 1989, p.14.

24 Doug Saunders, "The Social Work Wars: Social Workers Tried to Improve Their School — and Hit a Brick Wall," *Excalibur,* March 10, 1993, pp.17-18.

25 Ibid., p.17.

26 Narda Razack, "Anti-Discriminatory Practice: Pedagogical Struggles and Challenges," *British Journal of Social Work,* vol.29, no.2 (April 1999), pp.232, 245.

27 Ibid., p.234.

28 Accreditation Standards, Ottawa, Canadian Association of Schools of Social Work, June 1999, Section 6; these apply to social work programs at the Master's degree level; similar standards in Section 5 apply to programs at the Bachelor's degree level.

29 Barbara Riley, "Teachings from the Medicine Wheel: Theories for Practice," a commissioned paper for WUNSKA Network, Canadian Association of Schools of Social Work, Ottawa, 1994, p.8 (presented in part at the CASSW Conference, Calgary, June 16, 1994). See also Kathy Absolon, "Healing as Practice: Teachings from the Medicine Wheel," and Edward Connors, "The Role of Spirituality in Wellness or How Well We See the Whole Will Determine How Well We Are and How Well We Can Become," commissioned papers for the WUNSKA Network, Canadian Association of Schools of Social Work, Ottawa, 1994.

30 Fyre Jean Graveline, *Circle Works: Transforming Eurocentric Consciousness* (Halifax: Fernwood Publishing, 1998), p.133.

31 Ibid., p.195.

32 Ibid., pp.73, 124. Even when schools try to be inclusive, basic change is still elusive. See Gord Bruyere, "Living in Another Man's House: Supporting Aboriginal Learners in Social Work Education," *Canadian Social Work Review,* vol.15, no.2 (Summer 1998), pp.169-76.

33 Graveline, *Circle Works,* pp.199-200. See also website on Anti-Racist Training for Social Work Education <www.cassw-acess.ca>.

34 Ray J. Thomlison and Cathryn Bradshaw, "Canadian Political Processes and Social Work Practice," in *Social Work Practice: A Canadian Perspective,* ed. F. Turner (Scarborough, Ont.: Prentice Hall, Allyn and Bacon Canada, 1999), p.265.

35 Universities are also expected to increasingly serve the immediate needs of business. See Janice Newson and Howard Buchbinder, *The University Means Business: Universities, Corporations and Academic Work* (Toronto: Garamond Press, 1988).

CHAPTER 4: SOCIAL WORKERS: ON THE FRONT LINE

1 Elspeth Latimer, "An Analysis of the Social Action Behaviour of the Canadian Association of Social Workers, from Its Organizational Beginnings to the Modern Period," Ph.D. dissertation, Faculty of Social Work, University of Toronto, 1972, pp.52, 84. Correspondence from Manon Allaire, Canadian Association of Social Workers, Ottawa, June 3, 1999.

2 John McKnight, "Professionalized Service and Disabling Help," in Ivan Illich et al., *Disabling Professions* (London: Marion Boyars, 1977), pp.82-83.

3 Carolyne Gorlick and Guy Brethour, *Welfare-to-Work Programs in Canada: An Overview* (Ottawa: Canadian Council on Social Development, 1998), p.3.

4 Wanda Bernard, Lydia Lucas-White, and Dorothy Moore, "Two Hands Tied Behind Her Back: The Dual Negative Status of 'Minority Group' Women," paper

presented to CASSW Annual Conference, Dalhousie University, Halifax, June 1981, p.23.

5 Wanda Thomas Bernard, Lydia Lucas-White, and Dorothy Moore, "Triple Jeopardy: Assessing Life Experiences of Black Nova Scotian Women from a Social Work Perspective," *Canadian Social Work Review,* vol.10 (Summer, 1993), no.2, p.267.

6 Jill Abramczyk, "Why Schools of Social Work Must Challenge Heterosexism," student paper submitted to Challenging Heterosexism course, Faculty of Graduate Studies and Research, School of Social Work, Carleton University, March 1994, p.8.

7 Ibid., pp.11-12. See also Lee Blue (Project Co-ordinator), *Preparing for HIV and AIDS: Resource Kit for Social Workers,* Ottawa: Canadian Association of Social Workers, 1990, pp.112-14.

8 Ron Clarke, "Human Sexuality and the Social Work Program: A Reflection on the Paradigmatic Quality of AIDS," in *AIDS and Social Work Education in Canada* (Ottawa: Canadian Association of Schools of Social Work, 1991), p.54.

9 Bonnie Burstow, *Radical Feminist Therapy: Working in the Context of Violence* (London: Sage Publications, 1992), p.70.

10 Kathleen Bennett, "Feminist Bisexuality: A Both/And Option for an Either/Or World," in *Close to Home: Bisexuality and Feminism*, ed. Elizabeth Reba Weise (Seattle, Wash.: Seal, 1992), p.216.

11 Molly R. Hancock, *Principles of Social Work Practice: A Generic Practice Approach* (New York: Haworth Press, 1997), p.176.

12 Daphne Statham, *Radicals in Social Work* (London: Routledge & Kegan Paul, 1978), p.9.

13 Lawrence Shulman, *The Skills of Helping: Individuals, Families and Groups,* 3rd ed. (Itasca, Ill.: Peacock, 1992), p.44.

14 Jenny Morris, *Pride against Prejudice: Transforming Attitudes to Disability* (Philadelphia: New Society Publishers, 1991), p.176.

15 Neil Thompson, *Anti-Discriminatory Practice*, 2nd ed. (London: Macmillan, 1997), pp.102, 127.

16 Jennifer Dale and Peggy Foster, *Feminists and State Welfare* (London: Routledge & Kegan Paul, 1986), p.104.

17 Bob Mullaly, *Structural Social Work: Ideology, Theory and Practice*, 2nd ed. (Toronto: Oxford University Press, 1997), p.169.

18 Paul Kivel, *Uprooting Racism: How White People Can Work for Racial Justice* (Philadelphia: New Society, 1996), p.107.

19 Workfare Watch, *Broken Promises: Welfare Reform in Ontario* (Toronto: Ontario Social Safety Network and the Community Social Planning Council of Toronto, 1999), p.47.

20 Quoted in Marilyn Callahan, Barbara Field, Carol Hubberstey, and Brian Wharf, *Best Practices in Child Welfare: Perspectives from Parents, Social Workers and Community Partners,* Child, Family and Community Research Program, School of Social Work, University of Victoria, Victoria, B.C., June 1998, p.24.

21 Ibid., p.54.

22 Francis J. Turner, "The Theoretical Base of Practice," in *Social Work Practice: A Canadian Perspective*, ed. Francis J. Turner (Scarborough, Ont.: Prentice Hall Allyn and Bacon Canada, 1999), p.25.

23 Ray J. Thomlison and Cathryn Bradshaw, "Canadian Political Processes and Social Work Practice," in *Social Work Practice*, ed. Turner, pp.268-69.

24 See, for instance, Tony Clarke, *Silent Coup: Confronting the Big Business Takeover of Canada* (Ottawa and Halifax: Centre for Policy Alternatives and James Lorimer, 1997). See also Social Justice Committee, "Report on the Royal Bank of Canada," Church of the Holy Trinity, Toronto, March 1999; and here, ch.5, "Privatization of Social Services," ch.6, "Globalization and Social Programs," and ch.7, "Postmodernism."

25 Peter Clutterbuck, Elise Davis, Marvyn Novick, Richard Volpe, *Best Practice Survey,* a review prepared for the Children at Risk Subcommittee, Laidlaw Foundation, 1990, pp.23, 50.

26 Elizabeth Radian and her partner, Ken Lederer, worked on this project from 1994 to 1996. Correspondence from Elizabeth Radian, Red Deer, Alberta, Aug. 27, 1999.

27 Sandra Frosst, with assistance from Gwyn Frayne, Mary Hlywa, Lynne Leonard, Marilyn Rowell, *Empowerment II: Snapshots of the Structural Approach* (Ottawa: Carleton University, 1993), pp.106, 119, 120, 126.

28 Marilyn Callahan, Colleen Lumb, and Brian Wharf, *Strengthening Families by Empowering Women: A Joint Project of the Ministry of Social Services and the School of Social Work,* School of Social Work, University of Victoria, Victoria, B.C., 1994, p.20.

29 Correspondence with Kathryn McCannell, Director of Clinical Development, Pacific Spirit Family and Community Services, Vancouver, August 1994. David Hannis, Grant MacEwan College, Edmonton, Alta., notes in his correspondence, Sept. 16, 1999, that programs in Edmonton containing anti-oppressive practices include: Beverly Human Rights Project, Poverty in Action, Central Edmonton Community Land Trust, Third Stage Housing Project, Making Connections (advocacy training for women), Women's Economic and Business Solutions, and Edmonton Community Loan Fund.

30 Janis Fook, *Radical Casework: A Theory of Practice* (St. Leonards, Australia: Allen & Unwin, 1993), p.91. See also Jim Ife, *Rethinking Social Work: Towards Critical Practice* (South Melbourne, Australia: Longman, 1997).

31 Mullaly, *Structural Approach to Social Work*, p.186.

32 Bernard, Lucas-White, and Moore, "Triple Jeopardy," p.271. See also Carol R. Swenson, "Clinical Social Work's Contribution to a Social Justice Perspective," *Social Work*, vol.43, no.6 (November 1998), pp.527-37; Charlotte Williams, "Connecting Anti-Racist and Anti-Oppressive Theory and Practice: Retrenchment or Reappraisal?" *The British Journal of Social Work*, vol.29, no.2 (April 1999), pp.211-230.

33 Joan Pennell, "Honouring the Professing in the Profession," *Oval Works: Feminist Social Work Scholarship,* Social Work Discussion Papers, School of Social Work, Memorial University of Newfoundland, St. John's, 1992, p.4.

34 Michael Fabricant and Steve Burghardt, *The Welfare State Crisis and the Transformation of Social Service Work* (New York: M.E. Sharpe, 1992), pp.62-188. See also Elaine Rogala, "Why One Ontario Woman Left Her Job as a Social Worker," *The CCPA Monitor: Reporting on Business, Labour and Environment*, vol.5, no.8 (February 1999), p.7.

Chapter 5: Managing Social Work: From Top to Bottom

1 Elspeth Latimer, "An Analysis of the Social Action Behaviour of the Canadian Association of Social Workers, from Its Organizational Beginnings to the Modern Period," Ph.D. dissertation, Faculty of Social Work, University of Toronto, 1972, p.15.

2 C. Germain and A. Gitterman, *The Life Model of Social Work Practice* (New York: Columbia University Press, 1980), p.141.

3 Special Report of the Ombudsman, *An Investigation by the Alberta Ombudsman into the Foster Care Program,* Department of Social Services and Community Health, Edmonton, Alta., March 1981, p.22.

4 Carol T. Baines, "Women's Professions and an Ethic of Care," in *Women's Caring: Feminist Perspectives on Social Welfare*, 2nd ed., ed. Carol T. Baines, Patricia M. Evans, and Sheila M. Neysmith (Toronto: Oxford University Press, 1998), p.38.

5 Gail Kenyon, "Gender and Income among Ontario Social Workers: The Source of Disparity," *Canadian Social Work Review*, vol.14, no.2 (Summer 1997), p.161. The survey measured responses from over 1,300 members of the OASW.

6 Wanda Bernard, Lydia Lucas-White, and Dorothy Moore, "Two Hands Tied Behind Her Back: The Dual Negative Status of 'Minority Group' Women," paper presented to CASSW Annual Conference, Dalhousie University, Halifax, June 1981, p.23.

7 Robert Doyle and Livy Visano, *A Time for Action! Access to Health and Social Services for Members of Diverse Cultural and Racial Groups in Metropolitan Toronto,* Report 1, Social Planning Council of Metro Toronto, 1987, p.4.

8 Lena Dominelli, *Anti-Racist Social Work: A Challenge for White Practitioners and Educators,* 2nd ed. (London: Macmillan, 1997), p.130.

9 See, for instance: Canada, House of Commons, *Minutes of the Proceedings of the Special Committee on Indian Self-Government,* no.40, Oct. 12, 1983, pp.14-15; Patrick Johnston, *Native Children and the Child Welfare System* (Ottawa: Canadian Council on Social Development/James Lorimer, 1983).

10 Sid Fiddler "Genesis of Family Violence in Native Society," *WUNSKA Family Violence Project,* Ottawa: Canadian Association of Schools of Social Work, 1994, p.25.

11 Ibid.

12 Lauri Gilchrist and Kathy Absolon, "Social Work 354: An Introduction to First Nations Issues and Human Services: Study Guide and Course Manual," draft, School of Social Work, University of Victoria, Victoria, B.C., 1993, p.93.

13 Fiddler, "Genesis of Family Violence," p.48.

14 Peter C. McMahon, *Management by Objectives in the Social Services* (Ottawa: Canadian Association of Social Workers, 1981).

15 Neil Tudiver, "Ideology and Management in the Social Services," paper presented to the Conference of the Canadian Association of Schools of Social Work, Saskatoon, Sask., June 1979, pp.17, 28-29.

16 Lena Dominelli and Ankie Hoogvelt, "Globalization and the Technocratization of Social Work," *Critical Social Policy,* vol.16, no.47 (1996), pp.45-62.

17 James F. Gardner and Sylvia Nudler, *Quality Performance in Human Services: Leadership, Values and Vision* (Baltimore: Paul H. Brookes, 1999).

18 David Robertson et al., "The CAW Working Conditions Study: Benchmarking Auto Assembly Plants," North York, Ont.: CAW-Canada, 1996, cited in James Rinehart, "The International Motor Vehicle Program's Lean Production Benchmark: A Critique," in *Monthly Review,* vol.50, no.8 (January 1999), pp.22-23.

19 Neil Tudiver, "Employee Assistance Plans: Who Benefits?" *Canadian Review of Social Policy,* no.32 (1993), p.79.

20 Ernie S. Lightman, "The Impact of Government Economic Restraint on Mental Health Services in Canada," *Canada's Mental Health,* vol.34, no.1 (March 1986), p.26.

21 Neil Tudiver, *Universities for Sale: Resisting Corporate Control over Canadian Higher Education* (Toronto: James Lorimer, 1999).

22 Leah F. Vosko, "Workfare Temporaries: Workfare and the Rise of the Temporary Employment Relationship in Ontario," *Canadian Review of Social Policy,* no.42 (Winter 1998), pp.71, 68.

23 Ibid., p.66.

24 Ibid., p.63.

25 Adam Cohen, "When Wall Street Runs Welfare," *Time Magazine,* March 23, 1998, pp.64-66, only in the U.S. edition, accessible from http://www.epnet.com/ehost (search terms: welfare and Wall Street and time). See also Evelyn Shapiro, *The Cost of Privatization: A Case Study of Home Care in Manitoba* (Ottawa: Canadian Centre for Policy Alternatives, 1997); and Margaret Gibelman and Harold W. Demone Jr., eds., *The Privatization of Human Services: Policy and Practice Issues* (New York: Springer, 1998).

26 Thomas Walkom, "Money Woes Leave Home Care in Sad Shape," *The Toronto Star,* April 27, 1999, p.A2. See also Michael Scheinert, "The Catch-22 That Could End Non-profit Home Care," *The Toronto Star,* April 9, 1999, p.A25.

Chapter 6: Unemployment to Welfare to Poverty: Clients Speak Out

1 Linda McQuaig, *The Cult of Impotence: Selling the Myth of Powerlessness in the Global Economy* (Toronto: Penguin Books, 1998), p.47.

2 Armine Yalnizyan, *The Growing Gap: A Report on Growing Inequality between the Rich and Poor in Canada* (Toronto: Centre for Social Justice, 1998), p.57.

3 Mike Burke and John Shields, in consultation with Marvyn Novick, Susan Silver, and Sue Wilson, "The Job-Poor Recovery: Social Cohesion and the Canadian Labour Market," *Research Report of the Ryerson Social Policy Reporting Network*, Ryerson Polytechnic University, Toronto, May 1999, pp.16-18.

4 Dorothy O'Connell, "Poverty: The Feminine Complaint," in *Perspectives on Women in the 1980s,* ed. Joan Turner and Lois Emery (Winnipeg: University of Manitoba, 1983), p.47.

5 Margrit Eichler, "The Connection Between Paid and Unpaid Labour," in *Women's Paid and Unpaid Work: Historical and Contemporary Perspectives,* ed. Paula Bourne (Toronto: New Hogtown Press, 1985), p.62. See also *Who's Counting? Marilyn Waring on Sex, Lies and Global Economics*, directed by Terre Nash, National Film Board of Canada, Montreal, 1995, 94 minutes.

6 National Council of Welfare, *Who Are the People on Welfare?* Social Security Backgrounder, no.2, Ottawa, 1994, p.4.

7 Moira Welsh, "Jobless Sick Bill Hits $1 Billion: Real Unemployed Rate Likely 20% New Study Says," *The Toronto Star*, May 28, 1994, p.1.

8 Neil Tudiver, "Employee Assistance Plans: Who Benefits?" *Canadian Review of Social Policy*, no.32 (1993), p.76.

9 Gordon Ternowetsky, "Hunger in Regina: Where Do We Go from Here?" address to World Food Day Hunger Symposium, Regina and District Food Bank, Oct. 15, 1993, pp.3, 6.

10 Linda McQuaig, "The Debt Obsession," *The Toronto Star,* Feb. 18, 1995, pp.C1, C4.

11 *Paying for Canada: Perspectives on Public Finance and National Programs,* joint statement, Toronto Child Poverty Action Group and Citizens for Public Justice and Social Planning Council of Metropolitan Toronto, October 1994, p.4.

12 Kirk Falconer, "Corporate Taxation in Canada: A Background Paper," *Canadian Review of Social Policy,* vol.26 (1990), p.83; Ternowetsky, "Hunger in Regina," pp.3, 7; Marvyn Novick, "Societal Strategies to Promote Family Security," in *Social Security Reform: What Are the Issues?* Social Planning Council of Metro Toronto, March 1994, p.6. The failure of NDP governments to support a corporate minimum tax is illustrated by Brigitte Kitchen, *Fair Taxation in a Changing World: Report of the Ontario Fair Tax Commission* (Toronto: University of Toronto Press, 1993), p.1068. Kitchen was a commissioner of Ontario's Fair Tax Commission.

13 See, for instance, Canadian Centre for Policy Alternatives, "Poverty Could be Eliminated in Canada by Reducing Tax Breaks, Closing Loopholes," *CCPA Monitor,* vol.1, no.1 (May 1994), p.6, which shows that the total for selected tax expenditures is $19 billion while the total poverty gap (amount needed to bring all Canadians over the poverty line) is $13.4 billion.

14 Laura Karmatz and Aisha Labi, with research by Joan Levinstein, "Corporate Welfare: A System Exposed," *Time Magazine*, Canadian edition, Nov. 9, 1998, p.3.

15 Ibid., p.33.

16 Tony Clarke, *Silent Coup: Confronting the Big Business Takeover of Canada* (Ottawa and Halifax: Centre for Policy Alternatives and James Lorimer, 1997), Appendix III, "Business Organizations and the Support Groups," pp.249-52.

17 Canadian Association of Food Banks, *HungerCount 1998: Emergency Food Assistance*

in Canada, Toronto, September 1998, p.12. See also Website for the Canadian Association of Food Banks <www.icomm.ca/cafb>.

18 Graham Riches, "Hunger, Welfare and Food Security: Emergency Strategies," in *First World Hunger: Food Security and Welfare Politics,* ed. Graham Riches (London: Macmillan, 1997), p.173.

19 Ibid., pp.13, 174. See also Mustafa Koc, Rod MacRae, Luc J.A. Mougeot, and Jennifer Welsh, *For Hunger-Proof Cities: Sustainable Urban Food Systems* (Ottawa: International Development Research Centre, 1999).

20 Quoted in Graham Riches, "Fighting Hunger: The Struggle for Food Sovereignty," in *Civil Society and Global Change: Canadian Development Report 1999,* ed. Alison Van Rooy (Ottawa: North-South Institute, 1999), p.42.

21 Burke and Shields, *Job-Poor Recovery,* pp.3, 9; emphasis in original.

22 Maude Barlow and Tony Clarke, *MAI: The Multilateral Agreement on Investment and the Threat to American Freedom* (New York: Stoddart, 1998), p.3. See also Russell Mokhiber and Robert Weissman, *Corporate Predators: The Hunt for Mega-Profits and the Attack on Democracy* (Munroe, Maine: Common Courage Press, 1999); John McMurtry, *The Cancer Stage of Capitalism* (London: Pluto, 1999). Upward approaches to globalization and to other dimensions of exploitation are analysed in William K. Carroll, ed., *Organizing Dissent: Contemporary Social Movements in Theory and Practice,* 2nd ed. (Toronto: Garamond Press, 1997).

23 "The Siena Declaration: Leading World Activists Address the Global Economic Crisis," *CCPA Monitor,* vol.5, no.7 (December 1998/January 1999), p.26.

24 Ibid., p.26.

25 "Siena Declaration," p.27. See also Tony Clarke and Maude Barlow, *MAI Round 2: New Global and Internal Threats* (Toronto: Stoddart, 1998). For an analysis of how social justice movements can influence international affairs, see John Tirman, "How We Ended the Cold War: Peace Activists' Demand for an End to Nuclear Madness Played a Decisive Role," *The Nation,* Nov. 1, 1999, pp.13-21.

26 Quoted in Rose M. Raftus et al., "Centering the Cycle for the Able Bodied Unemployed: A Participatory Research Study," paper presented in partial fulfilment of requirements for M.S.W. degree, Dalhousie University, Halifax, 1992, p.57.

27 O'Connell, "Poverty," p.47.

28 Workfare Watch, *Broken Promises: Welfare Reform in Ontario* (Toronto: Ontario Social Safety Network and the Community Social Planning Council of Toronto, 1999), p.32.

29 Helen Levine, "The Personal Is Political: Feminism and the Helping Professions," in *Feminism in Canada: From Pressure to Politics,* ed. Angela R. Miles and Geraldine Finn (Montreal: Black Rose, 1982), p.191.

30 See Eli Zaretsky, "Rethinking the Welfare State: Independence, Economic Individualism and Family," in *Family, Economy and State: The Social Reproduction Process under Capitalism,* ed. James Dickinson and Bob Russell (Toronto: Garamond Press, 1986), p.93.

31 Levine, "Personal Is Political," p.192.

32 Report of the Special Senate Committee on Poverty, *Poverty in Canada* (Ottawa: Information Canada, 1971), p.83. These findings are confirmed by more recent studies on social assistance. For example, *Transitions: Summary,* report of the Social Assistance Review Committee prepared for the Ontario Ministry of Community and Social Services (Toronto: Queen's Printer for Ontario, 1988), ch.2; and Social Planning and Research Council of British Columbia, *Regaining Dignity 1989: An Examination of Costs and the Adequacy of Income Assistance Rates (GAIN) in British Columbia,* Vancouver, April 1989.

33 Erminie Joy Cohen, *Sounding the Alarm: Poverty in Canada,* Senate of Canada, Ottawa, 1997, p.44.

34 Hugh Shewell, "Canada," in *Poverty: A Persistent Global Reality,* ed. John Dixon and David Macarov (London: Routledge, 1998), p.69. This chapter by Hugh Shewell, pp.50-69, provides a historical analysis as to why Canada's social security programs have failed to respond effectively to poverty.

35 Pat Capponi, *The War at Home: An Intimate Portrait of Canada's Poor* (Toronto: Penguin, 1999); Daniel Broderick/Danny Downey, *Ear to the Streets: Straight Out of the Minds, Bodies, and Spirits of Canada's Street Youth* (Toronto: On the Path, 1999). See also Yves Vaillancourt, "Remaking Canadian Social Policy: A Quebec Viewpoint," in *Remaking Canadian Social Policy: Social Security in the Late 1990s,* ed. Jane Pulkingham and Gordon Ternowetsky (Halifax: Fernwood Publishing, 1996), pp.81-99; Nancy Pollack with Richard Vedan and Frank Tester, *Critical Choices, Turbulent Times: A Community Workbook on Social Programs,* 2nd ed. (Vancouver: School of Social Work, University of British Columbia, 1998); National Anti-Poverty Organization, *A Human Rights Meltdown in Canada: Submission to the Committee on Economic, Social and Cultural Rights,* Ottawa, 1998.

36 Louise Johnson, *Social Work Practice: A Generalist Approach* (Boston: Allyn and Bacon, 1983), p.283.

37 Solicitor General Canada, *Annual Report 1979-1980* (Ottawa: Ministry of Supply and Services, 1981), p.60.

38 Phyllis Chesler, *Women and Madness* (New York: Avon, 1972), p.165. See also Leah Cohen, *Small Expectations: Society's Betrayal of Older Women* (Toronto: McClelland and Stewart, 1984), pp.101-5, on nursing homes as abusive institutions.

39 Levine, "Personal Is Political," p.183.

40 Bonnie Burstow and Don Weitz, eds., *Shrink Resistant: The Struggle against Psychiatry in Canada* (Vancouver: New Star Books, 1988), pp.24, 25. See also Bonnie Burstow, *Radical Feminist Therapy: Working in the Context of Violence* (London: Sage Publications, 1992), pp.235-66; and Corey Weinstein, "Seeking Prison Madness," book review of *Prison Madness: The Mental Health Crisis behind Bars and What We Must Do about it,* by Terry Kupers, Jossey-Bass Publishers, 1999, in *Tikkun: A Bi-Monthly Jewish Critique of Politics, Culture and Society,* vol.14, no. 4 (July/August 1999), p.80.

41 Robb Travers, "The Needs of Lesbian, Gay and Bisexual Youth: Social Services' Next Challenge," *Ontario Association of Professional Social Workers' Newsmagazine,* vol.21, no.2 (Summer 1994), p.6.

42 Johnson, *Social Work Practice,* p.284.

43 Mike Oliver and Colin Barnes, "Discrimination, Disability and Welfare: From Needs to Rights," in *Disabling Barriers — Enabling Environments,* ed. J. Swain, V. Finkelstein, S. French, and M. Oliver (London: Sage Publications, 1993), p.273.

44 Jenny Morris, *Pride against Prejudice: Transforming Attitudes to Disability* (Philadelphia: New Society Publishers, 1991), p.33.

45 National Anti-Poverty Organization, *Human Rights Meltdown,* p.39.

46 Ibid., p.39.

47 Cohen, *Sounding the Alarm,* p.19.

48 Carolyne Gorlick and Guy Brethour, *Welfare-to-Work Programs in Canada: An Overview* (Ottawa: Canadian Council on Social Development, 1998), pp.7-8.

49 National Anti-Poverty Organization, *Human Rights Meltdown,* p.28.

50 Grant Schellenberg, *The Changing Nature of Part-Time Work,* Social Research Series, Canadian Council on Social Development, Ottawa, 1997, p.43.

51 National Anti-Poverty Organization, *Human Rights Meltdown,* p.42.

52 Interfaith Social Assistance Reform Coalition, *Our Neighbours' Voices: Will We Listen?* (Toronto: James Lorimer, 1998), pp.95, 97.

53 Eric Shragge, "Introduction," in *Workfare: Ideology of a New Under-Class,* ed. Eric Shragge (Toronto: Garamond Press, 1997), p.13.

54 Eric Shragge and Marc-Andre Deniger, "Workfare in Quebec," in *Workfare*, ed. Shragge, pp.71-83.

55 Statistics sent to me by Mike Farrell, National Anti-Poverty Organization, Ottawa, Aug. 3, 1999.

56 Barbara Blouin, "Below the Bottom Line: The Unemployed and Welfare in Nova Scotia," *Canadian Review of Social Policy,* no.29/30 (1992), pp.116, 121-31.

57 Jean Swanson, "Quick Analysis of the Report of the Ontario Social Assistance Review Committee, 'Transitions,'" *Canadian Review of Social Policy,* no.23 (May 1989), p.19. For another example of analysis emphasizing universal access to decent jobs at decent wages, see Marvyn Novick, "A New Work Agenda: Social Choices for a Healthy Society," in *Unemployment and Welfare,* ed. Riches and Ternowetsky.

58 Swanson, "Quick Analysis of the Report."

59 Telephone conversation with Ian Morrison, Executive Director, The Clinic Resource Office of the Ontario Legal Aid Plan, Toronto, Oct. 17, 1994.

60 Telephone conversation with Ian Morrison.

61 "Welfare Cops Saving Province $80 Million a Year: Bourbeau," *The Gazette* (Montreal), Nov. 10, 1993, p.A8.

62 Levine, "Personal Is Political," p.196.

63 Alberta Social Services and Community Health, *Child Welfare Programs,* 1 B.9, 1 C2(c); emphasis added.

64 National Council of Welfare, *In the Best Interests of the Child* (Ottawa: National Department of Health and Welfare, 1979), pp.17-18.

65 Marilyn Callahan, "Feminist Approaches: Women Recreate Child Welfare," in *Rethinking Child Welfare in Canada,* ed. Brian Wharf (Toronto: McClelland and Stewart, 1993), p.185.

66 Canada, House of Commons, *Indian Self-Government in Canada,* Ottawa, 1983, p.31; cited in *Taking Control Newsletter: A Review of Indian and Native Social Work Education in Canada,* no.2 (1985), Faculty of Social Work, University of Regina, p.4.

67 Brad McKenzie, "Social Work Practice with Native People," in *An Introduction to Social Work Practice in Canada,* ed. Shankar Yelaja (Toronto: Prentice-Hall, 1985), p.277.

68 Quoted in *Taking Control Newsletter,* p.10.

69 Quoted in *Say Hi to Julie: A Commentary from Children in Care in Alberta,* ed. Jim Allison and Janice Johnson (Calgary: Who Cares? 1981), p.49.

70 Ibid. For similar concerns expressed by fostered teens in Newfoundland, see Dean Stokes Sullivan, "Tough Talk from Fostered Teens," *Evening Telegram* (St. John's, Nfld.), June 11, 1997, pp.1-2.

71 Campaign 2000, *Child Poverty in Canada: Report Card 1999* (Toronto: Family Service Association, 1999), p.2.

72 Ibid., p.1.

73 Ibid., p.2.

74 Royal Commission on Aboriginal Peoples, "Current Realities — The Failure of the Justice System," in *Bridging the Cultural Divide: A Report on Aboriginal Peoples and Criminal Justice in Canada* (Ottawa: Minister of Supply and Services Canada, 1996), ch.2, p.29.

75 Marianne O. Nielsen, "Introduction," in *Aboriginal People and Canadian Criminal Justice,* ed. Robert A. Silverman and Marianne O. Nielsen (Toronto and Vancouver: Butterworths, 1992), pp.3-4.

76 Ibid., p.7.

77 Quoted in *What Was Said? Study Guide One,* ed. Harvey Stalwick (Regina: Faculty of Social Work, 1986), p.11.

78 Ibid., p.84.

79 Quoted in Joan Ryan, *Wall of Words: The Betrayal of the Urban Indian* (Toronto: Peter Martin, 1978), p.84.

Chapter 7: Social Work and Social Change: Breaking Out

1 Helen Levine, "Personal Is Political: Feminism and the Helping Professions," in *Feminism in Canada: From Pressure to Politics,* ed. Angela R. Miles and Geraldine Finn (Montreal: Black Rose, 1982), p.199.

2 Maurice Moreau, in collaboration with Lynne Leonard, *Empowerment Through a Structural Approach to Social Work: A Report from Practice* (Montreal and Ottawa: Ecole de service sociale, Université de Montréal and Carleton University School of Social Work, 1989), p.23.

3 Ibid., p.1.

4 George J. Sefa Dei, "The Challenges of Anti-Racist Education in Canada," *Canadian Ethnic Studies,* vol.25, no.2 (1993), p.42.

5 Howard Zinn, *You Can't Be Neutral on a Moving Train: A Personal History of Our Times* (Boston: Beacon, 1994), p.10. See also for a lyrical, self-reflective examination of resistance, dian marino, *Wild Garden: Art, Education, and the Culture of Resistance* (Toronto: Between the Lines, 1997).

6 Maurice Moreau, "Structural Social Work Practice: A Case Illustration," unpublished paper, Montreal, 1985, p.4. See also M. Moreau, "Structural Approach to Social Work," *Canadian Journal of Social Work Education,* vol.5, no.1 (1979), pp.78-94.

7 Correspondence with author, Aug. 24, 1989.

8 Karen J. Swift, *Manufacturing "Bad Mothers": A Critical Perspective on Child Neglect* (Toronto: University of Toronto Press, 1995), p.183. See also Karen Swift, "Contradictions in Child Welfare: Neglect and Responsibility," in *Women's Caring: Feminist Perspectives on Social Welfare,* 2nd ed., ed. Carol T. Baines, Patricia M. Evans, and Sheila M. Neysmith (Toronto: Oxford University Press, 1998), pp.160-87; and Betty Joyce Carter, *Who's To Blame? Child Sexual Abuse and Non-Offending Mothers* (Toronto: University of Toronto Press, 1999).

9 Marilyn Callahan, "Creating Second-Class Citizens in Child Welfare," in *Community Approaches to Child Welfare: International Perspectives*, ed. Lena Dominelli (Aldershot, Eng.: Ashgate, 1999), p.49.

10 Ibid., p.53. In the same chapter Callahan advocates a citizenship approach to reframing child welfare that would be more community-based, using a structural, feminist approach to practice. See also Lea Caragata, "How Should Social Work Respond? Deconstructing Practice in Mean Times," *Canadian Social Work Review,* vol.4, no.2 (Summer 1997), pp.139-54. For reconstructing conditions enabling children to thrive, see Marvyn Novick, "Prospects for Children: Life Chances and Civic Society," work in progress, Ryerson School of Social Work, Toronto, 1999.

11 See, for instance, Paulo Freire, *Pedagogy of the Oppressed*, new revised 20th anniversary edition, trans. Myra Bergman Ramos (New York: Continuum, 1999).

12 Joyce West Stevens, "A Question of Values in Social Work Practice: Working with the Strength of Black Adolescent Females," *Families in Society: The Journal of Contemporary Human Services,* vol.79, no.3 (May-June, 1998), p.292.

13 Janis Fook, "Radical Social Casework: A Theory of Practice," M.A. thesis, Department of Social Work, University of Sydney, Australia, 1986, pp.143, 251-53. See also Janis Fook, *Radical Casework: A Theory of Practice* (St. Leonards, Australia: Allen & Unwin, 1993), p.112; and Michael Lerner, *Surplus Powerlessness: The Psychodynamics of Everyday Life . . . and the Psychology of Individual and Social Transformation* (Oakland, Cal.: Institute of Labor and Mental Health, 1986), pp.281-99.

14 Nancy Adamson, Linda Briskin, and Margaret McPhail, *Feminist Organizing for Change: The Contemporary Women's Movement in Canada* (Toronto: Oxford University Press, 1988), p.101.

15 Ben Carniol, "Structural Social Work: Maurice Moreau's Challenge to Social Work Practice," *Journal of Progressive Human Services*, vol.3, no.1 (1992), p.15; see also pp.5-14.

16 Budd Hall, "Introduction," in *Voices of Change: Participatory Research in the United States and Canada*, ed. Peter Park, Mary Brydon-Miller, Budd Hall, and Ted Jackson (Toronto: Ontario Institute for Studies in Education, 1993), p.xvii.

17 Peter Park, "What Is Participatory Research? A Theoretical and Methodological Perspective," in *Voices of Change*, ed. Park et al., p.15.

18 Patricia Maguire, "Challenges, Contradictions and Celebrations: Attempting Participatory Research as a Doctoral Student," in *Voices of Change*, ed. Park et al., pp.162-63.

19 Mary Nomme Russell, "Feminist Social Work Skills," *Canadian Social Work Review*, vol.6, no.1 (Winter 1989), p.77.

20 Donna Baines, "Feminist Social Work in the Inner City: Challenges of Race, Class and Gender," *Affilia: Journal of Social Work and Women*, vol.12, no.3 (Fall 1997), p.306.

21 Marilyn Callahan, "Feminist Approaches: Women Recreate Child Welfare," ch.6 in *Rethinking Child Welfare in Canada*, ed. Brian Wharf (Toronto: McClelland and Stewart, 1993), p.198. For elaboration on policy communities and potential changes in child welfare, see Brian Wharf, "Rethinking Child Welfare," ch.7 of the same book, pp.210-30.

22 Yvonne Howse and Harvey Stalwick, "The First Nation Movement," ch.4 in *Social Work and Social Change in Canada*, ed. Wharf; see also ch.5.

23 Ann Charter "A Medicine Wheel Approach to Working with Men Who Batter," *A WUNSKA Discussion Paper,* Canadian Association of Schools of Social Work, Ottawa, 1994.

24 Ibid., pp.3, 4. See also Ontario Native Women's Association, "Breaking Free," *Perception*, vols.15-4/16-1 (Fall/Winter 1992), pp.40-43.

25 Jerome Schiele, "Afrocentricity as an Alternative World View for Equality," *Journal of Progressive Human Services*, vol.5, no.1 (1994), pp.5-25.

26 Ibid., p.15.

27 Ibid., p.19. See also Mekada J. Graham, "The African-Centred Worldview: Developing a Paradigm for Social Work," *British Journal of Social Work*, vol.29, no.2 (April 1999), pp.251-67.

28 Dei, "Challenges of Anti-Racist Education."

29 Brian O'Neill, "Social Work with Gay, Lesbian and Bisexual Members of Racial and Ethnic Minority Groups," in *Professional Service Delivery in a Multicultural World*, ed. Gwat-Yong Lie and David Este (Toronto: Canadian Scholars' Press, 1999), p.85.

30 London Edinburgh Weekend Return Group, *In and Against the State* (London: Pluto, 1979), p.83.

31 Callahan, "Feminist Approaches," p.199.

32 Michèle Kérisit and Nérée St-Amand, "Taking Risks with Families at Risk: Some Alternative Approaches with Poor Families in Canada," in *Child Welfare in Canada: Research and Policy Implications*, ed. Joe Hudson and Burt Galaway (Toronto: Thompson Educational Publishing, 1995), p.161. See also Melvin Delgado, *Social Work Practice in Nontraditional Urban Settings* (New York: Oxford University Press, 1999).

33 Kathryn McCannell, Colleen Lumb, and Paule McNicoll, "The Single Mothers' Housing Network," in *The Ecological Perspective in Family-Centered Therapy*, ed. M. Rodway and B. Trute (Lewiston, N.Y.: Edwin Mellen, 1993), pp.109, 112.

34 Ibid., p.107.

35 Jenny Morris, *Pride against Prejudice: Transforming Attitudes to Disability* (Philadelphia: New Society Publishers, 1991), p.184.

36 Sid Fiddler "Genesis of Family Violence in Native Society," *WUNSKA Family Violence Project,* Ottawa: Canadian Association of Schools of Social Work, 1994, pp.20, 21. See also Augie Fleras and Jean Leonard Elliott, *The Nations Within: Aboriginal-State Relations in Canada, the United States and New Zealand* (Toronto: Oxford University Press, 1992).

37 Vern Morrissette, Brad McKenzie, and Larry Morrissette, "Toward an Aboriginal Model of Social Work Practice: Cultural Knowledge and Traditional Practices," *Canadian Social Work Review,* vol.10, no.1 (Winter 1993), pp.91-108.

38 Jim Albert, "If We Don't Do It, It Won't Get Done: A Case Study from Nicaragua," *International Social Work: Special Issue on Poverty and Interventions,* vol.35, no.2 (April 1992), p.240.

39 Maureen Wilson and André Jacob, "International Development Through Community Action," presentation to Canadian Association of Schools of Social Work Conference, Calgary, June 1994, pp.2, 12. See also Rebecca Abers, "Learning Democratic Practice: Distributing Government Resources through Popular Participation in Porto Alegre, Brazil," in *Cities for Citizens: Planning and the Rise of Civil Society in a Global Age,* ed. Mike Douglass and John Friedmann (New York: John Wiley, 1998), pp.39-66.

40 Angela Miles, "Ideological Hegemony in Political Discourse: Women's Specificity and Equality," in *Feminism in Canada,* ed. Miles and Finn, p.220.

41 Callahan, "Feminist Approaches," p.198.

42 Jillian Ridington, "Providing Services the Feminist Way," in *Still Ain't Satisfied: Canadian Feminism Today,* ed. Maureen Fitzgerald, Connie Guberman, and Margie Wolfe (Toronto: Women's Press, 1982), p.96.

43 Correspondence with author, Aug. 24, 1989. See also Helen Levine, "The Impact of Feminist Theory on Social Work Practice," *Newsmagazine* (Ontario Association of Professional Social Workers), vol.21, no.1 (Summer 1994), pp.5-7.

44 Cindy Player, "Government Funding of Battered Women's Shelter, Feminist Victory or Co-optation?" in *Breaking the Silence: A Newsletter on Feminism in Social Welfare Research, Action, Policy and Practice,* vol.1, no.5 (1983), p.4.

45 National Clearinghouse on Family Violence, Health Promotions and Programs Branch, Health Canada, *Transition Houses and Shelters for Abused Women in Canada* (Ottawa: Minister of Supply and Services Canada, 1998), p.1.

46 Shirley Masada with Jillian Ridington for DAWN Canada, *Meeting Our Needs: Access Manual for Transition Houses* (Toronto: DisAbled Women's Network Canada, 1991); Leanne Cusitar, *Strengthening the Links — STOPPING THE VIOLENCE: A Guide to the Issue of Violence against Women with Disabilities* (Toronto: DAWN, 1994); Joanne Bacon, *Violence against Women with Disabilities: Practical Considerations for Health Care Professionals* (Toronto: DAWN, 1994).

47 Bob Mullaly, *Structural Social Work: Ideology, Theory and Practice,* 2nd ed. (Toronto: McClelland and Stewart, 1997), p.189.

48 Greg MacLeod, *From Mondragon to America: Experiments in Community Economic Development* (Sydney, N.S.: University College of Cape Breton Press, 1997), p.140. See also Eric Shragge, ed., *Community Economic Development: In Search of Empowerment,* 2nd ed. (Montreal: Black Rose Books, 1997); and Eric Shragge and Kathryn Church, "None of your Business?! Community and Economic Development and the Mixed Economy of Welfare," *Canadian Review of Social Policy,* no.41 (Spring 1998), pp.33-44.

49 See, for instance, Steve Wineman, *The Politics of Human Services: Radical Alternatives to the Welfare State* (Montreal: Black Rose Books, 1984), pp.59-79; and Shragge, *Community Economic Development.*

50 The phrase is from Greg McElligott, "The Shifting Boundaries of Industrial Citizenship," *Socialist Studies Bulletin,* no.57-58 (July-December 1999), p.5.

51 Sheila Baxter, *No Way to Live: Poor Women Speak Out* (Vancouver: New Star, 1988), p.204. See also Wanda MacNevin, *From the Edge: A Woman's Evolution from Abuse to Activism* (Toronto: Picas and Points Publishing, 1999).

52 Marilyn Callahan, "Creating Second-Class Citizens in Child Welfare," in *Community Approaches to Child Welfare*, ed. Dominelli, p.51.

53 Uma Narayan, "Working Together across Difference: Some Considerations on Emotions and Political Practice," *Hypatia,* vol.3, no.2 (Summer 1988), pp.35, 36.

54 Anne Bishop, *Becoming an Ally: Breaking the Cycle of Oppression* (Halifax: Fernwood Publishing, 1994), p.99.

55 John Gary Cameron, in John Gary Cameron and Patrick Kerans, "Social and Political Action," in *An Introduction to Social Work Practice,* ed. Shankar Yelaja (Toronto: Prentice-Hall, 1985), p.131.

56 Charlotte Bunch, "The Reformist Tool Kit," *Quest Magazine,* vol.1, no.1 (1974), p.48.

57 Roxana Ng, Gillian Walker, and Jake Muller, eds., *Community Organizing and the State* (Toronto: Garamond Press, 1988).

58 Cameron and Kerans, "Social and Political Action," p.117. See also Bill Lee, *Pragmatics of Community Organization* (Mississauga, Ont.: Common Act Press, 1986).

59 Diana Ralph, "Grim, But Not Hopeless: The Future of Canada's Social Programs," Canadian Centre for Policy Alternatives, Ottawa, 1994. See also Diana Ralph, "Strategies for the Post Harris Era," in *Open for Business, Closed to People: Mike Harris's Ontario,* ed. Diana Ralph, André Regimbald, and Nérée St-Amand (Halifax: Fernwood Publishing, 1997), pp.177-85.

60 Denise Kouri, "Getting Organized in Saskatchewan," in *Still Ain't Satisfied,* ed. Fitzgerald, Guberman, and Wolfe, p.167.

61 From a discussion, "What Are Our Options?" in *Still Ain't Satisfied,* ed. Fitzgerald, Guberman, and Wolfe, p.306.

62 Karen McNama is past president of CUPE Local 2316 and was interviewed for Ben Carniol, "Social Work and the Labour Movement," in *Social Work and Social Movements in Canada,* ed. Wharf.

63 Carniol, "Social Work and the Labour Movement," pp.129-30. See also Milton Lee Tambor, "Containment, Accommodation, and Participative Management in Agency Union Relations," *Journal of Progressive Human Services,* vol.5, no.1 (1994), pp.45-62.

64 Leo Panitch and Donald Swartz, *The Assault on Trade Union Freedoms: From Consent to Coercion Revisited* (Toronto: Garamond Press, 1988), p.111. See also Craig Heron, *The Canadian Labour Movement: A Brief History,* 2nd ed. (Toronto: James Lorimer, 1996).

65 Andy Banks, "The Power and Promise of Community Unionism," *Labour Research Review,* no.18 (Fall-Winter 1991-92), p.30.

66 For different currents in feminism, see Adamson, Briskin, and McPhail, *Feminist Organizing,* ch.1. These authors also analyse feminist struggles from both within and outside the system: see chs.5, 6, and 7.

67 Patricia M. Daenzer, "Challenging Diversity: Black Women and Social Welfare," in *Women and the Canadian Welfare State: Challenges and Change,* ed. Patricia M. Evans and Gerda R. Wekerle (Toronto: University of Toronto Press, 1997), p.282.

68 Ibid., p.281.

69 Shragge, "Foreword," in *Services and Circuses: Community and the Welfare State,* ed. Frédéric Lesemann (Montreal: Black Rose, 1984), pp.20-21.

70 George Ehring and Wayne Roberts, *Giving away a Miracle: Lost Dreams, Broken Promises and the Ontario NDP* (Oakville, Ont.: Mosaic Press, 1993), pp.303-4.

71 Reverend Susan Eagle, "Foreword," in Vincenzo Pietropaolo, *Celebration of Resistance: Ontario's Days of Action* (Toronto: Between the Lines, 1999), p.3.

72 Joan Gilroy, "Social Work and the Women's Movement," in *Social Work and Social Movements in Canada,* ed. Wharf, pp.69-70.

73 Peggy McIntosh, "White Privilege: Unpacking the Invisible Knapsack," in *Re-Visioning Family Therapy: Race, Culture and Gender in Clinical Practice,* ed. Monica McGoldrick (New York: Guilford, 1998), pp.147-50.

74 Janet Sawyer, "Internalized Dominance," *Quarterly Change,* vol.1, no.2 (1989), pp.16-23.

75 Dianne de Champlain and Rosalie Goldstein, "Reflections on Anti-Oppressive Practice in the Classroom," *Curriculum Comments,* School of Social Work, University of Victoria, 1999, p.4.

76 Lilla Watson, 1986 Newsletter of Canadians in Urban Training, Winnipeg, cited by Lib Spry, "Structures of Power: Toward a Theatre of Liberation," in *Playing Boal: Theatre, Therapy, Activism,* ed. Mary Schutzman and Jan Cohen-Cruz (New York: Routledge, 1994), pp.183-84.

77 Julie Salverson "The Mask of Solidarity," in *Playing Boal,* ed. Schutzman and Cohen-Cruz, pp.167, 168. See also a favourable assessment of forum theatre to address anti-racism approaches: Roopchand B. Seebaran and Susan P. Johnston, *Anti-Racism Theatre Projects for Youth,* Community Liaison Division, British Columbia Ministry Responsible for Multiculturalism and Immigration, Victoria, 1998.

78 Barbara Findlay, *With All of Who We Are: A Discussion of Oppression and Dominance* (Vancouver: Lazara Press, 1991), p.11.

79 Allan Irving, "Waiting for Foucault: Social Work and the Multitudinous Truth(s) of Life," in *Reading Foucault for Social Work,* ed. Adrienne S. Chambon, Allan Irving, and Laura Epstein (New York: Columbia University Press, 1999), p.29.

80 Adrienne S. Chambon, "Foucault's Approach," in *Reading Foucault for Social Work,* ed. Chambon, Irving, and Epstein, p.70.

81 Frank T.Y. Wang, "Resistance and Old Age: The Subject behind the American Seniors' Movement," in *Reading Foucault for Social Work,* ed. Chambon, Irving, and Epstein, p.192.

82 Michel Foucault, *Politics, Philosophy, Culture: Interviews and Other Writings, 1977-84,* ed. Lawrence D. Kritzman (New York: Routledge, 1988), p.123, quoted in Catherine E. Foote and Arthur W. Frank, "Foucault and Therapy," in *Reading Foucault for Social Work,* ed. Chambon, Irving, and Epstein, p.172.

83 Mullaly, *Structural Social Work,* p.113. Iara Lessa, Ryerson School of Social Work, through several consultations, helped me to clarify various concepts within postmodernism. June Yee, also from the Ryerson School of Social Work, helped me to clarify the definition of narrative therapy.

84 Mullaly, *Structural Social Work,* p.114.

85 Michael White and David Epston, *Narrative Means to Therapeutic Ends* (New York: W.W. Norton, 1990). See also Alan Parry and Robert E. Doan, *Story Re-Visions: Narrative Therapy in the Postmodern World* (New York: Guilford Press, 1994), chs.2, 3, pp.12-117.

86 Shari Brotman and Shoshana Pollack, "The Loss of Context: The Problem of Merging Postmodernism with Feminist Social Work," *Canadian Social Work Review,* vol.14, no.1 (Summer 1997), p.13.

87 Ibid., pp.20, 9-19.

88 Chambon, "Foucault's Approach," pp.51-81. See also Nancy Fraser and Linda Gordon, "A Genealogy of Dependency: Tracing a Keyword of the U.S. Welfare State," *Signs: Journal of Women in Culture and Society,* vol.19, no.2 (Winter 1994), pp.309-36, for a postmodern critique of the term "dependency." For a postmodern critique of the social control in welfare payments, see Ken Moffatt, "Surveillance and Government of the Welfare Recipient," in *Reading Foucault for Social Work,* ed. Chambon, Irving, and Epstein, ch.9, pp.219-45.

89 Bishop, *Becoming an Ally,* p.51.

90 Ibid., p.95. For useful, brief guidelines of how to become an effective ally, see "How to — Becoming an Ally," in the same book, pp.96-102. See also "Being a Strong White Ally," and "Basic Tactics," in Paul Kivel, *Uprooting Racism: How White People Can Work for Racial Justice* (Philadelphia: New Society Publishers, 1996), pp.102-4.

91 Bishop, *Becoming an Ally,* p.97. For a similar point, see bell hooks, *Killing Rage: Ending Racism* (New York: Henry Holt, 1995), p.173. For a family therapist's awareness of oppression via gender, race, and class, see Monica McGoldrick, "Belonging and Liberation," in *Re-Visioning Family Therapy,* ed. McGoldrick, pp.215-28.

92 Roland Chrisjohn and Sherri Young, with Michael Maraun, *The Circle Game: Shadows and Substance in the Indian Residential School Experience in Canada* (Penticton, B.C.: Theytus Books, 1997), pp.277-78.

93 Janet Conway, "Knowledge, Power, Organization: Social Justice Coalitions at a Crossroads," Occasional Paper no.1, Community Social Planning of Toronto, October 1999, p.22. See also Janet Conway, "Knowledge and the Impasse in Left Politics: Potentials and Problems in Social Movement Practice," *Studies in Political Economy,* 2000.

94 Labour Council of Metro Toronto and York Region, *Metro Toronto Labour Yearbook,* 1989, p.3. See also ch.6 here for resistance to globalization; websites <www.web.net/coc> for Council of Canadians and <www.web.net/dwatch> for Democracy Watch and other websites challenging corporate control, listed in *Exposing the Facts of Corporate Rule: A Handbook on How to Challenge the Big Business Agenda* (Toronto: Centre for Social Justice, 1999), pp.32-34, and its website <www.socialjustice.org>; Canadian Centre for Policy Alternatives website <www.policyalternatives.ca>; and Web Networks: Internet Solutions for People Not for Profit <www.web.net>.

95 Michael Lerner, *Jewish Renewal: A Path to Healing and Transformation* (New York: Harper Perennial, 1995), p.95. See also Abraham Joshua Heschel, *Moral Grandeur and Spiritual Audacity: Essays,* ed. Susannah Heschel (New York: Farrar, Straus and Giroux, 1996).

96 Michael Lerner, "Spirituality in America," *Tikkun,* vol.13, no.6 (November/December 1998), p.33.

97 Thich Nhat Hanh, *Peace Is Every Step: The Path of Mindfulness in Everyday Life* (New York: Bantam, 1991); Ruth Morris, *Listen Ontario: Faith Communities Speak Out* (Oakville, Ont.: Mosaic Press, 1995); bell hooks, *Remembered Rapture: The Writer at Work* (New York: Henry Holt, 1999), pp.108-23; Oscar Cole-Arnal, *To Set the Captives Free: Liberation Theology in Canada* (Toronto: Between the Lines, 1998).

98 hooks, *Killing Rage,* p.264. See also Brian K. Murphy, *Transforming Ourselves, Transforming the World: An Open Conspiracy for Social Change* (Halifax: Fernwood Publishing, 1999).

ABOUT THE AUTHOR

Ben Carniol is a professor at the School of Social Work at Ryerson Poly-technic University in Toronto, teaching in the areas of social work practice and social policy analysis. In addition to a Masters in Social Work from McGill University, he also holds a law degree from the University of Toronto.

As a practitioner in social services for thirty-five years, Carniol has worked in Montreal, Calgary, and Toronto. He is active with several social justice organizations, including the Metro Network for Social Justice, and is a former President of the Canadian Association of Schools of Social Work. Ben Carniol lives in Toronto.